High Score iBT TOEFL LISTENING For Junior

Beginner

2nd Edition

DARAKWON

Dear Teachers and Parents,

Welcome to Darakwon's *High Score iBT TOEFL Listening for Junior* series.

Today, many English textbooks focus on the same topics and follow similar study patterns. Students are able to learn basic conversation skills, but too often, that is about it. They are limited because many texts do not allow students the opportunity to take it to the next level. The *High Score iBT TOEFL Listening for Junior* series has been created to change the way students study English. This wonderful series focuses on teaching students English by introducing them to an exciting variety of topics. By studying fascinating subjects and topics, students will become more interested in the English language, enhance their English vocabulary, and broaden their overall knowledge.

The *High Score iBT TOEFL Listening for Junior* series is written as a junior iBT TOEFL textbook. The books in this series cover topics that appear on the actual iBT TOEFL test. The questions in the books are also phrased just like those that students will find on the iBT TOEFL test. This should help familiarize students with the iBT TOEFL test and prepare them for when they take it in the future. By learning as much as they can about the iBT TOEFL test prior to taking it, the students will ensure that they will have some knowledge of many of the topics on the test and will be comfortable with the style of the test and the questions on it. All of these factors should lead to higher scores for the students.

Students will be able to use this series as a kind of stepping-stone for the actual iBT TOEFL test. The lectures and conversations have been written at a level they will be able to understand and follow. They are also filled with real-world situations and interesting facts and information. I believe that students will find the content stimulating, and it will help them become familiar and comfortable with what to expect on the actual iBT TOEFL test. Furthermore, I hope this series will ignite a passion for the English language, one which will remain with each student for a lifetime.

Henry William Link, VI

Table of CONTENTS

About the TOEFL 4

How to Use This Book 8

Chapter 1	**Weather** (Focusing on Content Words) 13
Chapter 2	**Office Hours & Service Encounters** (Linking) 29
Chapter 3	**Music** (Focusing on Structure Words) 45
Chapter 4	**Office Hours & Service Encounters** (Chunking) 61
Chapter 5	**Office Hours & Service Encounters** (Pitch and Intonation) 77
Chapter 6	**Education** (Signal Words and Phrases) 93
Chapter 7	**Nutrition** (Distinguishing Consonants) 109
Chapter 8	**Endangered Animals** (Listening for Numbers) 125

Actual Test 141

Appendix: Dictation Exercises 155

About the TOEFL

The TOEFL iBT

TOEFL is the Test of English as a Foreign Language. It measures the test taker's ability in English. Foreign students often need to take the TOEFL to get into an American college or university. For that reason, the TOEFL exam is very important.

The TOEFL iBT is an Internet-based test (iBT). Students take the TOEFL iBT on a computer at one of the test centers.

The TOEFL iBT tests four language skills. These skills are reading, listening, speaking, and writing. There are many different kinds of passages, lectures, conversations, and questions. Many sections combine two or more of these skills. So students must be capable in several English skills to get high scores on the exam.

The Format of the TOEFL iBT

There are four sections on the TOEFL iBT. These sections are Reading, Listening, Speaking, and Writing.

The Reading section has two passages. These passages are around 700 words long with 10 questions per passage. The Reading section of the test takes 35 minutes.

The Listening section has two types of passages. They are lectures and conversations. Each Listening section has 3 lectures. The lectures are 3-5 minutes each with 6 questions per lecture. Each listening section has 2 conversations. The conversations are 3 minutes each with 5 questions per conversation. The Listening section of the test takes 36 minutes.

The Speaking section has two types of questions. They are independent and integrated questions. There is 1 independent question. The independent question asks about your own ideas, opinions, and experiences. There are 3 integrated questions. The integrated questions consist of conversations, reading passages, lectures, or combinations of them—just as you would see in or out of a classroom. They ask questions based on the reading and listening passages. The Speaking section of the test takes 16 minutes.

The Writing section has two types of questions: 1 integrated task and 1 academic discussion task. The integrated task combines a short reading passage and a short lecture. The test taker must then write an essay about these two. The academic discussion task asks a question about a personal experience or opinion. The test taker must then write an essay about this question. The Writing section of the test takes 29 minutes.

The Test Format

Test Section	Number of Questions	Timing	Score
Reading	• 2 passages, 10 questions each	35 minutes	30
Listening	• 3 lectures, 6 questions each • 2 conversations, 5 questions each	36 minutes	30
Speaking	• 1 independent task • 3 integrated tasks	16 minutes	30
Writing	• 1 integrated task • 1 academic discussion task	29 minutes	30

The Listening Section

There are 8 different kinds of questions in the Listening section. Each question appears a different number of times.

The different kinds of questions are:

1 Gist-Content Questions

These ask about the main idea of the lecture.
There is one of these questions for each lecture.

2 Gist-Purpose Questions

These ask about the reason why the speakers are talking.
There is one of these questions for each conversation.

3 Detail Questions

These ask about the main facts in the lecture or conversation.
There are 0-2 of these questions in each lecture or conversation.

4 Understanding Function of What Is Said Questions

These ask about the reason why the speaker says or mentions something.
There are 0-1 of these questions in each lecture or conversation.

5 Understanding Speaker's Attitude Questions

These ask about the attitude of the speaker.
There are 0-1 of these questions in each lecture or conversation.

About the TOEFL

6. Understanding Organization Questions
These ask about the overall organization of the lecture.
There are 0-1 of these questions in each lecture.

7. Connecting Content Questions
These ask about the understanding of the relationships among ideas in a lecture.
There are 0-1 of these questions in each lecture.

8. Making Inferences Questions
These ask about the conclusion based on information.
There are 0-1 of these questions in each lecture or conversation.

How to Use This Book

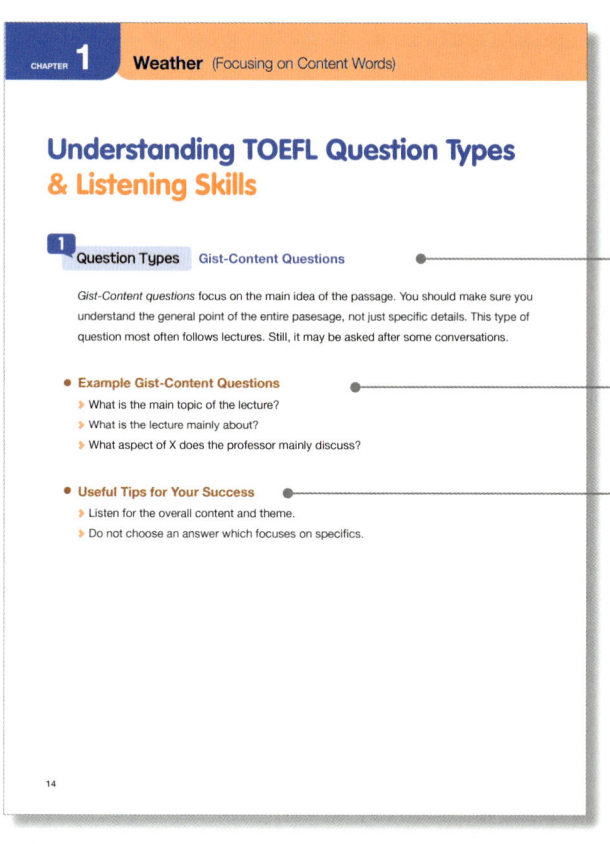

Question Types
This section describes the question or questions covered in the chapter. It provides an explanation of each question and how to try to answer it.

Example Questions
This section shows the different ways that the questions appear on the TOEFL test. Students can learn how to recognize the different types of question in this section.

Useful Tips for Your Success
This section provides various tips on how to answer the questions properly. It also provides hints on the right and wrong approaches to answering each question.

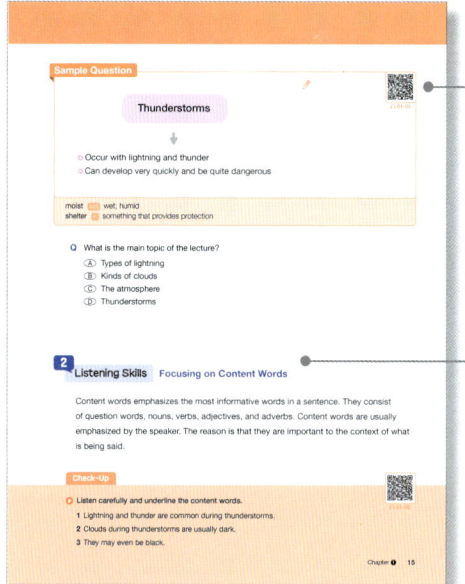

Sample Lecture or Conversation
This is a short 25-30 second lecture or conversation on one of the topics in the unit. It has one TOEFL question and one listening skills question.

Listening Skills
This is an explanation of the listening skill that the chapter covers.

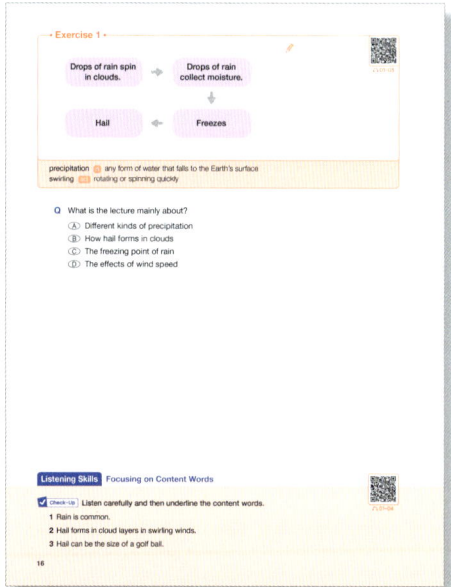

Short Lectures or Conversations
There are four short lectures or conversations. The conversations are between 35 and 40 seconds long. The lectures are 25-35 seconds long. Each passage is on a topic that concerns the subject of the unit and has one TOEFL question and one listening skills question.

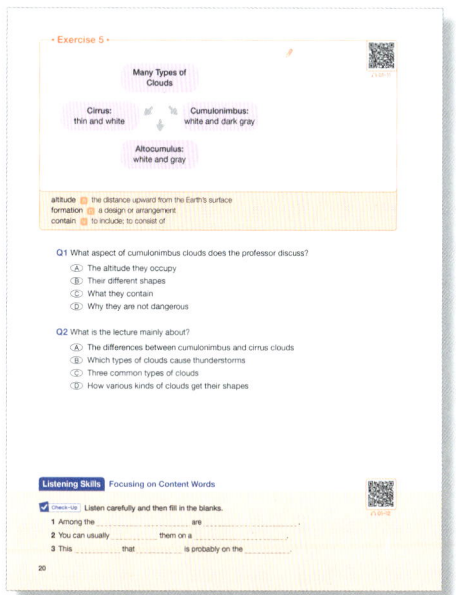

Medium Lectures or Conversations
There are four medium lectures or conversations. The conversations are between 45 and 60 seconds long. The lectures are 45-65 seconds long. Each passage is on a topic that concerns the subject of the unit and has two TOEFL questions and one listening skills question.

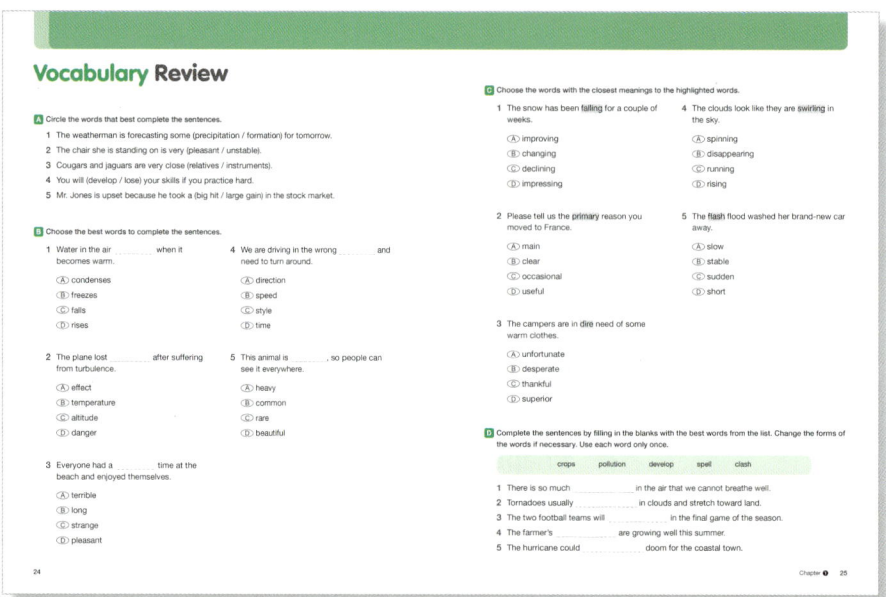

Vocabulary Review

This section provides a comprehensive review of the vocabulary found in the various passages in the unit. Each unit has twenty vocabulary review questions, and all of the answer choices are words that appear in the passages in the unit.

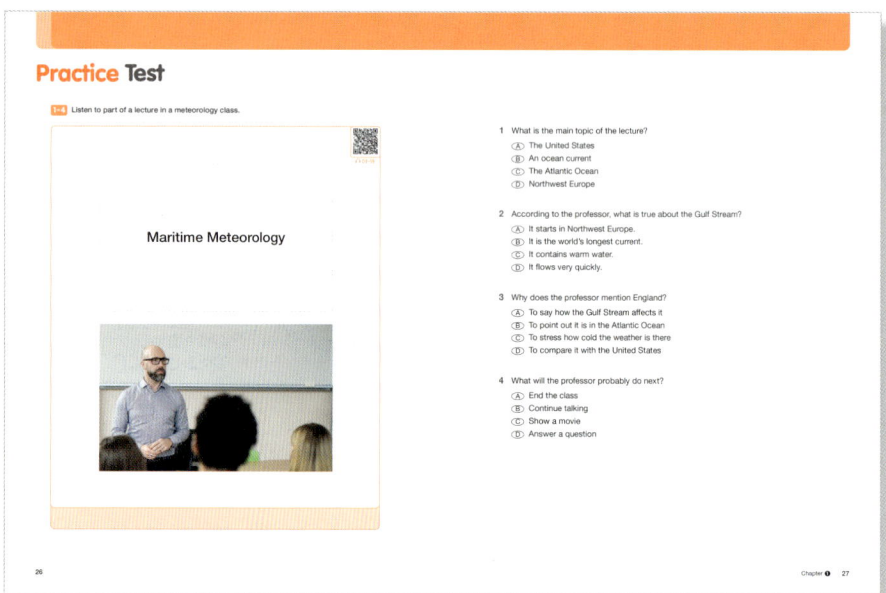

Practice Test

There is one lecture or conversation with 150-180 words. The lecture or conversation is on a topic that concerns the subject of the unit and has four TOEFL questions.

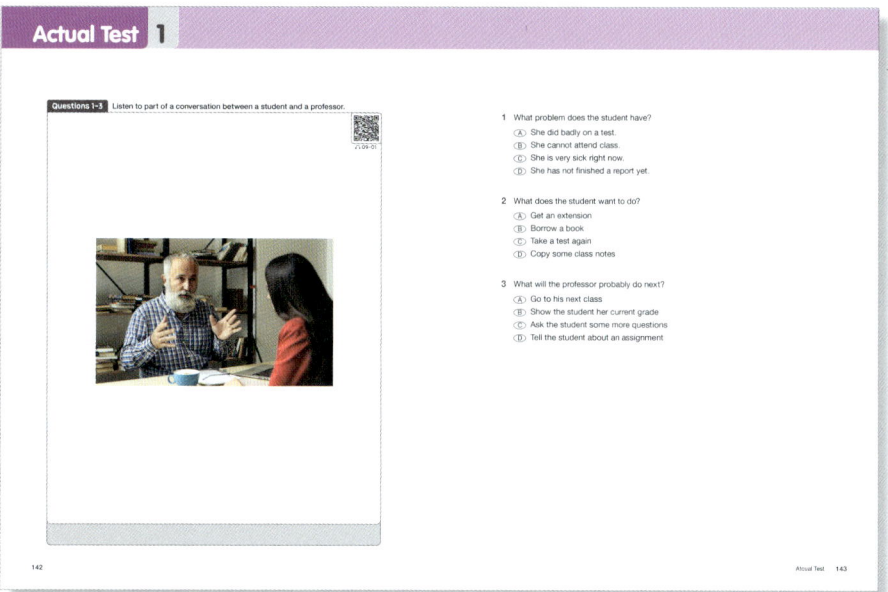

Actual Test

The actual test includes both lectures and conversations. The lectures are between 65 and 85 seconds long and include 4 questions each. The conversations are between 60 and 75 seconds long and include 3 questions each. There are different types of questions for each lecture or conversation. The questions are from all 8 types found in the listening section. Additionally, the lectures are from topics that appear in the book while the conversations are new office hours or service encounters. These lectures and conversations as well as the questions are shorter versions of a typical TOEFL iBT Listening section.

CHAPTER

01

Weather
(Focusing on Content Words)

CHAPTER 1 Weather (Focusing on Content Words)

Understanding TOEFL Question Types & Listening Skills

1 Question Types — Gist-Content Questions

Gist-Content questions focus on the main idea of the passage. You should make sure you understand the general point of the entire pasesage, not just specific details. This type of question most often follows lectures. Still, it may be asked after some conversations.

- **Example Gist-Content Questions**
  - What is the main topic of the lecture?
  - What is the lecture mainly about?
  - What aspect of X does the professor mainly discuss?

- **Useful Tips for Your Success**
  - Listen for the overall content and theme.
  - Do not choose an answer which focuses on specifics.

Sample Question

🎧 01-01

Thunderstorms

⬇

- Occur with lightning and thunder
- Can develop very quickly and be quite dangerous

moist `adj` wet; humid
shelter `n` something that provides protection

Q What is the main topic of the lecture?

- Ⓐ Types of lightning
- Ⓑ Kinds of clouds
- Ⓒ The atmosphere
- Ⓓ Thunderstorms

2 Listening Skills   Focusing on Content Words

Content words emphasizes the most informative words in a sentence. They consist of question words, nouns, verbs, adjectives, and adverbs. Content words are usually emphasized by the speaker. The reason is that they are important to the context of what is being said.

Check-Up

▶ Listen carefully and underline the content words.

1. Lightning and thunder are common during thunderstorms.
2. Clouds during thunderstorms are usually dark.
3. They may even be black.

🎧 01-02

Chapter ❶   15

Exercise 1

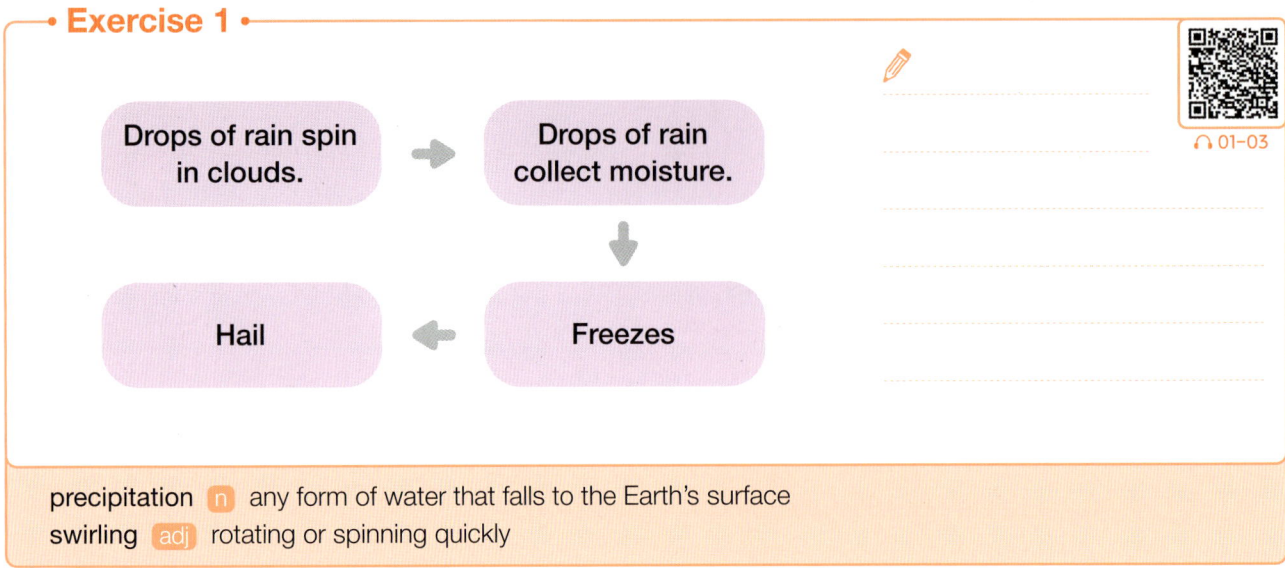

precipitation n   any form of water that falls to the Earth's surface
swirling adj rotating or spinning quickly

Q What is the lecture mainly about?
- Ⓐ Different kinds of precipitation
- Ⓑ How hail forms in clouds
- Ⓒ The freezing point of rain
- Ⓓ The effects of wind speed

Listening Skills   Focusing on Content Words

✓ **Check-Up**   Listen carefully and then underline the content words.

1 It it very common.
2 Hail forms in cloud layers in swirling winds.
3 Some hail can be the size of a golf ball.

• Exercise 2 •

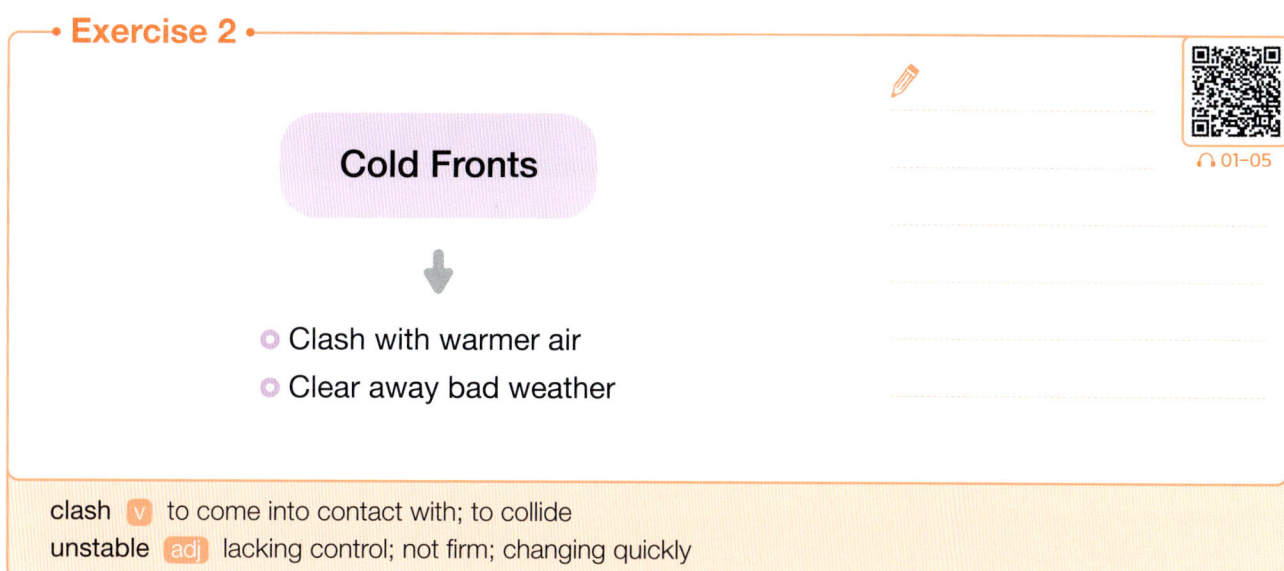

🎧 01-05

Cold Fronts

⬇

- Clash with warmer air
- Clear away bad weather

clash v to come into contact with; to collide
unstable adj lacking control; not firm; changing quickly

Q What aspect of cold fronts does the professor mainly discuss?
  Ⓐ The way they affect the weather
  Ⓑ Where they come from
  Ⓒ Which season they occur in
  Ⓓ How they are different from warm fronts

Listening Skills   Focusing on Content Words

🎧 01-06

✓ **Check-Up** Listen carefully and then underline the content words.

1 It depends on the season and the area.
2 The weather then becomes dry and cool.
3 This happens because high pressure follows the cold front.

Chapter ❶   17

• **Exercise 3** •

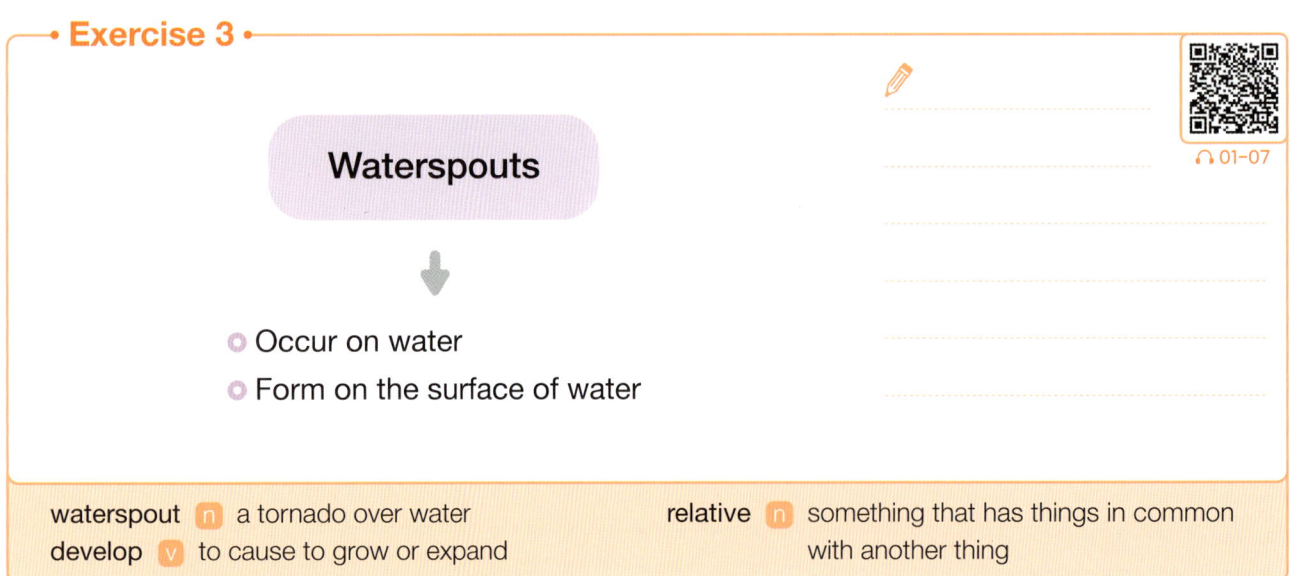

Waterspouts

- Occur on water
- Form on the surface of water

waterspout n a tornado over water	**relative** n something that has things in common
develop v to cause to grow or expand	with another thing

Q What is the main topic of the lecture?

Ⓐ The formation of tornadoes
Ⓑ How waterspouts typically form
Ⓒ Where waterspouts usually form
Ⓓ The differences between waterspouts and tornadoes

Listening Skills **Focusing on Content Words**

 Listen carefully and then underline the content words.

1 Waterspouts form on water.
2 Waterspouts form on the surface of the water.
3 There's another difference between the two.

• **Exercise 4** •

The Effects of Droughts

⬇

○ Lakes begin to dry up.
○ Agriculture takes a big hit.
○ Fires destroy vegetation.

spell v to promise or indicate
big hit n a great amount of damage
vegetation n any kind of plant

Q What is the lecture mainly about?
- Ⓐ A lack of rainfall
- Ⓑ Forest fires
- Ⓒ Lake water levels
- Ⓓ Agricultural problems

Listening Skills   Focusing on Content Words

 **Check-Up**   Listen carefully and then underline the content words.

1 It may rain during that time.
2 Lakes begin to dry up.
3 Agriculture takes a big hit.

• **Exercise 5** •

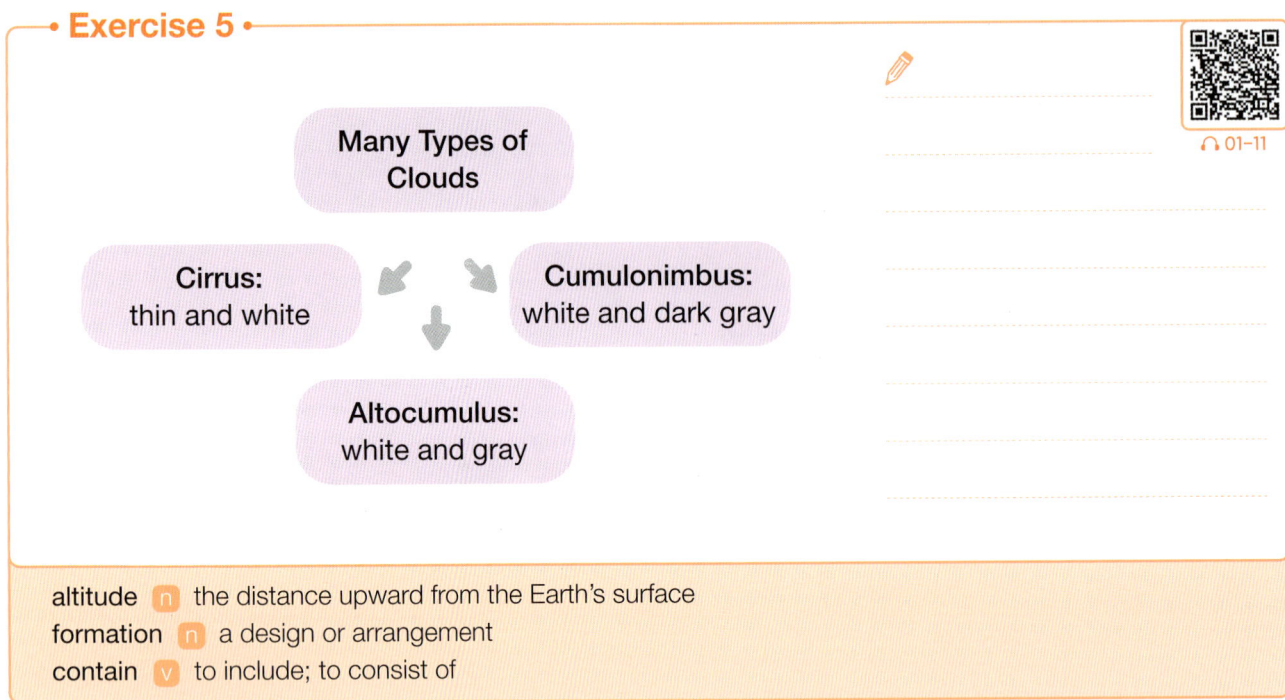

altitude n the distance upward from the Earth's surface
formation n a design or arrangement
contain v to include; to consist of

Q1 What aspect of cumulonimbus clouds does the professor discuss?
- Ⓐ The altitude they occupy
- Ⓑ Their different shapes
- Ⓒ What they contain
- Ⓓ Why they are not dangerous

Q2 What is the lecture mainly about?
- Ⓐ The differences between cumulonimbus and cirrus clouds
- Ⓑ Which types of clouds cause thunderstorms
- Ⓒ Three common types of clouds
- Ⓓ How various kinds of clouds get their shapes

Listening Skills Focusing on Content Words

✓ **Check-Up** Listen carefully and then fill in the blanks.

1 Among the _____ are _____.
2 You can usually _____ them on a _____.
3 This _____ that _____ is probably on the _____.

• **Exercise 6** •

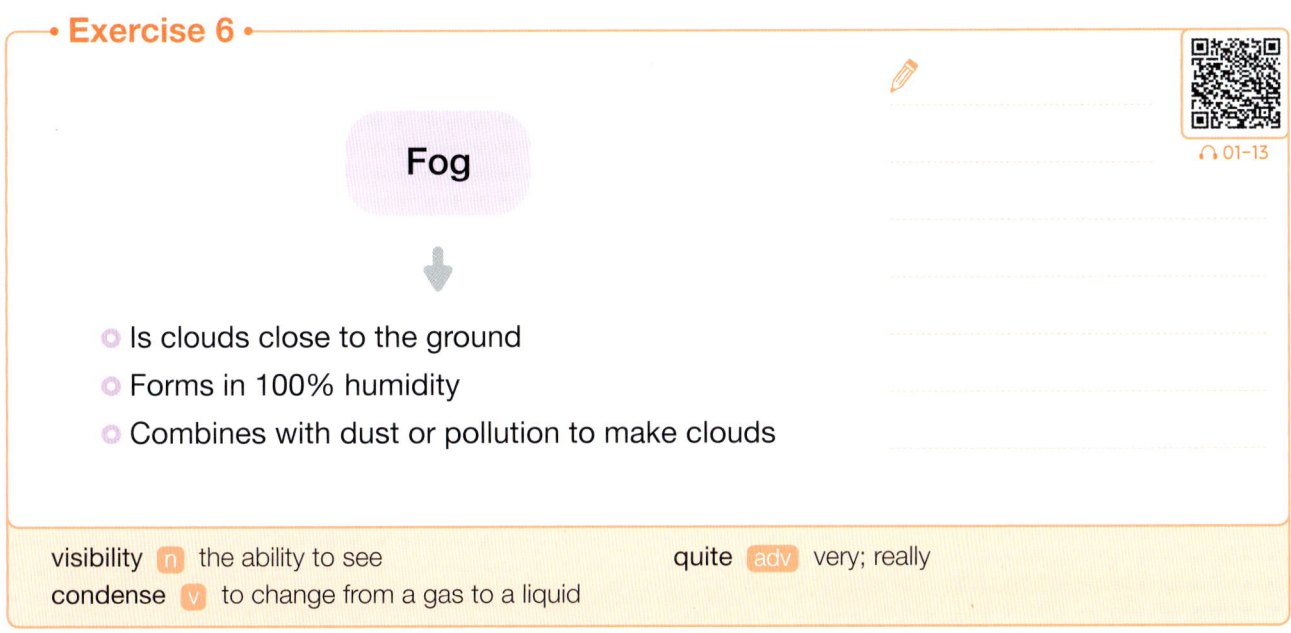

- Is clouds close to the ground
- Forms in 100% humidity
- Combines with dust or pollution to make clouds

visibility n the ability to see
condense v to change from a gas to a liquid
quite adv very; really

Q1 What is the lecture mainly about?
- Ⓐ What fog looks like
- Ⓑ Where fog is common
- Ⓒ When fog appears
- Ⓓ How fog forms

Q2 What aspect of water vapor does the professor mainly discuss?
- Ⓐ How it helps create fog
- Ⓑ What creates it
- Ⓒ How it is different from liquid water
- Ⓓ Why it can float in the air

Listening Skills   Focusing on Content Words

✓ **Check-Up** Listen carefully and then fill in the blanks.

1 So _____ can _____ for _____.
2 First, _____ need _____.
3 The _____ then _____ with _____ or _____ to _____.

Chapter ❶ 21

Exercise 7

Weather Forecast Tools

⬇

- Thermometer: tells the temperature
- Barometer: measures the air pressure
- Windsock: tells which direction the wind is blowing
- Rain Gauge: measures the amount of rain that falls

forecast [v] to make a prediction about the future	pleasant [adj] nice
instrument [n] a tool; a device	primary [adj] main; major

🎧 01-15

Q1 What is the main topic of the lecture?
- Ⓐ Tools for forecasting the weather
- Ⓑ Thermometers and barometers
- Ⓒ The usage of the windsock
- Ⓓ Rising and falling air pressure

Q2 What aspect of rain gauges does the professor mainly discuss?
- Ⓐ When they are needed
- Ⓑ Why they are hard to use
- Ⓒ Where to find them
- Ⓓ Who uses them

Listening Skills Focusing on Content Words

✅ **Check-Up** Listen carefully and then fill in the blanks. 🎧 01-16

1 _____ to _____ about the _____.

2 The _____ is _____.

3 They _____ the _____ of _____ that _____ during a _____.

• Exercise 8 •

🎧 01-17

How Floods Occur

⬇

- Flash floods
- Hurricanes
- Everyday thunderstorms

flash adj sudden
dire   adj urgent or desperate

Q1 What is the lecture mainly about?
- Ⓐ The causes of floods
- Ⓑ Where flash floods occur
- Ⓒ The effects of hurricanes
- Ⓓ Types of heavy rainfall

Q2 What aspect of river floods does the professor mainly discuss?
- Ⓐ How serious they are
- Ⓑ When they occur
- Ⓒ Why they occur
- Ⓓ How long they last

Listening Skills Focusing on Content Words

🎧 01-18

✓ **Check-Up** Listen carefully and then fill in the blanks.

1 There are two _____ _____ of _____.
2 A _____ _____ can have _____ _____ on a region.
3 Long-lasting _____, _____, and _____ _____ can cause _____ _____.

Vocabulary Review

A Circle the words that best complete the sentences.

1 The weatherman is forecasting some (precipitation / formation) for tomorrow.
2 The chair she is standing on is very (pleasant / unstable).
3 Cougars and jaguars are very close (relatives / instruments).
4 You will (develop / lose) your skills if you practice hard.
5 Mr. Jones is upset because he took a (big hit / large gain) in the stock market.

B Choose the best words to complete the sentences.

1 Warm air _____ when it becomes cold.
   A condenses
   B freezes
   C falls
   D rises

2 The plane lost _____ after suffering from turbulence.
   A effect
   B temperature
   C altitude
   D danger

3 Everyone had a _____ time at the beach and enjoyed themselves.
   A terrible
   B long
   C strange
   D pleasant

4 We are driving in the wrong _____ and need to turn around.
   A direction
   B speed
   C style
   D time

5 This animal is _____, so people can see it everywhere.
   A heavy
   B common
   C rare
   D beautiful

C Choose the words with the closest meanings to the highlighted words.

1 The snow has been falling for a couple of weeks.
   A improving
   B changing
   C declining
   D impressing

2 Please tell us the primary reason you moved to France.
   A main
   B clear
   C occasional
   D useful

3 The campers are in dire need of some warm clothes.
   A unfortunate
   B desperate
   C thankful
   D superior

4 The clouds look like they are swirling in the sky.
   A spinning
   B disappearing
   C running
   D rising

5 The flash flood washed her brand-new car away.
   A slow
   B stable
   C sudden
   D short

D Complete the sentences by filling in the blanks with the best words from the list. Change the forms of the words if necessary. Use each word only once.

| crops | pollution | develop | spell | clash |

1 There is so much _____ in the air that we cannot breathe well.
2 Tornadoes usually _____ in clouds and stretch toward land.
3 The two football teams will _____ in the final game of the season.
4 The farmer's _____ are growing well this summer.
5 The hurricane could _____ doom for the coastal town.

Practice Test

1-4 Listen to part of a lecture in a meteorology class.

Meteorology

1. What is the main topic of the lecture?
   - Ⓐ The United States
   - Ⓑ An ocean current
   - Ⓒ The Atlantic Ocean
   - Ⓓ Northwest Europe

2. According to the professor, what is true about the Gulf Stream?
   - Ⓐ It starts in Northwest Europe.
   - Ⓑ It is the world's longest current.
   - Ⓒ It contains warm water.
   - Ⓓ It flows very quickly.

3. Why does the professor mention England?
   - Ⓐ To say how the Gulf Stream affects it
   - Ⓑ To point out it is in the Atlantic Ocean
   - Ⓒ To stress how cold the weather is there
   - Ⓓ To compare it with the United States

4. What will the professor probably do next?
   - Ⓐ End the class
   - Ⓑ Continue talking
   - Ⓒ Show a movie
   - Ⓓ Answer a question

CHAPTER 02

Office Hours & Service Encounters
(Linking)

CHAPTER 2   **Office Hours & Service Encounters** (Linking)

Understanding TOEFL Question Types & Listening Skills

1 Question Types   **Gist-Purpose Questions**

Gist-Purpose questions ask about the reasons why people are having a conversation. Listen to the reasons why the student and the other person are meeting. The reason usually appears at the beginning of the conversation.

● **Example Gist-Purpose Questions**
- Why does the student visit the professor?
- Why did the professor ask to see the student?
- Why does the professor explain X?

● **Useful Tips for Your Success**
- Listen for → the main theme of the conversation.
   → the problem the student is trying to solve.
- Don't → focus on the facts of the conversation.
   → ignore the beginning of the conversation.

Sample Question

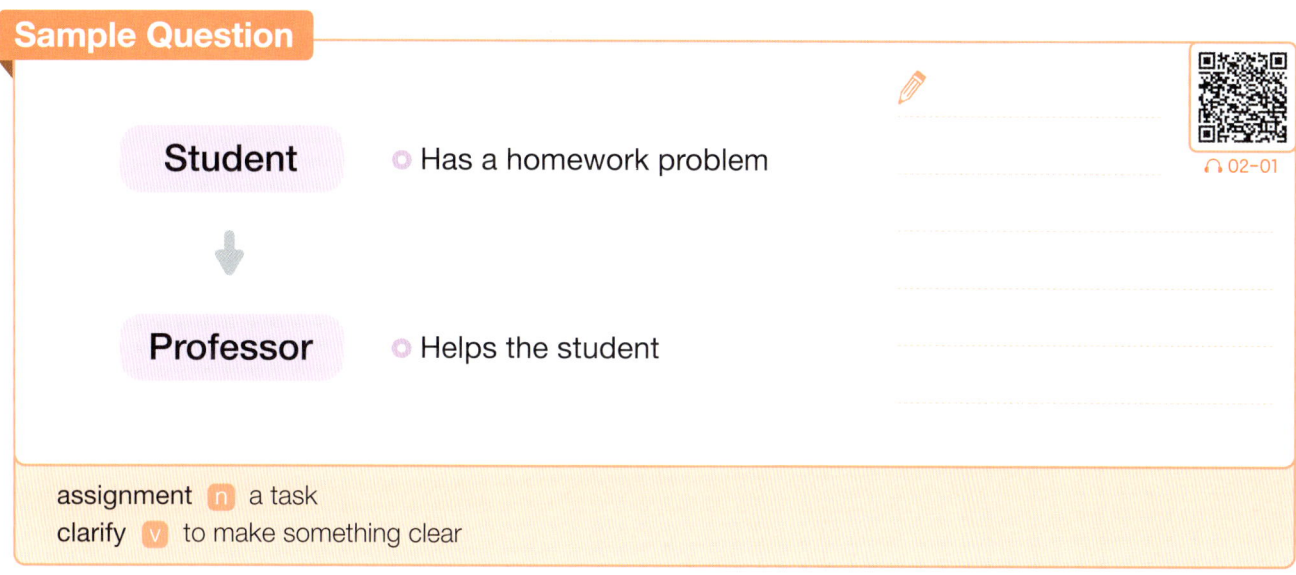

Student — Has a homework problem

Professor — Helps the student

02-01

assignment n a task
clarify v to make something clear

Q Why does the student visit the professor?

Ⓐ To ask about her homework grade
Ⓑ To get some help on her homework
Ⓒ To ask what her assignment is
Ⓓ To talk about her latest problem

2 Listening Skills   Linking

Linking is joining the pronunciation of two words when speaking. This makes the words easier to speak. The words also flow more smoothly. By using linking, you can speak more clearly and fluently. You should learn to recognize linking when people use it. This will allow you to understand people much better.

Check-Up

▶ Listen carefully and write the words you hear.

02-02

1 _____

2 _____

3 _____ begun

4 _____

Chapter ❷ 31

• **Exercise 1** •

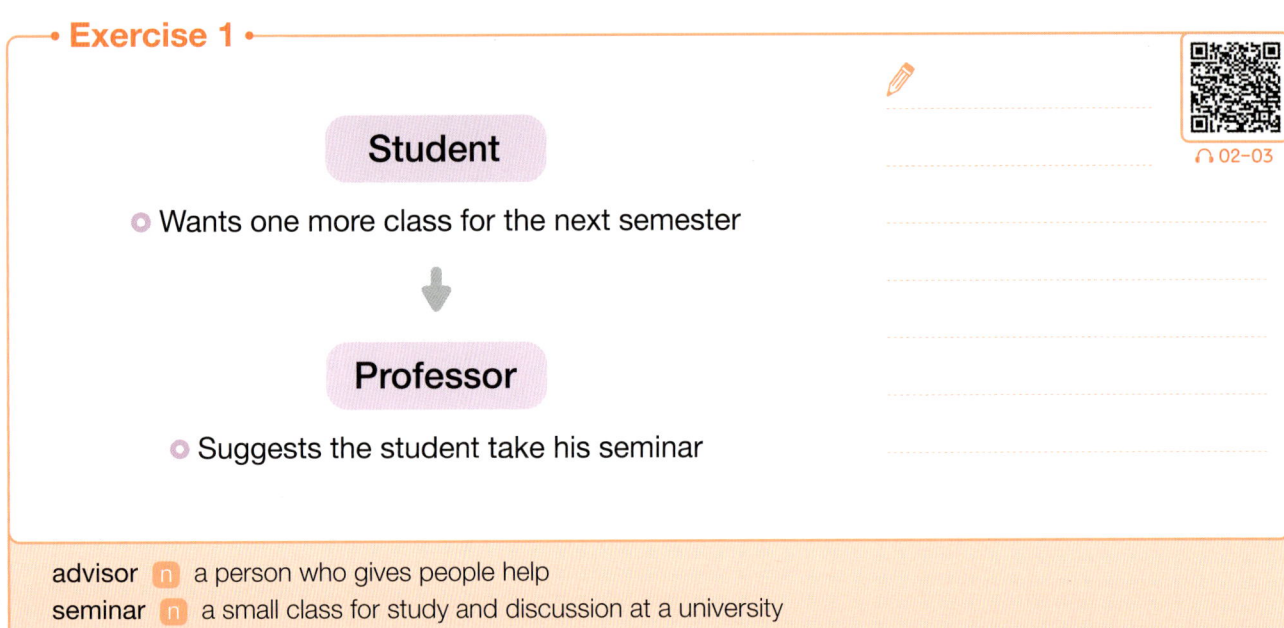

advisor n a person who gives people help
seminar n a small class for study and discussion at a university

Q Why does the student visit the professor?
  Ⓐ To ask about the professor's seminar
  Ⓑ To enroll in the professor's new class
  Ⓒ To get some advice on his schedule
  Ⓓ To discuss his plans for this semester

Listening Skills Linking

✓ Check-Up Listen carefully and write the words you hear.

1 _____
2 _____
3 you _____ me
4 have _____

• **Exercise 2** •

Student
- Needs help finding library books

⬇

Librarian
- Shows how to find the call numbers of books

click v to press a button, especially on a mouse
call number n a number on a library book that shows its location

Q Why does the librarian explain the library's computer system?
- Ⓐ To show the student how to find books
- Ⓑ To find the call number of the student's book
- Ⓒ To locate the title and the author of a book
- Ⓓ To tell the student how easy a system is

Listening Skills | Linking

✅ **Check-Up** Listen carefully and write the words you hear.

1 _____ books
2 _____ really easy.
3 _____
4 _____ .

Exercise 3

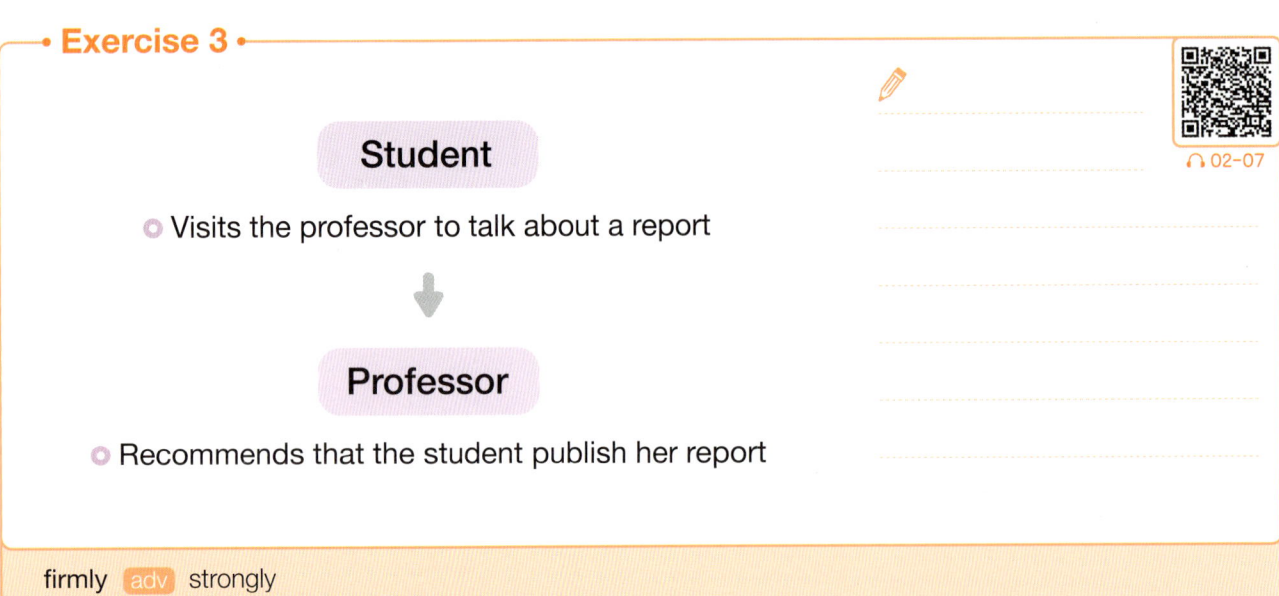

Student
- Visits the professor to talk about a report

Professor
- Recommends that the student publish her report

firmly *adv* strongly
publish *v* to print something in a book, newspaper, or magazine

Q Why did the professor ask to see the student?
- Ⓐ To compliment her on her latest work
- Ⓑ To ask her to read a certain magazine
- Ⓒ To criticize a report that she just wrote
- Ⓓ To assign her a journal to look over

Listening Skills Linking

Check-Up Listen carefully and write the words you hear.

1 you _____
2 _____ so sorry.
3 _____
4 _____ I can help you with that.

Exercise 4

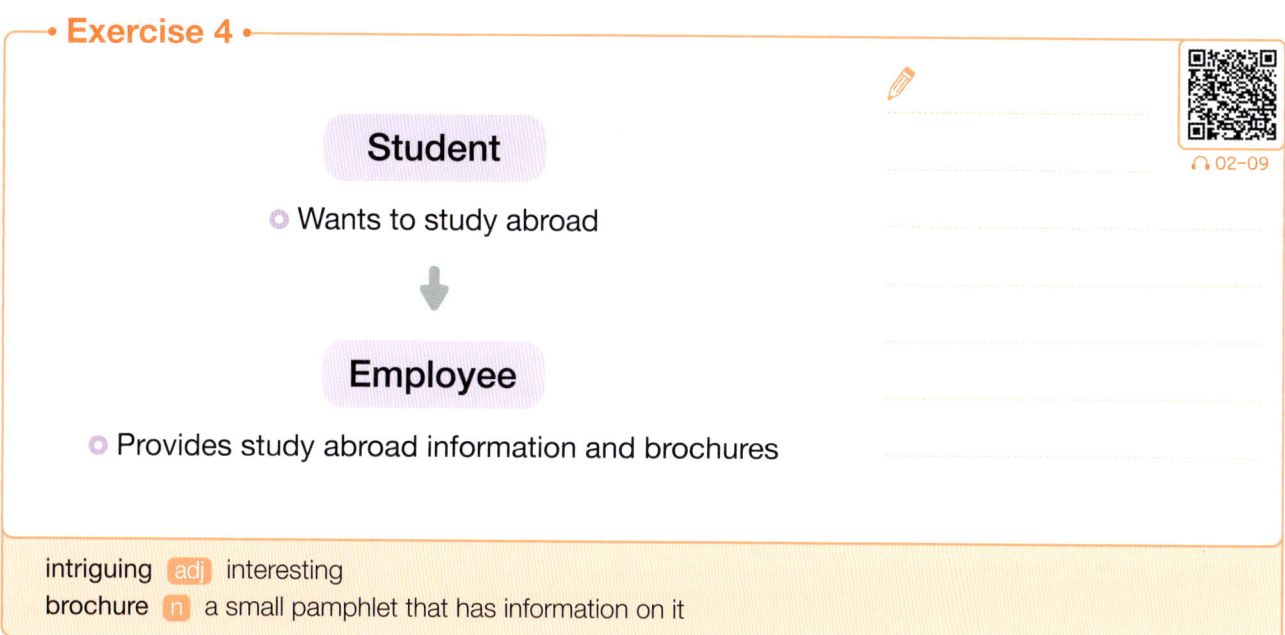

Student
- Wants to study abroad

↓

Employee
- Provides study abroad information and brochures

intriguing adj interesting
brochure n a small pamphlet that has information on it

Q Why does the student visit the study abroad office?
- Ⓐ She wants to know the prices to visit different countries.
- Ⓑ She would like to get some brochures on traveling abroad.
- Ⓒ She wants to improve her foreign language abilities.
- Ⓓ She is considering studying in a different country.

Listening Skills **Linking**

✓ **Check-Up** Listen carefully and write the words you hear.

1 _____

2 _____

3 _____ good choice

4 the _____ going to each country

Chapter ❷ 35

• Exercise 5 •

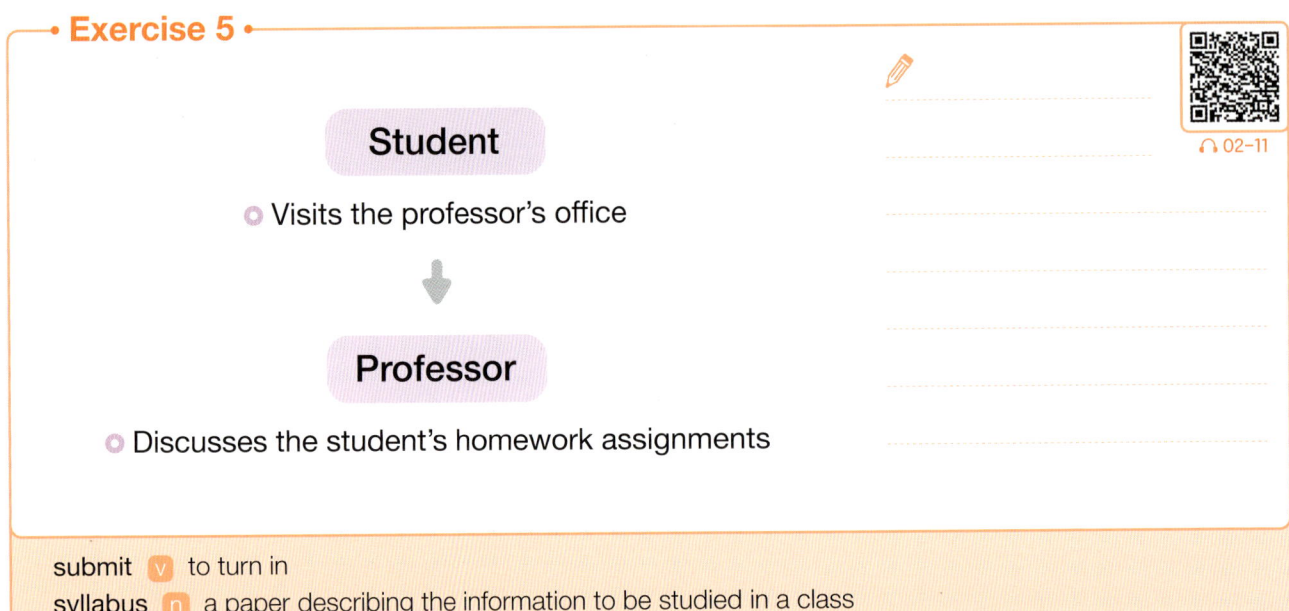

Student
- Visits the professor's office

↓

Professor
- Discusses the student's homework assignments

submit v to turn in
syllabus n a paper describing the information to be studied in a class

Q1 Why did the professor ask to see the student?
- Ⓐ To tell the student he is getting a zero in her class
- Ⓑ To complain about the quality of his homework
- Ⓒ To insist that he read the syllabus more carefully
- Ⓓ To ask why he has turned in none of his assignments

Q2 Why does the professor explain her grading system?
- Ⓐ To let the student know how low his grade is
- Ⓑ To tell the student how many points he will lose
- Ⓒ To say that the student will fail the class
- Ⓓ To give the student a chance to make up his grade

Listening Skills | Linking

✓ **Check-Up** Listen carefully and write the words you hear.

1 _____ your grade
2 _____
3 _____ want
4 _____ not good

• **Exercise 6** •

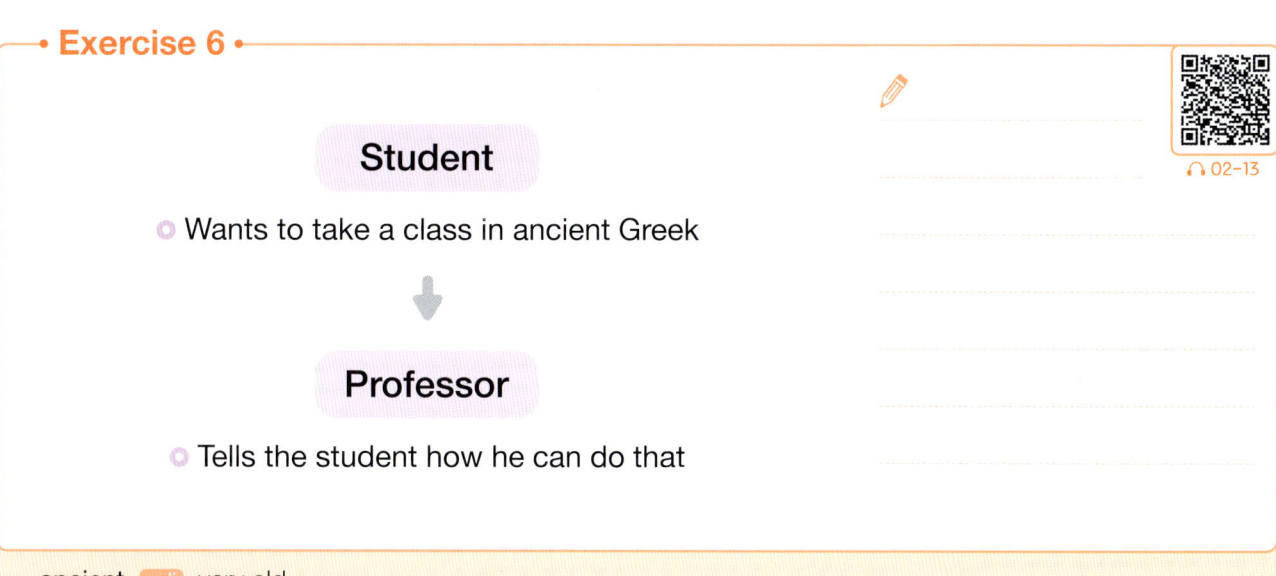

ancient adj very old
agreement n a deal or understanding between two or more people

Q1 Why did the professor ask to see the student?
 Ⓐ To discuss his grade in her class
 Ⓑ To introduce him to her colleague
 Ⓒ To encourage him to change his major
 Ⓓ To tell him about an opportunity

Q2 Why does the professor explain the agreement with Central University?
 Ⓐ To answer the student's question about it
 Ⓑ To state her opposition to the agreement
 Ⓒ To say how the student can take a class
 Ⓓ To advise the student to transfer to the school

Listening Skills Linking

✓ Check-Up Listen carefully and write the words you hear.

1 why _____
2 remember _____ wanted
3 we _____ doing that
4 fifteen _____

• **Exercise 7** •

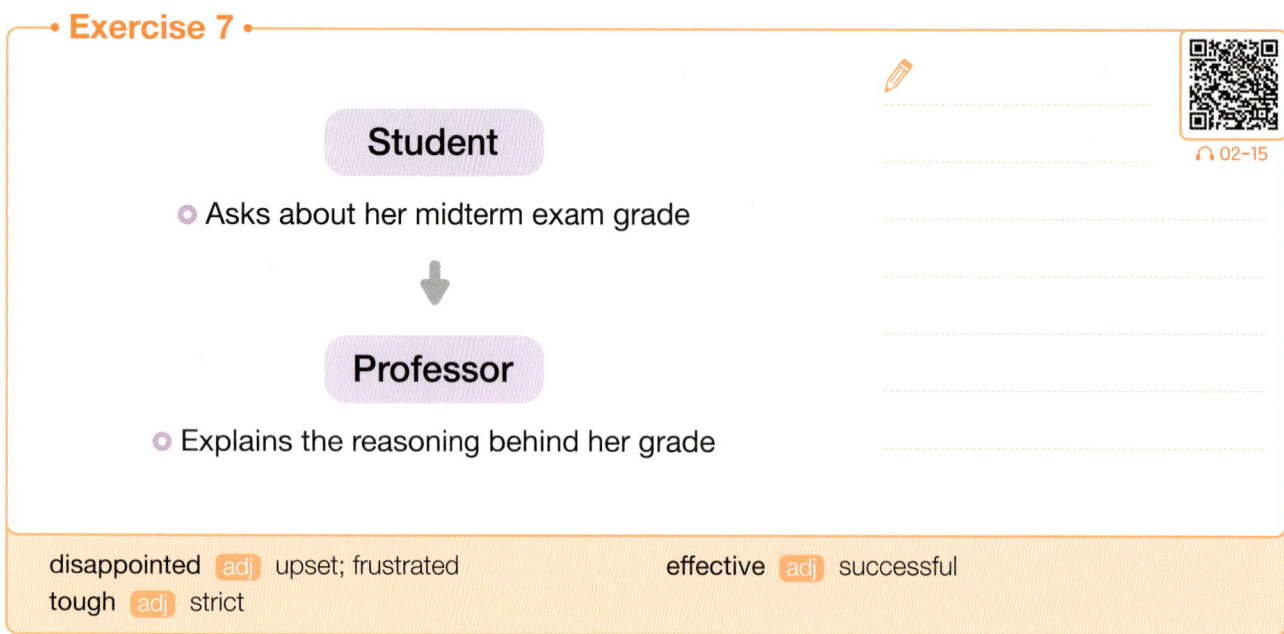

🎧 02-15

disappointed adj upset; frustrated
tough adj strict
effective adj successful

Q1 Why does the student visit the professor?
  Ⓐ To complain about her recent grade
  Ⓑ To ask the professor to raise her grade
  Ⓒ To understand why her grade was low
  Ⓓ To state that her grade is unfair

Q2 Why does the professor explain the student's grade?
  Ⓐ He wants her to know why she lost some points.
  Ⓑ He would like to help her improve on her next test.
  Ⓒ She can improve her grade by knowing her mistakes.
  Ⓓ He believes she needs to get her facts correct.

Listening Skills Linking

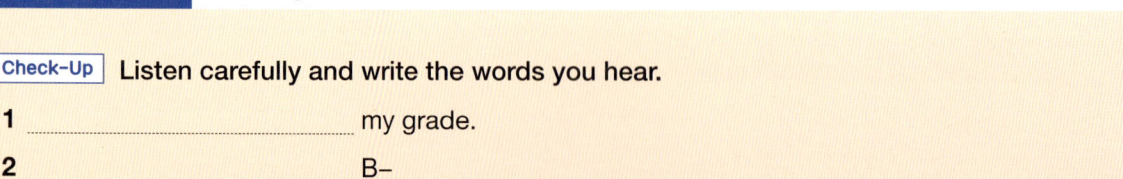

✓ Check-Up Listen carefully and write the words you hear.

🎧 02-16

1 _____ my grade.
2 _____ B–
3 _____ a very tough grader.
4 you _____

Exercise 8

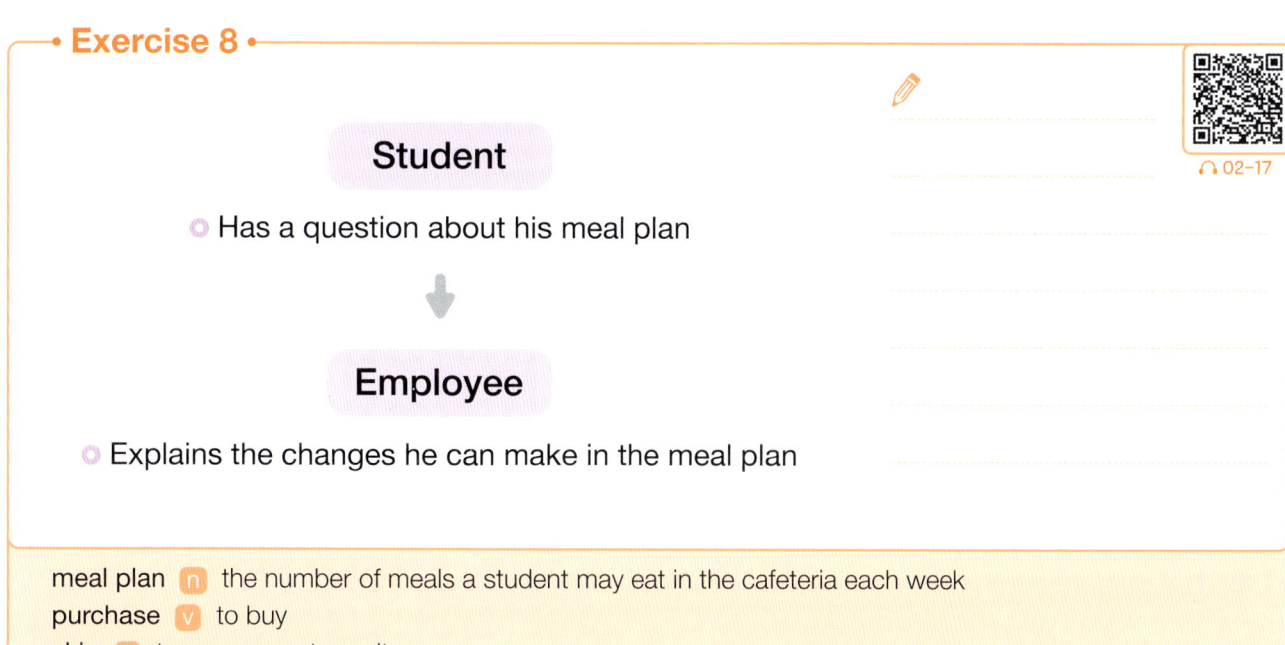

Student
- Has a question about his meal plan

↓

Employee
- Explains the changes he can make in the meal plan

---

meal plan n the number of meals a student may eat in the cafeteria each week
purchase v to buy
skip v to pass over; to omit

Q1 Why does the student visit the cafeteria?
- Ⓐ He needs to purchase a meal plan.
- Ⓑ He would like to eat lunch.
- Ⓒ He wants to change his meal plan.
- Ⓓ He thinks his meal plan is too expensive.

Q2 Why does the employee explain the meal plans?
- Ⓐ To encourage the student not to change his
- Ⓑ To give the student some possible choices
- Ⓒ To provide the student with some prices
- Ⓓ To persuade the student to get ten meals a week

Listening Skills Linking

✓ Check-Up   Listen carefully and write the words you hear.

1 I _____ here
2 _____
3 _____ day
4 _____ each

Vocabulary Review

A Circle the words that best complete the sentences.

1 The professor is teaching three classes during the fall (semester / seminar).
2 John (purchased / skipped) lunch because he was too busy to eat.
3 Everyone (explained / expected) Mary to get the highest grade in the class.
4 Please check your (advisor / syllabus) for information on this class.
5 The student purchased a (meal plan / call number) from the cafeteria.

B Choose the best words to complete the sentences.

1 Greg needed some help, so we all _____ him.
   A assisted
   B expected
   C disappointed
   D rented

2 The students in the literature class had to write many _____.
   A seminars
   B schedules
   C essays
   D midterm exams

3 The two groups made an _____ and solved their problem.
   A agreement
   B example
   C exam
   D approach

4 I was very _____ because I got a low grade on my test.
   A busy
   B disappointed
   C interested
   D fascinating

5 Please turn in your homework _____ by the end of the week.
   A assignments
   B questions
   C replacements
   D semesters

C Choose the words with the closest meanings to the highlighted words.

1 The students were reading some magazines in the library.
   - Ⓐ books
   - Ⓑ plans
   - Ⓒ grades
   - Ⓓ journals

2 Visitors are not permitted to stay in the museum after it closes.
   - Ⓐ expected
   - Ⓑ allowed
   - Ⓒ reported
   - Ⓓ trusted

3 The company publishes many different kinds of books.
   - Ⓐ writes
   - Ⓑ starts
   - Ⓒ thinks
   - Ⓓ prints

4 Everyone was upset because the test was too tough.
   - Ⓐ easy
   - Ⓑ factual
   - Ⓒ difficult
   - Ⓓ recent

5 He gave me a full explanation of his activities.
   - Ⓐ twice
   - Ⓑ complete
   - Ⓒ effective
   - Ⓓ comfortable

D Complete the sentences by filling in the blanks with the best words from the list. Change the forms of the words if necessary. Use each word only once.

submit   instructor   tough   fit   purchase

1 They must _____ new books, not used ones, for the class.
2 He wants to take the class, but it does not _____ his schedule.
3 Professor Marrone wants the students to _____ their papers on Monday.
4 Exam week was very _____ for many of the students.
5 Kate Smith was hired to be the _____ for an engineering class.

Practice Test

1-3 Listen to part of a conversation between a student and a student services center employee.

02-19

1   Why does the student visit the student ID office?
    A   To get a duplicate ID card
    B   To get his first student ID card
    C   To look for his ID card
    D   To pick up a friend's ID card

2   What form of identification does the employee accept from the student?
    A   A driver's license
    B   A university meal card
    C   A library card
    D   A gym membership card

3   What will the student probably do next?
    A   Make a payment
    B   Submit a picture
    C   Fill out a form
    D   Leave the office

CHAPTER 03

Music
(Focusing on Structure Words)

CHAPTER 3 Music (Focusing on Structure Words)

Understanding TOEFL Question Types & Listening Skills

1 Question Types — Detail Questions

Detail questions test your understanding of the details and the facts in the passage. They often support the main idea of the listening passage. However, you may be asked about some details which are not related to the main topic.

- **Example Detail Questions**
  - What are X?
  - How did X . . . ?
  - How did X affect Y?

- **Useful Tips for Your Success**
  - Focus on major points and check your notes for the right answer.
  - Never choose an answer just because it appears in the passage.

Sample Question

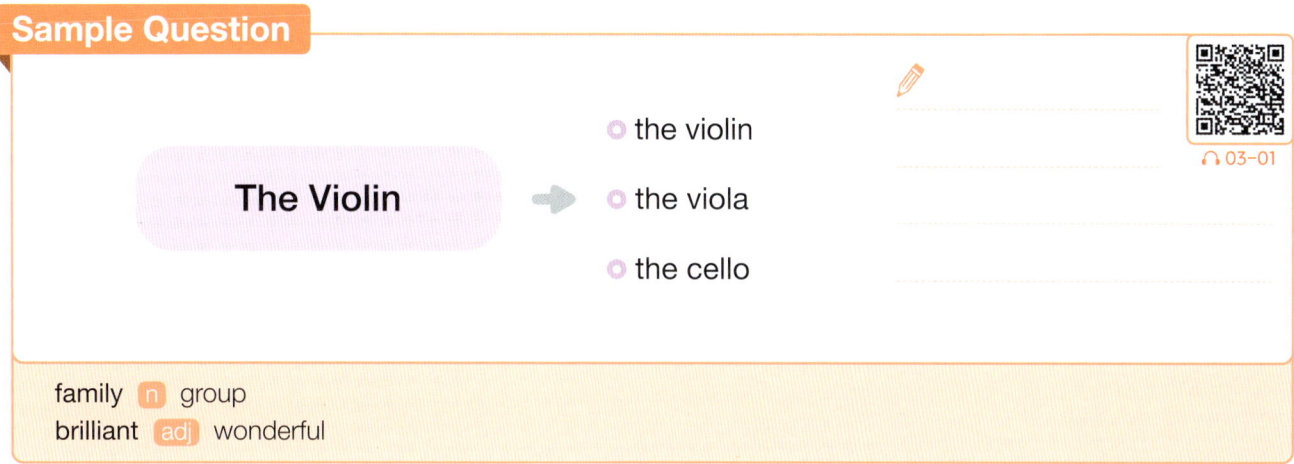

🎧 03-01

family n group
brilliant adj wonderful

Q   What is the smallest instrument in the violin family?
   Ⓐ The bass
   Ⓑ The cello
   Ⓒ The viola
   Ⓓ The violin

2 Listening Skills   Focusing on Structure Words

Structure words are all of the words in a sentence that are not nouns, verbs, adjectives, and adverbs. They are pronouns, prepositions, be verbs, and articles. They mostly indicate grammatical relations.

Check-Up

🎧 03-02

▶ Listen carefully and underline the structure words.

1 It is a family of instruments.
2 They are all made of wood.
3 The violin is the smallest.
4 It produces a variety of brilliant sounds.

Chapter ❸   47

• **Exercise 1** •

John Philip Sousa

- Was an American composer
- Composed *Semper Fidelis* and *The Stars and Stripes Forever*

compose v to make; to create
tune n a song

Q What kind of music did John Philip Sousa compose?

Ⓐ Symphonies
Ⓑ Dance music
Ⓒ Operas
Ⓓ Military songs

Listening Skills Focusing on Structure Words

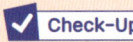 Listen carefully and underline the structure words.

1 He wasn't a singer though.
2 He was a composer.
3 He also composed *The Stars and Stripes Forever*.
4 Let's listen to it now.

• **Exercise 2** •

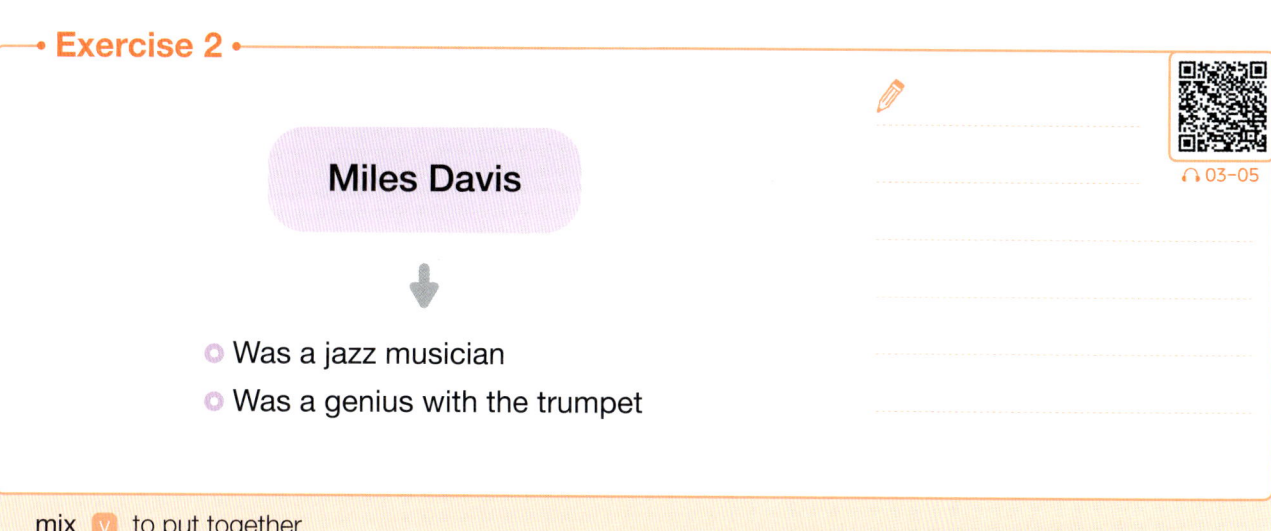

Miles Davis

⬇

- Was a jazz musician
- Was a genius with the trumpet

🎧 03-05

| mix | v | to put together |

Q How did Miles Davis affect jazz music?

Ⓐ He made it easier.
Ⓑ He changed it to rock music.
Ⓒ He developed cool jazz.
Ⓓ He created the jazz trumpet.

Listening Skills | Focusing on Structure Words

✓ **Check-Up** | Listen carefully and underline the structure words.

1 Miles Davis was one of the coolest jazz musicians ever.
2 Actually, he helped develop a new style of jazz.
3 He was a genius with the trumpet.
4 He started to mix jazz with rock music.

🎧 03-06

• **Exercise 3** •

The *Gayageum*

- Is the best-known Korean instrument
- Is made of wood

hollow adj empty; vacant
relaxed adj soothing; even

Q How do musicians play the *gayageum*?

Ⓐ They pluck it.
Ⓑ They blow into it.
Ⓒ They beat it.
Ⓓ They push it.

Listening Skills | **Focusing on Structure Words**

 Check-Up Listen carefully and underline the structure words.

1 It is a string instrument.
2 The body of the *gayageum* is made of wood.
3 The musician plucks the strings.
4 The *gayageum* is used for traditional Korean folk music.

• **Exercise 4** •

Gregorian Chants

- Were music from the Middle Ages
- Had no musical instruments

chant n a short, simple melody
in unison phr together; as one

Q Where were Gregorian chants sung?

Ⓐ At festivals
Ⓑ At churches
Ⓒ At people's homes
Ⓓ At holiday celebrations

Listening Skills Focusing on Structure Words

✓ Check-Up Listen carefully and underline the structure words.

1 They were first sung in the ninth or tenth century.
2 This was during the Middle Ages in Europe.
3 As you heard, there were no musical instruments.
4 So I guess nobody understood the words, right?

• Exercise 5 •

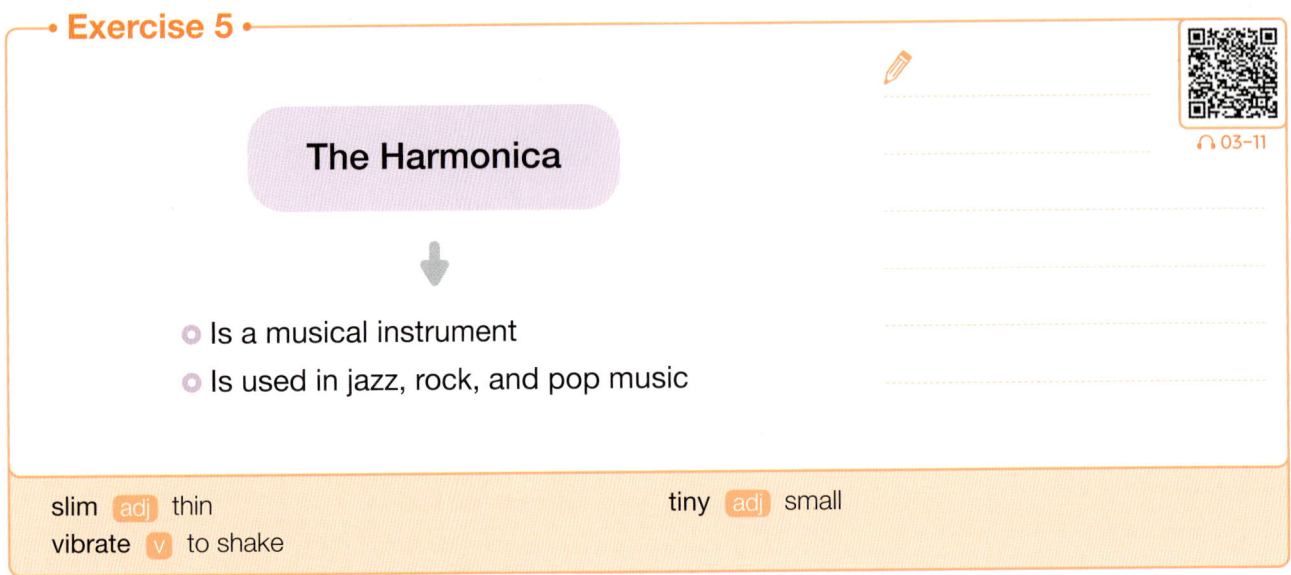

○ 03-11

- Is a musical instrument
- Is used in jazz, rock, and pop music

slim **adj** thin   tiny **adj** small
vibrate **v** to shake

Q1 What kind of instrument is the harmonica?
- Ⓐ A percussion instrument
- Ⓑ A wind instrument
- Ⓒ A string instrument
- Ⓓ A brass instrument

Q2 How does air create sound in the harmonica?
- Ⓐ It uses a small motor.
- Ⓑ It creates pressure.
- Ⓒ It vibrates with reeds.
- Ⓓ It stays inside for a long time.

Listening Skills Focusing on Structure Words

✓ **Check-Up** Listen carefully. Write the contractions and the complete sentences.

○ 03-12

1 _____ .... _____ always _____ .
2 _____ .... _____ _____ , _____ ?
3 _____ .... _____ also _____ it in _____ , _____ , and _____ .
4 _____ .... _____ one of the _____ .

• **Exercise 6** •

The Beatles

⬇

- Formed in the late 1950s
- Consisted of John Lennon, Paul McCartney, George Harrison, and Ringo Starr

| club | n | a place for music and dancing |
| glimpse | n | look |

Q1 Who influenced the Beatles?
- Ⓐ Ringo Starr
- Ⓑ Paul McCartney
- Ⓒ John Lennon
- Ⓓ Elvis Presley

Q2 How did the British Invasion affect the United States?
- Ⓐ Fewer Americans listened to British music.
- Ⓑ Americans loved the music.
- Ⓒ England became very popular.
- Ⓓ American music got better.

Listening Skills   Focusing on Structure Words

Check-Up Listen carefully. Write the contractions and the complete sentences.

1 _____ .... _____ for the Beatles.
2 _____ .... Their fans just _____.
3 _____ .... _____ like the Beatles.
4 _____ .... So they _____ the United States.

Exercise 7

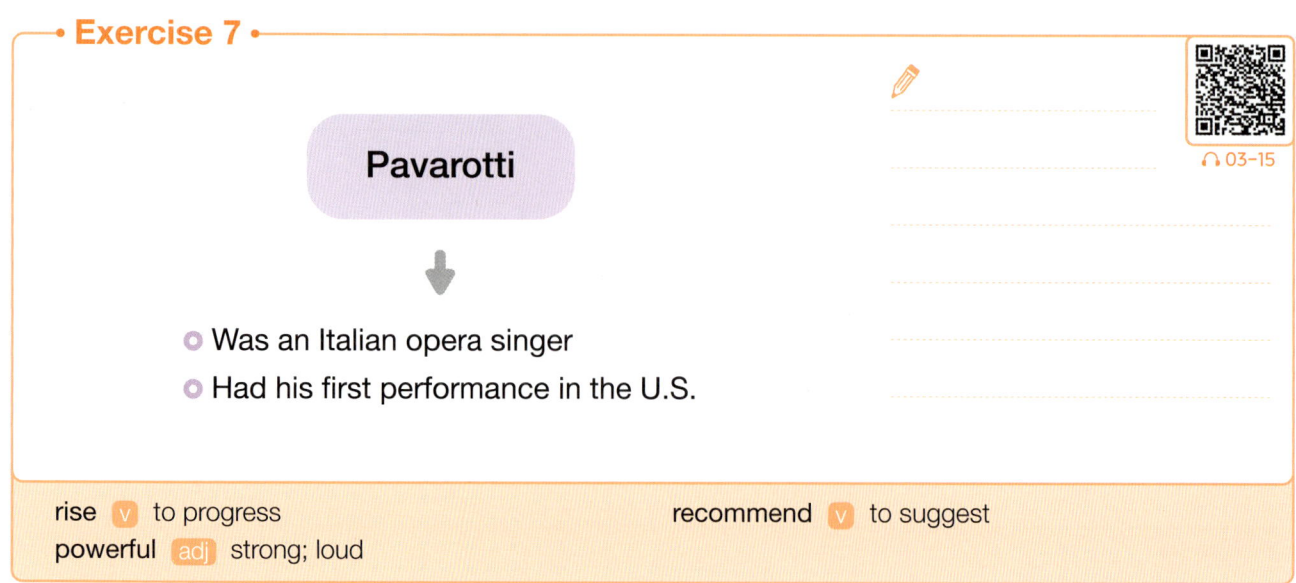

🎧 03-15

- Was an Italian opera singer
- Had his first performance in the U.S.

rise [v] to progress   recommend [v] to suggest
powerful [adj] strong; loud

Q1 What kind of singer was Pavarotti?
- Ⓐ A bass
- Ⓑ An alto
- Ⓒ A tenor
- Ⓓ A baritone

Q2 How did Pavarotti's career in the United States begin?
- Ⓐ He replaced another singer.
- Ⓑ He studied at a music school.
- Ⓒ He became sick.
- Ⓓ He debuted in New York City.

Listening Skills   Focusing on Structure Words

🎧 03-16

✓ **Check-Up**   Listen carefully. Write the contractions and the complete sentences.

1 _____ .... _____ a _____ at singer Luciano Pavarotti.
2 _____ .... The _____ .
3 _____ .... He _____ .
4 _____ .... He _____ any _____ .

• **Exercise 8** •

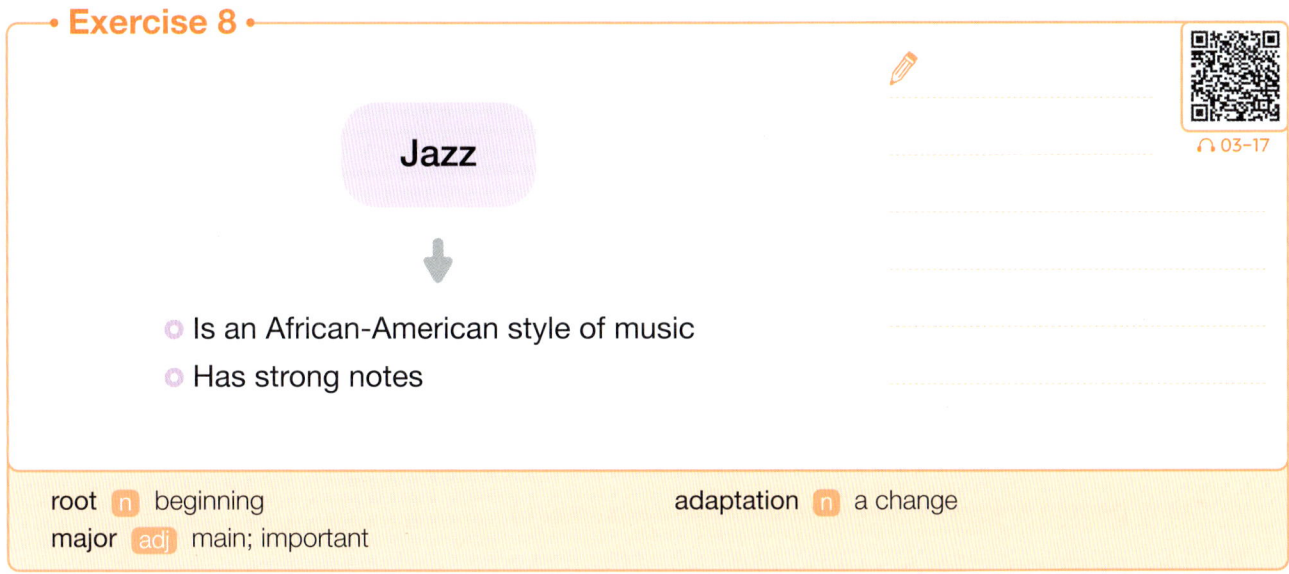

Jazz
- Is an African-American style of music
- Has strong notes

🎧 03-17

| root | n | beginning | adaptation | n | a change |
| major | adj | main; important |

Q1 Who started jazz music?
- Ⓐ Mexicans
- Ⓑ Europeans
- Ⓒ African-Americans
- Ⓓ South Americans

Q2 How is jazz different from other kinds of music?
- Ⓐ It is not very loud.
- Ⓑ It relies on adaptation.
- Ⓒ It did not begin in the United States.
- Ⓓ It does not use the piano.

Listening Skills Focusing on Structure Words

✓ **Check-Up** Listen carefully. Write the contractions and the complete sentences.

🎧 03-18

1 _____ .... _____ _____ .
2 _____ .... The _____ a _____ _____ .
3 _____ .... Actually, _____ _____ .
4 _____ .... _____ what makes jazz _____ _____ to many people.

Chapter ❸ 55

Vocabulary Review

A Circle the words that best complete the sentences.

1 The wonderful sunrise made the clouds turn (brilliant / dull) colors.
2 Some of the (native / major) highways flooded during the storm.
3 The (rise / fall) of the leader made the citizens happy.
4 Many people enjoyed dancing at the new (club / store).
5 The fans struggled for a (variety / glimpse) of the rock star.

B Choose the best words to complete the sentences.

1 She often hums her favorite _____ on the bus.
  A band
  B tune
  C composer
  D word

2 The crowd was a _____ of supporters and protesters.
  A drop
  B creature
  C note
  D mix

3 The strings on the guitar _____ together.
  A break
  B vibrate
  C improvise
  D leave

4 The _____ of his health problem is his poor diet.
  A root
  B danger
  C combination
  D real

5 The couple _____ the new restaurant to us.
  A perfomed
  B decided
  C separated
  D recommended

C Choose the words with the closest meanings to the highlighted words.

1. This family of instruments is important in the orchestra.
   - Ⓐ size
   - Ⓑ group
   - Ⓒ sound
   - Ⓓ prepare

2. The dog's adaptation to the house happened quickly.
   - Ⓐ adjustment
   - Ⓑ experience
   - Ⓒ nervousness
   - Ⓓ protection

3. A powerful storm destroyed the village.
   - Ⓐ weak
   - Ⓑ lightning
   - Ⓒ interesting
   - Ⓓ strong

4. New forms of dance develop every year.
   - Ⓐ sounds
   - Ⓑ styles
   - Ⓒ discoveries
   - Ⓓ relations

5. She found a tiny butterfly in her purse.
   - Ⓐ colorful
   - Ⓑ sick
   - Ⓒ small
   - Ⓓ easy

D Complete the sentences by filling in the blanks with the best words from the list. Change the forms of the words if necessary. Use each word only once.

| document | slim | adaptation | unison | hollow |

1. The reporter wanted to _____ the tragedy.
2. The tree was _____ on the inside.
3. Everyone must sing in _____ for the song to sound good.
4. Jazz musicians use _____ to make the music fresh and new.
5. Sam became very _____ thanks to his diet.

Practice Test

1-4 Listen to part of a lecture in an art class.

Art

1. What is the lecture mainly about?
   - Ⓐ Johann Sebastian Bach
   - Ⓑ A classical music period
   - Ⓒ Some famous composers
   - Ⓓ *Water Music*

2. What musical instrument was common during the Baroque Period?
   - Ⓐ The piano
   - Ⓑ The guitar
   - Ⓒ The trumpet
   - Ⓓ The organ

3. What is the professor's opinion of George Frideric Handel?
   - Ⓐ She enjoys his concertos very much.
   - Ⓑ She thinks Bach was better than him.
   - Ⓒ She likes him the most of all composers.
   - Ⓓ She does not think he was very good.

4. What will the professor probably do next?
   - Ⓐ Show a movie
   - Ⓑ Take a break
   - Ⓒ Listen to some music
   - Ⓓ Ask some questions

CHAPTER

04

Office Hours & Service Encounters
(Chunking)

CHAPTER 4 Office Hours & Service Encounters (Chunking)

Understanding TOEFL Question Types & Listening Skills

1 Question Types — Understanding Function of What Is Said Questions

Understanding Function of What Is Said questions test your understanding of what the speaker states or is asking about. It tests your knowledge of the speaker's intention, not simply the statement the speaker makes.

- **Example Understanding Function of What Is Said Questions**
  - What does the professor imply when he says this: (replay)
  - Why does the student say this: (replay)
  - What is the purpose of the woman's response: (replay)

- **Useful Tips for Your Success**
  - What the speaker says and what the speaker really means may be different.
  - Pay close attention to the overall gist of the dialogue.

Sample Question

🎧 04-01

Student
- Is having trouble with her essay

⬇

Professor
- Suggests an idea

trouble [n] a problem; a difficulty
decide [v] to choose

Q   Why does the student say this: "I'm having trouble with my essay."
   Ⓐ Her essay has many mistakes.
   Ⓑ She cannot finish her essay.
   Ⓒ She has no time to write an essay.
   Ⓓ She cannot think of a topic.

2 Listening Skills Chunking

Chunking is a way to sort and organize information. There are two kinds of signals to mark the end of a thought group: pause and falling pitch. A pause gives listeners time to understand what was said.

Check-Up

▶ Listen to the sentences and put / marks to divide the sentences into chunks.
   1 I'm having trouble with my essay.
   2 I cannot decide on a topic.
   3 I think I'll write about dolphin communication.
   4 Well, why don't you choose a topic you are interested in?

🎧 04-02

• **Exercise 1** •

```
        Student
  ○ Needs a new student ID card
          ↓
        Employee
  ○ Helps him make a new ID card
```

04-03

license n a permit; a certificate
extra adj more; another

Q   Why does the student want a new picture?
    Ⓐ He lost the first one.
    Ⓑ He doesn't like his old picture.
    Ⓒ He needs a new student ID.
    Ⓓ His girlfriend needs one.

Listening Skills **Chunking**

 Check-Up Listen to the sentences and put / marks to divide the sentences into chunks.

1 I need a new student ID card.
2 I also need to see another form of photo ID.
3 Would you like to use your old picture?
4 Um, I look terrible in that one. Can you take a new one?

04-04

• **Exercise 2** •

Student
○ Wants to know about a study abroad program

⬇

Professor
○ Explains what the student wants

sophomore n a second-year student
qualify v to prepare successfully

Q   Why does the professor say this: "Well, you need to have at least a B+ average."

   Ⓐ To see if the student qualifies for her class
   Ⓑ To check if the student can study abroad
   Ⓒ To find out whether the student has good grades
   Ⓓ To question the student about her interests

Listening Skills   **Chunking**

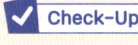 Listen to the sentences and put / marks to divide the sentences into chunks.

1 I want to ask you about the study-abroad program.
2 Well, you need to have at least a B+ average.
3 If that program is full, what is your next choice?
4 Bring it back tomorrow.

• Exercise 3 •

Student
- Has a broken heater in his dorm room

⬇

Employee
- Says that someone can fix it soon

04-07

dorm n a building in which students live on a school campus
pretty adv very; quite

Q Why does the student say this: It's going to get really cold tonight."

Ⓐ To ask when someone is available to help him
Ⓑ To stress the need to fix his problem quickly
Ⓒ To give the woman a weather update
Ⓓ To complain about the recent cold weather

Listening Skills Chunking

 Check-Up Listen to the sentences and put / marks to divide the sentences into chunks.

1 I have a problem with my dorm room.
2 The heater is broken.
3 We can send someone to fix it soon.
4 Hopefully, somebody can visit your room this afternoon.

04-08

66

• **Exercise 4** •

Student
- Wants to decide what to major in

⬇

Professor
- Suggests that she major in literature

| prepare | v | to get ready |
| major in | v | to focus one's studies on a certain subject |

Q Why does the professor say this: "I think you should major in literature."

Ⓐ The student wants the professor to decide.
Ⓑ The professor believes the student wants to teach.
Ⓒ The professor knows the student is a good writer.
Ⓓ The professor does not think the student is good at math.

Listening Skills **Chunking**

✓ **Check-Up** Listen to the sentences and put / marks to divide the sentences into chunks.

1 I cannot decide what to major in, writing or literature.
2 You want to be a teacher, right?
3 You will do a lot of writing as a literature major.
4 I think the literature major prepares students better for teaching.

• **Exercise 5** •

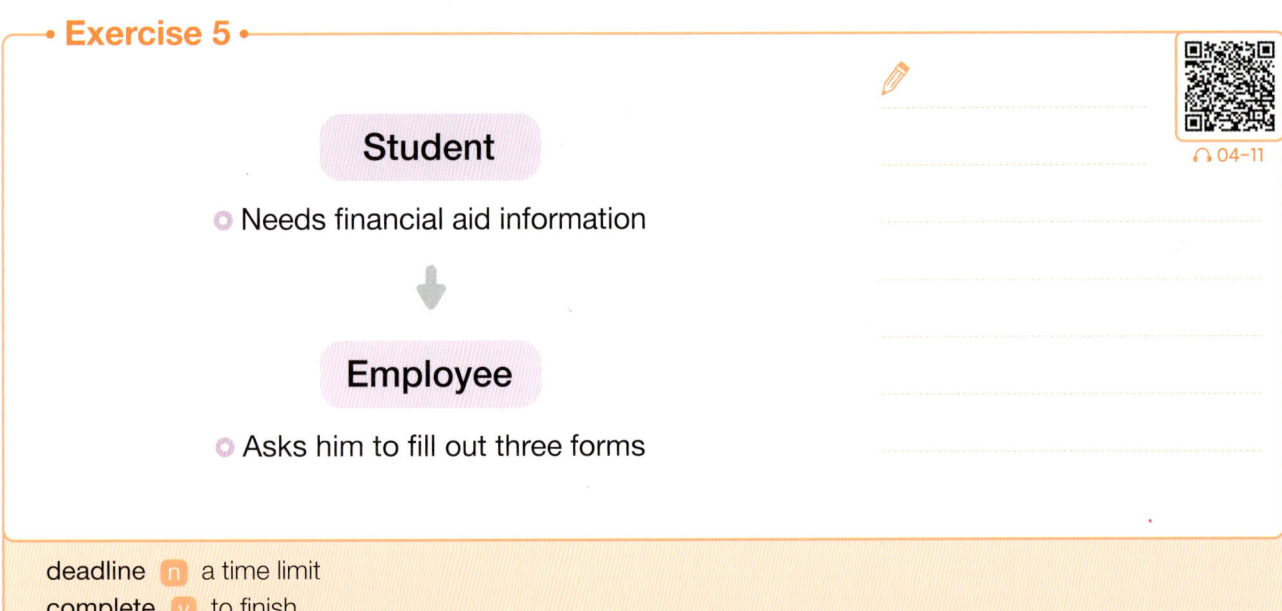

| deadline | n | a time limit |
| complete | v | to finish |

Q1 Why does the employee want the student to bring him some forms?

- Ⓐ The clerk is too busy.
- Ⓑ There is not much time.
- Ⓒ The clerk does not have them.
- Ⓓ The student needs a transcript.

Q2 What is the purpose of the student's response: "Really? That fast?"

- Ⓐ He is surprised some money will arrive soon.
- Ⓑ He thinks a decision will be slow.
- Ⓒ He did not expect a quick result.
- Ⓓ He did not have to wait in line long.

Listening Skills Chunking

 Check-Up Listen to the sentences and put / marks to divide the sentences into chunks.

1 I want to apply for financial aid.
2 Last, you should complete the white one.
3 As soon as you finish, bring them to me.
4 You will receive a response within two weeks.

• **Exercise 6** •

Student
- Wants to talk about her midterm exam

Professor
- Gives some tips for the final exam

04-13

| bulk | n | the majority of something |
| read over | v | to review |

Q1 What does the professor imply when he says this: "That was a good start."
- Ⓐ The student has a lot more to do.
- Ⓑ The student studies online.
- Ⓒ The student should come to class more.
- Ⓓ The student finally started her essay.

Q2 Why does the professor tell the student to study the notes?
- Ⓐ The test questions come from the book.
- Ⓑ They will help her understand the book.
- Ⓒ The test questions come from the notes.
- Ⓓ The student never takes notes in class.

Listening Skills Chunking

04-14

✓ **Check-Up** Listen to the sentences and put / marks to divide the sentences into chunks.

1 In addition, read over the notes each night.
2 I take the bulk of the questions from the class lectures.
3 Well, I didn't do too well on the midterm exam.
4 That should help you do much better on the final exam.

Chapter ❹ 69

• Exercise 7 •

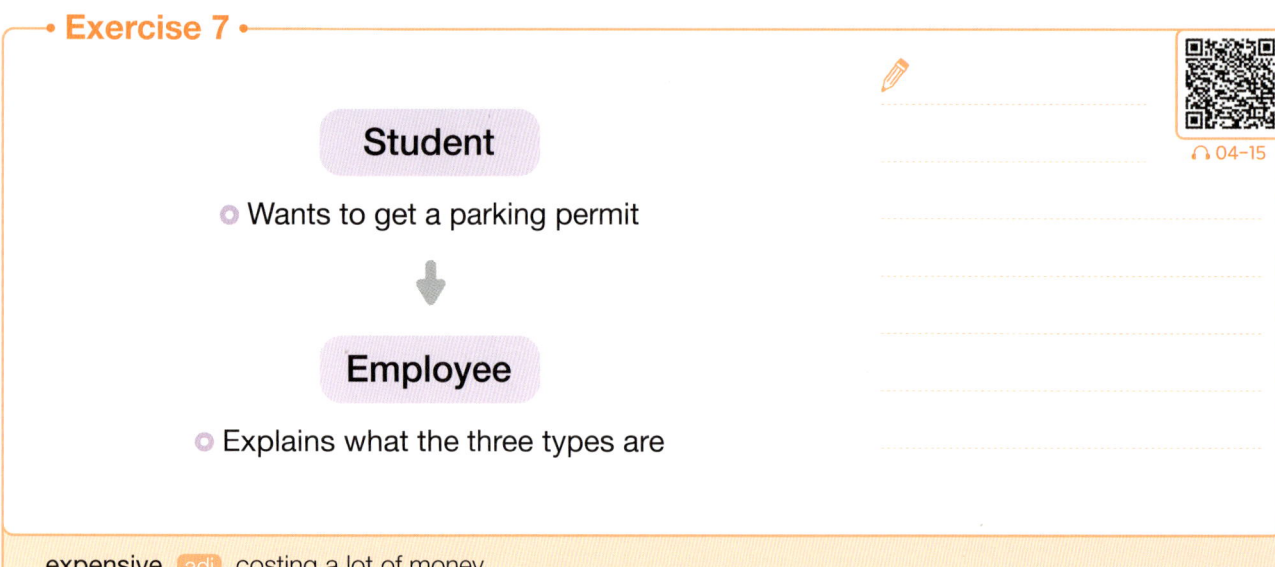

Student
○ Wants to get a parking permit

⬇

Employee
○ Explains what the three types are

expensive adj costing a lot of money

Q1 What does the employee imply when he says this: "Which kind would you like?"
- Ⓐ The student cannot decide on a permit.
- Ⓑ There is more than one type of permit.
- Ⓒ The permits are expensive.
- Ⓓ The student is not patient.

Q2 Why does the student choose the bronze permit?
- Ⓐ It is the cheapest one.
- Ⓑ She can park in every lot.
- Ⓒ The clerk suggests getting it.
- Ⓓ She can park near her department.

Listening Skills **Chunking**

✓ **Check-Up** Listen to the sentences and put / marks to divide the sentences into chunks.

1 I would like to get a student parking permit.
2 There are three types: bronze, silver, and gold.
3 You may park in bronze and silver parking areas.
4 Now I need your license plate number and student ID.

70

Exercise 8

Professor
- Asks the student to help during summer

⬇

Student
- Wants to help the professor

relief n comfort
pick up v to get; to find

Q1 Why does the student say this: "That's a relief."
- Ⓐ He is happy about the class.
- Ⓑ He thought he was in trouble.
- Ⓒ He is glad he got a good grade.
- Ⓓ He is thankful there is no homework.

Q2 Why does the professor want to see the student the next day?
- Ⓐ To begin working with the student
- Ⓑ To check on the student's progress
- Ⓒ To discuss a job some more
- Ⓓ To have the student work at the library

Listening Skills   Chunking

✓ **Check-Up**   Listen to the sentences and put / marks to divide the sentences into chunks.

1 I want to know your plans for summer.
2 I'll be working on my new book all summer.
3 Oh, just pick up books at the library for me.
4 I'm attending summer school.

Vocabulary Review

A Circle the words that best complete the sentences.

1 The student got into (class / **trouble**) for cheating.
2 David had to pay (**extra** / free) for the expensive bike.
3 The college senior (**majored in** / desired to) sociology.
4 It takes many months to (locate / **prepare**) for the exam.
5 Matt needs to buy a new parking (**permit** / plan) for his car.

B Choose the best words to complete the sentences.

1 Their _____ exam is on the day after Christmas.
   A present
   B complete
   C response
   D final

2 The editor wants to _____ her article.
   A read over
   B begin with
   C cram for
   D turn on

3 Many workers receive very low _____.
   A side
   B job
   C pay
   D money

4 Jimmy had to fill out many _____.
   A forms
   B information
   C attentions
   D decisions

5 His family is having some _____ problems.
   A broken
   B marked
   C financial
   D high

C Choose the words with the closest meanings to the highlighted words.

1 Suzy did not buy the expensive watch.
   - Ⓐ costly
   - Ⓑ new
   - Ⓒ stylish
   - Ⓓ famous

2 The writer's deadline is next Friday at noon.
   - Ⓐ meeting
   - Ⓑ limit
   - Ⓒ appointment
   - Ⓓ decision

3 Mr. Johnson does not qualify for the job.
   - Ⓐ find
   - Ⓑ look
   - Ⓒ ask
   - Ⓓ fit

4 Signs mark the rooms where students should go for their exams.
   - Ⓐ draw
   - Ⓑ remove
   - Ⓒ show
   - Ⓓ cancel

5 The policeman asked the woman to step into the building.
   - Ⓐ join
   - Ⓑ go
   - Ⓒ mean
   - Ⓓ respond

D Complete the sentences by filling in the blanks with the best words from the list. Change the forms of the words if necessary. Use each word only once.

> bulk   deadline   abroad   heater   turn on

1 The _____ of the test comes from the textbook.
2 Please _____ the lights so that we can see better.
3 Use the _____ in order to make the room warm.
4 We need to hurry up to meet the _____.
5 The family lived _____ for twelve years.

Practice Test

1-3 Listen to part of a conversation between a student and a professor.

1. Why does the professor want to see the student?
    - Ⓐ To find out why he did not do his report
    - Ⓑ To give him a letter of recommendation
    - Ⓒ To ask him why he missed class
    - Ⓓ To discuss a job opportunity

2. What will the student probably do next?
    - Ⓐ Go to the hospital
    - Ⓑ Go to the library
    - Ⓒ Go to an interview
    - Ⓓ Go to class

3. Why does the professor say this: "Yes, I heard a bad bug was going around."
    - Ⓐ The professor dislikes insects.
    - Ⓑ Many students were sick.
    - Ⓒ There are bugs in the office.
    - Ⓓ The professor heard a noise.

CHAPTER 05

Office Hours & Service Encounters
(Pitch and Intonation)

Office Hours & Service Encounters (Pitch and Intonation)

Understanding TOEFL Question Types & Listening Skills

1 Question Types — Understanding Speaker's Attitude Questions

Understanding Speaker's Attitude questions test how well you understand the attitude or opinion of the speaker. They are usually concerned with how the speaker feels or why the speaker is expressing him or herself in a certain way.

- **Example Understanding Speaker's Attitude Questions**
  - What can be inferred about the student?
  - What does the woman mean when she says this: (replay)
  - What can be inferred about the student when he says this: (replay)

- **Useful Tips for your Success**
  - Pay attention to the speaker's tone of voice.
  - Pay attention to the speaker's general attitude during the talk.

Sample Question

Student
- Wants to take a scuba diving class

↓

Employee
- Says what the student should do

🎧 05-01

register _v_ to sign up
fill out _v_ to complete

Q What can be inferred about the student when he says this: "Wow, fifty, huh . . . ?"

Ⓐ He is disappointed.
Ⓑ He is happy.
Ⓒ He is sad.
Ⓓ He is surprised.

2 Listening Skills — Pitch and Intonation

Pitch and intonation are the ways that your voice rises and falls as you speak. A fall in pitch helps listeners recognize the end of a thought group. However, a question may end with rising or falling pitch.

Check-Up

▶ Listen to the following dialogue and underline the high-pitched words.

Student: Do you take checks?
Employee: Sure. Is it from a local bank?
Student: Yes. When is the first class?
Employee: Next Wednesday at the student union pool at 2 PM.

🎧 05-02

Chapter ❺ 79

• **Exercise 1** •

Professor
o Asks what happened to the student

Student
o Misunderstood about the class

| miss | v | not to come or attend |
| fill in | v | to explain |

Q What is the professor's attitude toward the student?

Ⓐ He does not care about her.
Ⓑ He is upset with her.
Ⓒ He is supportive of her.
Ⓓ He is disappointed in her.

Listening Skills Pitch and Intonation

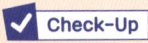 Listen to the following dialogue and underline the high-pitched words.

Professor: Why did you miss class last week?
Student: I thought you canceled it.
Professor: No. We had class.
Student: I'm sorry, Professor Green.

• **Exercise 2** •

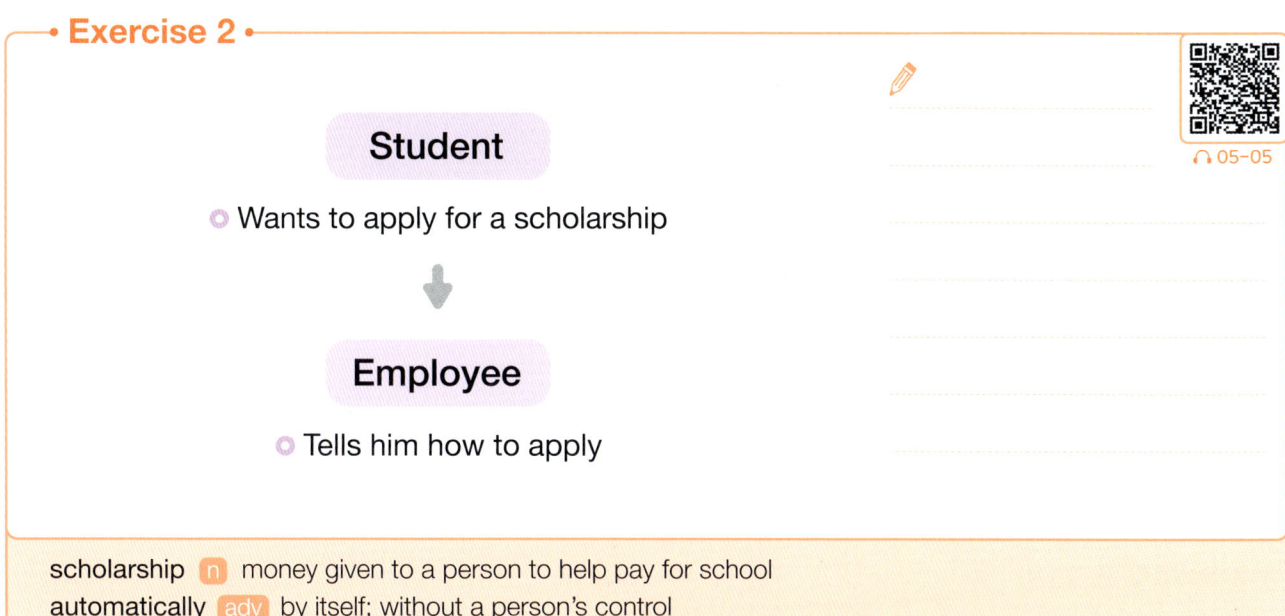

scholarship n money given to a person to help pay for school
automatically adv by itself; without a person's control

Q What can be inferred about the student?
    Ⓐ He is upset.
    Ⓑ He is relieved.
    Ⓒ He is in a difficult position.
    Ⓓ He does not like computers.

Listening Skills Pitch and Intonation

 Check-Up Listen to the following dialogue and underline the high-pitched words.

Employee: The computer will match your records with the scholarships.
Student: What does that mean?
Employee: That means it automatically applies for you.
Student: Wow. That's great!

Chapter ❺ 81

• Exercise 3 •

Professor
- Wants to tell the student about winning first prize

⬇

Student
- Is congratulated on winning

contest n a competition
forget v not to remember

Q What does the student mean when she says this: "I can't believe it."

Ⓐ She is shocked.
Ⓑ She is confused.
Ⓒ She is stressed.
Ⓓ She is disappointed.

Listening Skills Pitch and Intonation

 Check-Up Listen to the following dialogue and underline the high-pitched words.

Student: Really? How do you know?
Professor: I was one of the judges.
Student: Oh, that's wonderful.
Professor: Congratulations. We will publish it in the university magazine, too.

• **Exercise 4** •

Student
- Cannot work a weekend shift

⬇

Librarian
- Says she needs to find a substitute worker

shift n a period of time when a person works at a job
substitute n a person who does something in place of another

Q   What is the librarian's attitude toward the student?
   Ⓐ She is surprised by his comments.
   Ⓑ She is concerned about his family.
   Ⓒ She is happy with his actions.
   Ⓓ She is displeased with him.

Listening Skills   Pitch and Intonation

✓ Check-Up   Listen to the following dialogue and underline the high-pitched words.

Student: Yes, ma'am. It's about my shift this weekend.
Librarian: Do you mean the shift you work on Saturday evening?
Student: Yes, that's correct.
Librarian: So . . . what about it?

Chapter ❺ 83

• **Exercise 5** •

Student
o Wants to know how his paper is

⬇

Professor
o Gave the student an A-

second n a short time or moment
chance n an opportunity

Q1 What can be inferred about the professor when she says this: "It looks like you spent a lot of time on it."

    Ⓐ She thinks the student is lying.
    Ⓑ She does not understand the student.
    Ⓒ She believes the student worked hard.
    Ⓓ She hopes the student will do better.

Q2 What does the student mean when he says this: "Not an A."

    Ⓐ He is surprised by his grade.
    Ⓑ He did not study enough.
    Ⓒ He does not believe the professor.
    Ⓓ He hopes to get an A the next time.

Listening Skills Pitch and Intonation

 **Check-Up** Listen to the following dialogue and underline the high-pitched words.

Student: By the way, what grade did I get?
Professor: Let me see. I have it right here . . . Yes, an A–.
Student: An A–! Are you sure?
Professor: Yes. Why? What did you expect?

• Exercise 6 •

Student
○ Wants to start a new club

Employee
○ Tells the student how to do that

05-13

assist v to help
get in shape phr to be in good physical condition

Q1 What is the employee's attitude toward the student?
- Ⓐ He is helpful to her.
- Ⓑ He is concerned about her.
- Ⓒ He is uninterested in her.
- Ⓓ He is upset with her.

Q2 What can be inferred about the student?
- Ⓐ She does not have much free time.
- Ⓑ She enjoys doing exercise.
- Ⓒ She is already a member of a club.
- Ⓓ She is a first-year student.

Listening Skills | Pitch and Intonation

 Check-Up Listen to the following dialogue and underline the high-pitched words.

05-14

Student: Oh, no. I want to start my own club.
Employee: I see. What kind of club?
Student: I want to start a hiking club.
Employee: Interesting. We haven't had a hiking club here in years.

Chapter ❺ 85

• **Exercise 7** •

Student
○ Wants to join a history class

↓

Professor
○ Permits the student to take the class

🎧 05-15

join v to enter   show up v to come or attend
advanced adj developed; difficult

Q1 What can be inferred about the professor when she says this: "I'll see what I can do."
- Ⓐ She wants to help the student.
- Ⓑ She expects the student to try hard.
- Ⓒ She is unable to see anything.
- Ⓓ She has found a solution.

Q2 What can be inferred about the student?
- Ⓐ He has taken class with the professor before.
- Ⓑ He is very shy around the professor.
- Ⓒ He is thankful to the professor.
- Ⓓ He thinks the professor is a good teacher.

Listening Skills | Pitch and Intonation

✓ Check-Up Listen to the following dialogue and underline the high-pitched words.

Student: Excuse me, Professor Lansing. Can I speak with you?

Professor: Sure, I have a minute or two.

Student: I was hoping I could join your history class.

Professor: Are you a history major?

🎧 05-16

• **Exercise 8** •

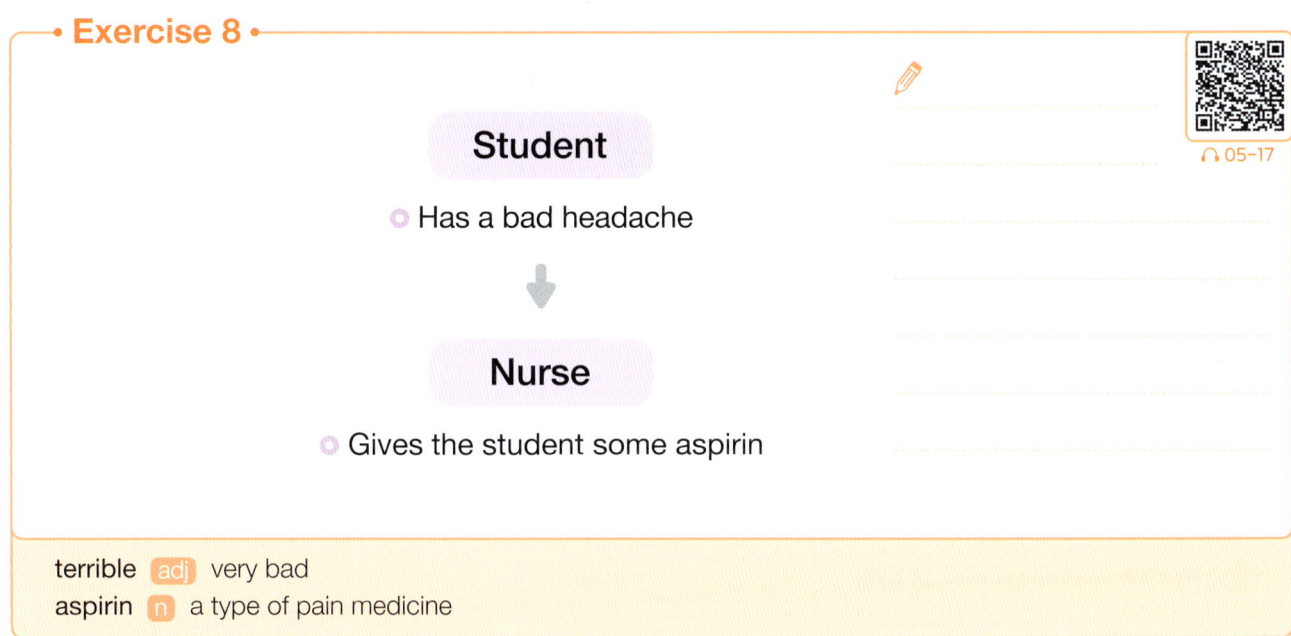

Student
○ Has a bad headache

⬇

Nurse
○ Gives the student some aspirin

terrible adj very bad
aspirin n a type of pain medicine

Q1 What is the nurse's attitude toward the student?
  Ⓐ She is happy to help him.
  Ⓑ She thinks he should go to the hospital.
  Ⓒ She is not concerned about him.
  Ⓓ She is too busy to help him.

Q2 What can be inferred about the nurse when she says this: "You should let the doctor look at you."
  Ⓐ She thinks the student is not sick.
  Ⓑ She hopes the student returns later.
  Ⓒ She does not want to take any chances.
  Ⓓ She believes aspirin will cure the student.

Listening Skills Pitch and Intonation

✓ Check-Up Listen to the following dialogue and underline the high-pitched words.

Student: I feel terrible. I was hoping to get some medicine before the test.
Nurse: Do you have a fever?
Student: No. Just a bad headache.
Nurse: Here is some aspirin. That should help.

Vocabulary Review

A Circle the words that best complete the sentences.

1 Alice works the morning (shift / hour) at her job.
2 Jason won a (scholarship / leadership) to go to college.
3 You must (fill in / take in) your name on the application.
4 How about taking a walk for a (second / time)?
5 Brooke was shocked at her science (grade / class).

B Choose the best words to complete the sentences.

1 The new course is an _____ math class.
   - Ⓐ advanced
   - Ⓑ able
   - Ⓒ applying
   - Ⓓ automatical

2 Take some _____ for your headache.
   - Ⓐ money
   - Ⓑ fever
   - Ⓒ list
   - Ⓓ aspirin

3 Avery wants another _____ to try out for the football team.
   - Ⓐ research
   - Ⓑ substitute
   - Ⓒ chance
   - Ⓓ judge

4 He often _____ students who need help in the class.
   - Ⓐ assists
   - Ⓑ changes
   - Ⓒ cares
   - Ⓓ tries

5 Students from another school will _____ the camp.
   - Ⓐ join
   - Ⓑ pay
   - Ⓒ appreciate
   - Ⓓ tear

C Choose the words with the closest meanings to the highlighted words.

1 His mother felt terrible about the dinner.
- Ⓐ bad
- Ⓑ full
- Ⓒ delicious
- Ⓓ wonderful

2 Please fill out this form and sign it at the bottom.
- Ⓐ card
- Ⓑ paper
- Ⓒ test
- Ⓓ sign

3 My brother always assists me with my homework.
- Ⓐ helps
- Ⓑ gives
- Ⓒ needs
- Ⓓ ends

4 All applicants must register in the main office.
- Ⓐ sign up
- Ⓑ find
- Ⓒ graduate
- Ⓓ meet

5 Nobody showed up for the speech.
- Ⓐ clapped
- Ⓑ came
- Ⓒ reminded
- Ⓓ sat down

D Complete the sentences by filling in the blanks with the best words from the list. Change the forms of the words if necessary. Use each word only once.

> individual   automatically   substitute   miss   fill out

1 He might _____ the first week of class.
2 Find a _____ if you do not have time to work tonight.
3 The computer _____ connects to our network.
4 Group tickets are often cheaper than _____ tickets.
5 People must _____ many forms to get a loan.

Practice Test

1-3 Listen to part of a conversation between a student and a student services center employee.

05-19

1 Why does the student visit the student services center?
   - Ⓐ To get a parking sticker
   - Ⓑ To pick up her car
   - Ⓒ To pay for a parking ticket
   - Ⓓ To apply for a job

2 What can be inferred about the student?
   - Ⓐ She has little cash.
   - Ⓑ She is a bad driver.
   - Ⓒ She does not like cars.
   - Ⓓ She seldom goes to class.

3 What does the employee imply when he says this: "You know, you're pretty lucky."
   - Ⓐ The student's fine is small.
   - Ⓑ The student still has her car.
   - Ⓒ The student has a lot of money.
   - Ⓓ The student has a local bank account.

CHAPTER 06

Education
(Signal Words and Phrases)

CHAPTER 6 Education (Signal Words and Phrases)

Understanding TOEFL Question Types & Listening Skills

1 Question Types Understanding Organization Questions

Understanding Organization questions check how well you understanding the overall organization and relationship between ideas in the passage. Some questions test general understanding, and others test more detailed understanding.

● **Example Understanding Organization Questions**
  ▸ How does the professor organize the information about X?
  ▸ How is the discussion organized?
  ▸ Why does the professor mention X?

● **Useful Tips for your Success**
  ▸ Listen carefully for transitions that indicate a sequence.
  ▸ Pay attention to comparisons made by the professor.

Sample Question

```
        Rote Learning
        ↙         ↘
    Method        Alphabet
○ Repeating     ○ An example of rote
  something       learning
  enough times
  to learn it
```

memorization n the act of remembering something exactly
alphabet n all the letters in a written language
repeat v to say something again

Q Why does the professor mention the alphabet?
   Ⓐ To ask the students to recite it
   Ⓑ To say it is an example of rote learning
   Ⓒ To state that learning it is important
   Ⓓ To show that he knows it well

2 Listening Skills — Signal Words and Phrases

Signal words and phrases are words that provide clues in a lecture. Their purpose is to help you organize information and recognize key ideas. Signal words and phrases also point to concept shifts in the passage.

Check-Up

▶ Listen carefully and fill in the blanks.

1 _____ _____ learning methods.
2 _____, it involves learning through memorization.

🎧 06-02

Chapter 6   95

Exercise 1

Language Education in Europe

- Students begin from a young age.
- English or French is required.

rare *adj* not usual
mandatory *adj* required

Q How is the discussion organized?

Ⓐ The professor discusses English and French.
Ⓑ The professor compares language education in two places.
Ⓒ The professor only discusses language education in Europe.
Ⓓ The professor talks about her language experiences.

Listening Skills | **Signal Words and Phrases**

✓ **Check-Up** Listen carefully and fill in the blanks.

1 _____ _____, in the U.S., this is rare.

2 _____ _____ _____, in Europe, languages like English and French are required courses through high school.

96

• **Exercise 2** •

Homeschooling

⬇

- Good Point: learn more from parents
- Bad Point: can't interact with others

🎧 06-05

participate v to take part in; to do
interact v to connect

Q Why does the professor mention clubs and sports?

Ⓐ To question homeschooling
Ⓑ To support an expert's argument
Ⓒ To explain that they are necessary
Ⓓ To note they are not important

Listening Skills   Signal Words and Phrases

✓ **Check-Up**   Listen carefully and fill in the blanks.

1 _____ _____ , they think their children learn more.
2 _____ _____ _____ a couple of reasons why.

🎧 06-06

• Exercise 3 •

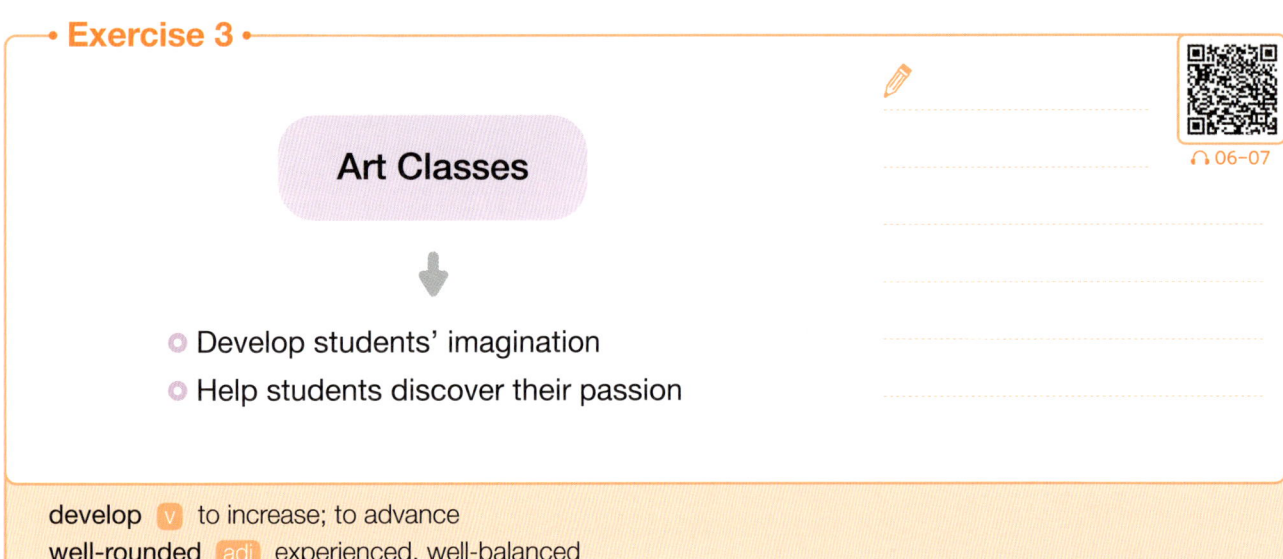

Art Classes

- Develop students' imagination
- Help students discover their passion

develop v to increase; to advance
well-rounded adj experienced, well-balanced

Q Why does the professor mention students' imaginations?

Ⓐ To discuss a benefit of fine arts classes
Ⓑ To note that students do not develop it
Ⓒ To explain how science classes are not enough
Ⓓ To question what teachers do in class

Listening Skills Signal Words and Phrases

✓ **Check-Up** Listen carefully and fill in the blanks.

1 _____ _____, they help develop students' imaginations.

2 Now, _____ _____ _____ _____ _____ some examples of fine arts classes.

• **Exercise 4** •

Kindergarten

⬇

○ Helps students adjust to school life
○ Allows to students make lots of new friends

06-09

adjust v to change
introduction n a start; a beginning

Q How is the discussion organized?

Ⓐ The professor compares kindergarten and middle school.
Ⓑ The professor describes some benefits of kindergarten.
Ⓒ The professor provides different opinions about kindergarten.
Ⓓ The professor talks about drawing and painting.

Listening Skills Signal Words and Phrases

✓ **Check-Up** Listen carefully and fill in the blanks.

1 _____ _____ _____, of course, students make lots of new friends.

2 _____ _____ _____ _____ kindergarten is a great way for children to begin their educations.

06-10

Chapter ❻ 99

• **Exercise 5** •

Online Learning

⬇

○ Students and teacher are in different locations.
○ There are several types of online programs.

compare v to show a similarity or difference between two things
assignment n work a student must do
lecture v to teach a class

Q1 Why does the professor discuss traditional learning?
- Ⓐ To explain her support for it
- Ⓑ To say it is no longer useful
- Ⓒ To point out some problems with it
- Ⓓ To explain how it happens

Q2 How does the professor organize the information about online learning?
- Ⓐ By describing several different types of it
- Ⓑ By talking about the online learning she prefers
- Ⓒ By discussing important events in chronological order
- Ⓓ By showing slides and then talking about them

Listening Skills Signal Words and Phrases

✓ **Check-Up** Listen carefully and fill in the blanks.

1 Now, uh, _____ traditional classes so that you can understand it.

2 _____, the teacher's lecture is recorded.

3 _____, they do various assignments and submit them.

• **Exercise 6** •

Prenatal Education

⬇

- Talking to the baby in the mother's belly
- Reading books to the baby
- Playing music

prenatal adj relating to the time before birth
comfort v to relax or ease
naturally adv normally; freely

Q1 Why does the professor mention books?
- Ⓐ To note that reading to babies does little
- Ⓑ To suggest that babies can read at an early age
- Ⓒ To refer the students to some new information
- Ⓓ To show a common form of prenatal education

Q2 How does the professor organize the information about prenatal education?
- Ⓐ He shows pictures as he talks.
- Ⓑ He uses chronological order.
- Ⓒ He compares it with art.
- Ⓓ He gives many examples of it.

Listening Skills Signal Words and Phrases

Check-Up Listen carefully and fill in the blanks.

1. _____ early education.
2. _____. Many parents play music for their unborn babies.
3. _____, songs help develop trust between the mother and her baby.

• **Exercise 7** •

Education for Physically Disabled People

↓

- Teaching Braille to the blind
- Teaching sign language to the deaf

accident [n] an event that may cause a problem
disabled [adj] handicapped

Q1 Why does the professor mention accidents?
- Ⓐ To show how the disabled learn
- Ⓑ To note how people may become disabled
- Ⓒ To explain why they are dangerous
- Ⓓ To have the students think about them

Q2 How does the professor organize the discussion?
- Ⓐ She discusses one type of disability.
- Ⓑ She talks about how the blind and the deaf learn.
- Ⓒ She presents new ideas for disabled education.
- Ⓓ She explains how Braille was created.

Listening Skills Signal Words and Phrases

✓ **Check-Up** Listen carefully and fill in the blanks.

1 _____ this happens. Some people are born that way.
2 _____ the deaf?
3 _____, people form words with their fingers and hands.

Exercise 8

One-Room Schools

- Existed in rural places
- All students learned in the same room

rural *adj* relating to the countryside
focus on *v* to pay close attention to

Q1 Why does the professor mention his school?
- Ⓐ To say it is a good school
- Ⓑ To note how many students go there
- Ⓒ To talk about its size
- Ⓓ To state the number of buildings it has

Q2 Why does the professor discuss one-room schools?
- Ⓐ To state that students could not learn well in them
- Ⓑ To say how students learned in them
- Ⓒ To point out why people studied at them
- Ⓓ To argue in favor of building more of them today

Listening Skills | Signal Words and Phrases

✓ **Check-Up** Listen carefully and fill in the blanks.

1. _____ _____ _____ _____ in the past, one-room schools existed?
2. _____, there was just one teacher.
3. _____ _____, older students were expected to help younger ones.

Vocabulary Review

A Circle the words that best complete the sentences.

1 The boys (participated / educated) in the class.
2 It does not (matter / care) what time you finish.
3 The teacher (excites / expects) the students to help her.
4 Children should (interact / avoid) with the teacher more.
5 The best students these days are (various / well-rounded) individuals.

B Choose the best words to complete the sentences.

1 _____ students have special needs in the classroom.
   Ⓐ Average
   Ⓑ Disabled
   Ⓒ Forgetful
   Ⓓ Amazing

2 There are many small schools in _____ areas these days.
   Ⓐ rural
   Ⓑ online
   Ⓒ popular
   Ⓓ learning

3 That animal _____ sleeps all day long.
   Ⓐ early
   Ⓑ naturally
   Ⓒ physically
   Ⓓ accidentally

4 Her father was in a car _____ on his way to work.
   Ⓐ speed
   Ⓑ sale
   Ⓒ price
   Ⓓ accident

5 The teacher gave a(n) _____ to the class on Friday.
   Ⓐ introduction
   Ⓑ campus
   Ⓒ subject
   Ⓓ experience

C Choose the words with the closest meanings to the highlighted words.

1 Please submit your homework by tomorrow morning.
   - Ⓐ check
   - Ⓑ finish
   - Ⓒ turn in
   - Ⓓ grade

2 Reading helps develop knowledge.
   - Ⓐ complete
   - Ⓑ erase
   - Ⓒ find
   - Ⓓ increase

3 The teacher uses a popular learning method.
   - Ⓐ style
   - Ⓑ example
   - Ⓒ speech
   - Ⓓ lecture

4 Comfort is very important on long trips.
   - Ⓐ Ease
   - Ⓑ Fuel
   - Ⓒ Sense
   - Ⓓ Mind

5 Please repeat that comment one more time.
   - Ⓐ compare
   - Ⓑ consider
   - Ⓒ say again
   - Ⓓ understand

D Complete the sentences by filling in the blanks with the best words from the list. Change the forms of the words if necessary. Use each word only once.

| adjust | form | gesture | traditional | prenatal |

1 They will have a _____ meal for Thanksgiving.
2 It is difficult to _____ to a new school.
3 The children are able to _____ words with letters.
4 _____ education is becoming very popular.
5 He used a _____ to help her park the car.

Practice Test

1-4 Listen to part of a lecture in an education class.

Education

1 What is the main topic of the lecture?

- Ⓐ The benefits of school
- Ⓑ The importance of homework
- Ⓒ Why students get burned out
- Ⓓ Changes in teaching methods

2 What is the professor's attitude toward homework?

- Ⓐ It is useless.
- Ⓑ It is good for parents.
- Ⓒ It develops character.
- Ⓓ It is too difficult.

3 How does the professor organize the discussion?

- Ⓐ He refers to the book.
- Ⓑ He discusses everyday situations.
- Ⓒ He looks into the future.
- Ⓓ He uses points written on the chalkboard.

4 Are the following advantages or disadvantages of homework?
Click in the correct box for each sentence.

	Advantage	Disadvantage
1 Students get burned out.		
2 Students become independent.		
3 Parents can do all of the homework.		
4 Students learn self-discipline.		

CHAPTER

07

Nutrition
(Distinguishing Consonants)

CHAPTER 7 Nutrition (Distinguishing Consonants)

Understanding TOEFL Question Types & Listening Skills

1 Question Types — Connecting Content Questions

Connecting Content questions test your ability to relate ideas in the passage. The ideas may be obvious or implied. You may be asked to fill in a chart which classifies items in categories.

- **Example Connecting Content Questions**
  - What can be inferred about X?
  - What does the professor imply about X?
  - What is the likely outcome of doing procedure X before procedure Y?
  - Are the following characteristics of X or Y?
  Click in the correct box for each sentence.

- **Useful Tips for your Success**
  - Pay close attention to how you organize your notes.
  - Identify terms and details as well as definitions.

Sample Question

Vitamins
⬇
- Vitamin C from fruits
- Vitamin A from vegetables

🎧 07-01

important *adj* necessary
weak *adj* not strong

Q Do the following foods contain vitamin A or vitamin C?

	Vitamin A	Vitamin C
1 Oranges		
2 Green vegetables		
3 Tangerines		
4 Lettuce		

2 Listening Skills — Distinguishing Consonants

A consonant is a sound such as *p*, *f*, *n*, and *t*. It is import to distinguish consonants like *r* from *l*, *v* from *w*, and *f* from *p* in passages.

Check-Up

▶ Listen carefully and then circle the words you hear.

1 very - berry   2 peel - feel

3 we - vee   4 will - win

🎧 07-02

Chapter 7   111

• **Exercise 1** •

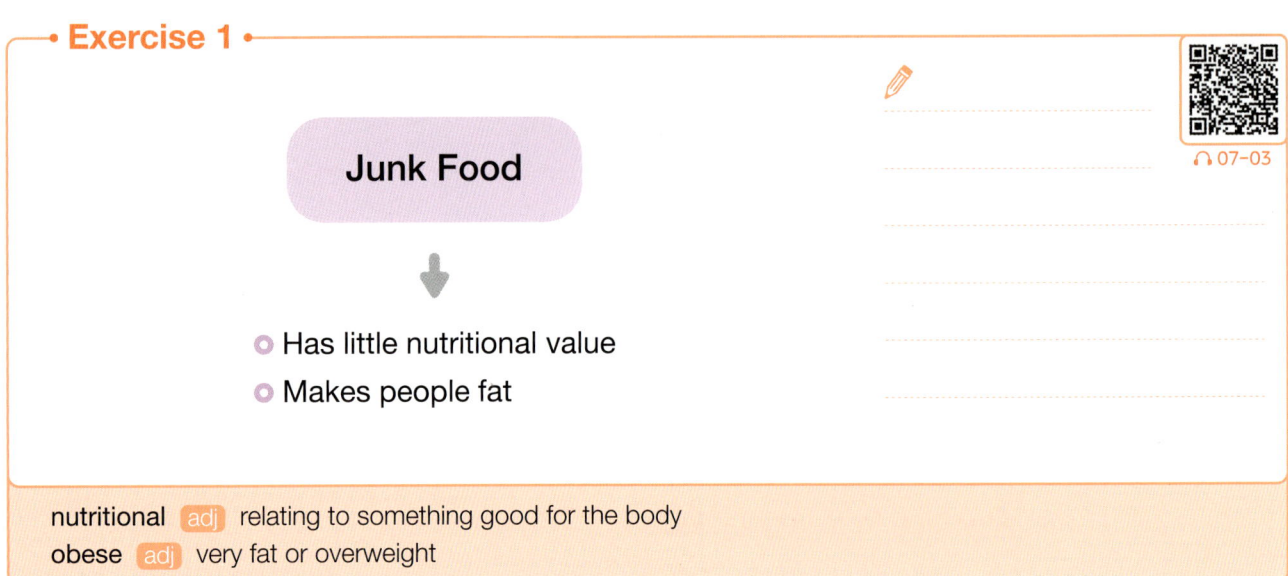

🎧 07-03

| nutritional | adj | relating to something good for the body |
| obese | adj | very fat or overweight |

Q What does the professor imply about junk food?

- Ⓐ It is delicious.
- Ⓑ It is good for people.
- Ⓒ It should be avoided.
- Ⓓ It is high in vitamins.

Listening Skills | **Distinguishing Consonants**

 Listen carefully and then circle the words you hear.

1 lot - not   2 know - low
3 fat - pat   4 tank - thank

🎧 07-04

• **Exercise 2** •

Protein

⬇

o Heals human body's tissues
o Gives energy to people

07-05

source n the start of something; a root

Q The professor mentions many foods. Check the ones which are good sources of protein.

	High in Protein
1 Cheese	
2 Tomatoes	
3 Tofu	
4 Meat	

Listening Skills **Distinguishing Consonants**

 Listen carefully and then circle the words you hear.

1 need - lead   2 food - good
3 hear - heal   4 ten - tell

07-06

Chapter 7   113

• **Exercise 3** •

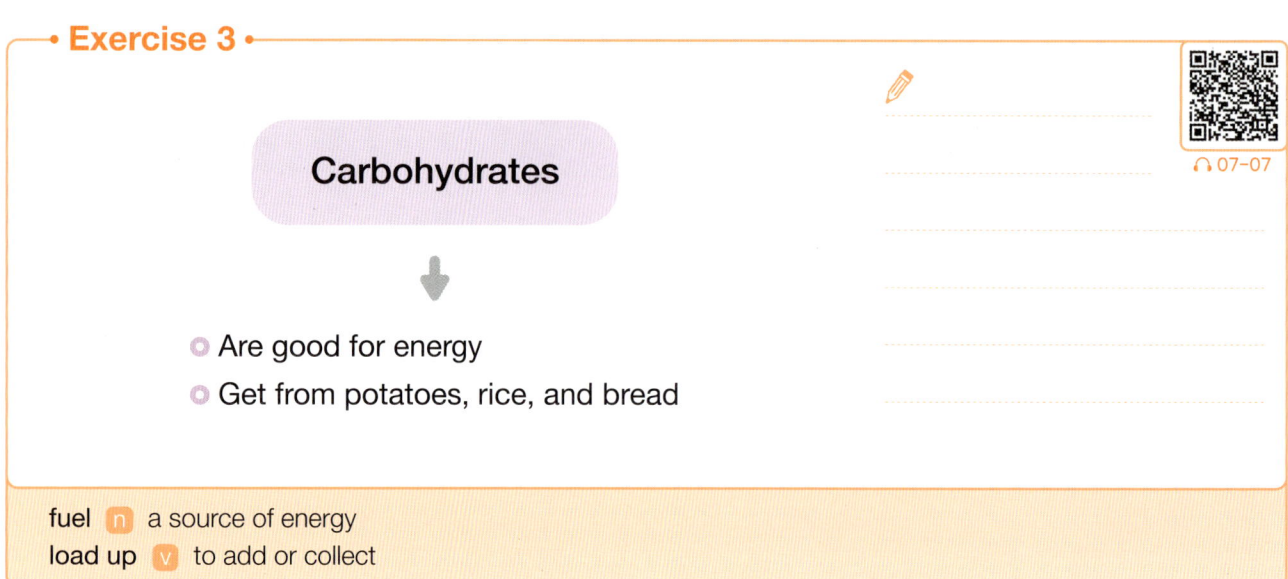

Carbohydrates

- Are good for energy
- Get from potatoes, rice, and bread

fuel n a source of energy
load up v to add or collect

Q What can be inferred about athletes?

Ⓐ They are good at sports.
Ⓑ They need carbohydrates to be successful.
Ⓒ They enjoy Italian food.
Ⓓ They do not need rice or bread.

Listening Skills Distinguishing Consonants

 **Check-Up** Listen carefully and then circle the words you hear.

1 vest - best   **2** load - road
3 rice - lice   **4** carve - carb

• **Exercise 4** •

Potassium
⬇
○ Helps with digestion
○ Allows the muscles to work

nutrient n a substance that helps plants and animals to grow
allow v to let or help

Q What will probably happen if a person does not get enough potassium?

Ⓐ The person might have poor digestion.
Ⓑ The person might have no body fluids.
Ⓒ The person might lose energy.
Ⓓ The person might not see well.

Listening Skills Distinguishing Consonants

✓ **Check-Up** Listen carefully and then circle the words you hear.

1 lot - not   2 fine - file
3 lice - nice   4 knife - life

• **Exercise 5** •

 07-11

Supplements

- Provide proper amounts of vitamins and minerals
- Make healthier, manage weight, and prevent disease

poorly adv badly; not well
consume v to eat or drink
moderation n the act of doing something a medium amount

Q1 What is the likely outcome of a person taking multivitamins?
  Ⓐ The person will gain weight.
  Ⓑ The person will stop eating a lot of junk food.
  Ⓒ The person will be able to drink soda.
  Ⓓ The person will improve in health.

Q2 Are the following advantages or disadvantages of taking supplements?

	Advantage	Disadvantage
1 Can avoid certain diseases		
2 Take large amounts of them		
3 Take them in moderation		
4 Can manage weight better		

Listening Skills Distinguishing Consonants

 07-12

✓ **Check-Up** Listen carefully and then circle the words you hear.

1 fast - past   2 lots - rots
3 poor - for   4 pine - fine

• **Exercise 6** •

Eight Foods for Health

- Spinach
- Tomatoes
- Blueberries
- Walnuts
- Yogurt
- Carrots
- Beans
- Oats

disease [n] a sickness	increase [v] to add to or develop
vision [n] the ability to see	

Q1 What can be inferred about blackberries?
- Ⓐ They can be helpful to students.
- Ⓑ They can cure blindness.
- Ⓒ They can reduce heart problems.
- Ⓓ They can help with breathing.

Q2 What are the benefits of the following foods?

	Tomatoes	Carrots	Beans	Walnuts
1 High in protein				
2 Good for vision				
3 Good for the heart				
4 Help fight diseases				

Listening Skills Distinguishing Consonants

✓ **Check-Up** Listen carefully and then circle the words you hear.

1 when - well   2 list - wrist
3 cancer - cancel   4 leave - reeve

Chapter ❼   117

• Exercise 7 •

> **Vegetarians**
> ↓
> ○ Experience fewer diseases
> ○ Have less cholesterol
> ○ Are low in protein, calcium, and iron

07-15

advantage n a benefit
risk n a chance or danger
rarely adv almost never

Q1 What does the professor imply about vegetarians?
- Ⓐ They are healthier than nonvegetarians.
- Ⓑ They never need to go on a diet.
- Ⓒ They often need extra vitamins to stay healthy.
- Ⓓ They are fatter than most people.

Q2 Are the following advantages or disadvantages of being a vegetarian?

	Advantage	Disadvantage
① Diet low in cholesterol		
② Diet high in most vitamins		
③ Diet low in protein		
④ Diet low in iron		

Listening Skills Distinguishing Consonants

✓ **Check-Up** Listen carefully and then circle the words you hear.

1 name - lame   2 main - mail
3 low - no   4 fast - past

07-16

• **Exercise 8** •

```
              Cooking Methods
                ↙         ↘
            Frying       Steaming
```

○ Not good for the body   ○ Healthy cooking method
○ Can cause weight gain   ○ Can help food keep nutrients

🎧 07-17

method n   a way of doing something
cut back on phr to reduce; to do something less often
digest v   to break down food in the body

Q1 What is the likely outcome of a person eating a lot of fried food?
  Ⓐ The person will be happy.
  Ⓑ The person will gain weight.
  Ⓒ The person will become healthy.
  Ⓓ They person will get many nutrients.

Q2 Are the following effects of frying or steaming food?

	Frying	Steaming
① Helps food keep nutrients		
② Is not good for the body		
③ Makes vegetable fibers soft		
④ May cause heart disease		

Listening Skills   Distinguishing Consonants

 **Check-Up** Listen carefully and then circle the words you hear.

1 prying - frying   2 but - putt
3 gain - cane   4 pack – back

🎧 07-18

Vocabulary Review

A Circle the words that best complete the sentences.

1 You should always eat in (moderation / medium) during meals.
2 People go on diets in order to lose (sight / weight).
3 Some people (ruin / risk) their lives to save others.
4 They can (resume / consume) lots of food.
5 Many animals have better (vision / session) than people.

B Choose the best words to complete the sentences.

1 The number of people will _____ next year.
   A increase
   B follow
   C begin
   D hurry

2 A car needs _____ to run.
   A heat
   B fuel
   C race
   D calorie

3 Jessica's parents did not _____ her to go to the party.
   A cause
   B provide
   C allow
   D forget

4 The workers must _____ the truck.
   A load up
   B fall down
   C prevent
   D soften

5 The body must _____ food in order to get nutrients from it.
   A remove
   B digest
   C waste
   D cook

120

C Choose the words with the closest meanings to the highlighted words.

1 Many of the people there were obese.
   - Ⓐ fat
   - Ⓑ afraid
   - Ⓒ rich
   - Ⓓ smart

2 Jonathan was very weak after his sickness.
   - Ⓐ strong
   - Ⓑ tired
   - Ⓒ happy
   - Ⓓ active

3 Spaghetti contains a lot of vitamins and minerals.
   - Ⓐ tastes
   - Ⓑ heals
   - Ⓒ has
   - Ⓓ avoids

4 Eggs are a very good source of protein.
   - Ⓐ result
   - Ⓑ nutrient
   - Ⓒ supply
   - Ⓓ requirement

5 Some vitamins actually repair the body.
   - Ⓐ fix
   - Ⓑ explore
   - Ⓒ develop
   - Ⓓ leave

D Complete the sentences by filling in the blanks with the best words from the list. Change the forms of the words if necessary. Use each word only once.

| advantage | stay away | important | rarely | nutritional |

1 It is best to _____ from junk food.
2 They _____ go out to dinner anymore.
3 One _____ of carbohydrates is energy.
4 That vegetable has little _____ value.
5 Vitamin C is one of the most _____ vitamins.

Practice Test

1-4 Listen to part of a lecture in a nutrition class.

Nutrition

1. What aspect of caffeine does the professor mainly discuss?
   - Ⓐ Where it comes from
   - Ⓑ Its advantages
   - Ⓒ Its side effects
   - Ⓓ The number of customers who use it

2. What is the professor's opinion of caffeine?
   - Ⓐ It is dangerous.
   - Ⓑ Everyone should consume it.
   - Ⓒ A little is good for people.
   - Ⓓ It tastes terrible in coffee.

3. Do the following sentences refer to the pros or cons of caffeine?
   Click in the correct box for each sentence.

	Pro	Con
1 It makes people jumpy.		
2 It gives people a boost.		
3 It causes sleep disorders.		
4 It keeps people alert.		

4. What percentage of Americans consume caffeine?
   - Ⓐ 70%
   - Ⓑ 80%
   - Ⓒ 90%
   - Ⓓ 95%

CHAPTER

Endangered Animals
(Listening for Numbers)

CHAPTER 8 Endangered Animals (Listening for Numbers)

Understanding TOEFL Question Types & Listening Skills

1 Question Types — Making Inferences Questions

Making Inferences questions are based on the facts in the listening passage. In many cases, the professor may imply something without directly stating it.

- **Example Making Inferences Questions**
  - What does the professor imply about X?
  - What can be inferred about X?
  - What does the professor imply when he says this: (replay)

- **Useful Tips for your Success**
  - Pay attention to what the professor implies.
  - The correct answer choice will usually use vocabulary not in the passage.

Sample Question

The Gray Wolf

- Is three feet high and four feet long
- Can expect to live about six to eight years

🎧 08-01

extinct adj gone forever
harsh adj hard; difficult

Q What does the professor imply about wolves?
- Ⓐ They are beautiful.
- Ⓑ They are extinct.
- Ⓒ They are often hungry.
- Ⓓ They have easy lives.

2 Listening Skills — Listening for Numbers

We often hear numbers in lectures. A pause is especially important when you are listening to numbers in addresses, telephone numbers, and other figures. Notice how spaces and punctuation are used to group the numbers.

Check-Up

▶ Listen and fill in the blanks with suitable numbers.

1. One foot is a bit more than _____ centimeters.
2. Hunters nearly made it extinct in the _____.
3. Most gray wolves live in the wild for only about _____ to _____ years.

🎧 08-02

Chapter ❽ 127

• **Exercise 1** •

> **The Hippopotamus**
>
>
>
> - Weighs more than 7,000 pounds
> - Is dangerous and attacks humans and boats

🎧 08-03

prefer *v* to like one thing more than another
aggressive *adj* being violent

Q What can be inferred about the hippopotamus?

Ⓐ It eats meat and plants.
Ⓑ It cannot live on land.
Ⓒ It sometimes kills people.
Ⓓ It is larger than an elephant.

Listening Skills | **Listening for Numbers**

🎧 08-04

✓ **Check-Up** Listen and fill in the blanks with suitable numbers.

1 It can weigh more than _____ pounds.
2 It can also be around _____ feet long.
3 And it can grow up to _____ feet high at the shoulder.

128

• **Exercise 2** •

```
         The Bald Eagle
              ↓
  ○ Has a white head and brown feathers
  ○ Was almost all killed by hunters
```

comeback n a recovery; a return
wingspan n the length of a bird's wings

Q What does the professor imply when he says this: "It's too bad that hunters almost killed them all."

Ⓐ She does not agree with hunting eagles.
Ⓑ She thinks it is okay to hunt eagles.
Ⓒ She hopes that eagle hunting will continue.
Ⓓ She believes hunters killed all the eagles.

Listening Skills   Listening for Numbers

✓ **Check-Up** Listen and fill in the blanks with suitable numbers.

1 That's about _____ centimeters.
2 Females are often _____ percent larger than males.
3 The average female's weight is around _____ pounds. That's about _____ kilograms.

• **Exercise 3** •

Blue Whales

○ Can reach 100 feet in length
○ Are only about 10,000 left

reach v to become
protected adj kept safe

Q   What does the professor imply about whale hunting?

   Ⓐ It did not affect blue whales.
   Ⓑ It hurt the blue whale population.
   Ⓒ It does not occur anymore.
   Ⓓ It is getting worse each year.

Listening Skills Listening for Numbers

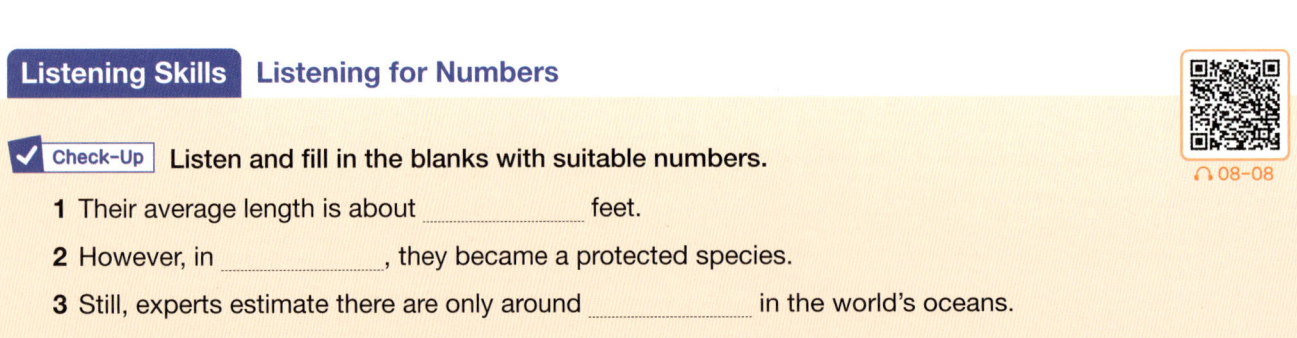

✓ **Check-Up** Listen and fill in the blanks with suitable numbers.

1 Their average length is about _____ feet.
2 However, in _____, they became a protected species.
3 Still, experts estimate there are only around _____ in the world's oceans.

• **Exercise 4** •

Grizzly Bears

- Are big and powerful bears
- Can be more than two meters tall

threatened adj being in danger
powerful adj strong

Q What can be inferred about grizzly bears?
- Ⓐ They live in caves.
- Ⓑ They are not found near sea level.
- Ⓒ They must live near streams or rivers.
- Ⓓ They can be found in South America.

Listening Skills Listening for Numbers

✓ **Check-Up** Listen and fill in the blanks with suitable numbers.
1. When they are standing, they can be about _____ meters in height.
2. Males weigh _____ times as much as females.
3. Adult males average about _____ kilograms in weight.

• Exercise 5 •

Pink River Dolphins

⬇

- Can be over 12 meters long
- Are in danger nowadays

🎧 08-11

species n a group of living things

Q1 What does the professor imply about the pink river dolphin?

Ⓐ Pollution can harm it.
Ⓑ It is nearly extinct.
Ⓒ It hunts fish and other animals.
Ⓓ Dams provide it with deep water.

Q2 What does the professor imply when she says this: "The pink river dolphin is the largest river dolphin species in the world."

Ⓐ Not much is known about the pink river dolphin.
Ⓑ The pink river dolphin can live in the ocean.
Ⓒ The pink river dolphin is bigger the ocean dolphins.
Ⓓ There are several species of river dolphins.

Listening Skills Listening for Numbers

✓ **Check-Up** Listen and fill in the blanks with suitable numbers.

🎧 08-12

1 It grows to be around _____ meters in length.
2 Males can weigh more than _____ kilograms.
3 Some of them can also live in the wild for around _____ years.

• **Exercise 6** •

Pandas

- Can be only found in China
- Eat bamboo
- Can live for up to fifteen years in wild

08-13

| **furry** adj covered with fur | **habitat** n a home in nature |
| **paw** n the foot of an animal | |

Q1 What does the professor imply about pandas?
- Ⓐ People enjoy seeing them.
- Ⓑ They are not endangered.
- Ⓒ They do not like zoos.
- Ⓓ They are found in several countries.

Q2 What can be inferred about where pandas live?
- Ⓐ They once lived in China.
- Ⓑ They no longer live in Vietnam.
- Ⓒ They only live in zoos.
- Ⓓ They live by themselves.

Listening Skills Listening for Numbers

08-14

✓ **Check-Up** Listen and fill in the blanks with suitable numbers.
1 Adults can weigh around _____ kilograms.
2 In _____, there were _____ pandas in the wild.
3 They can live to be about _____ in zoos though.

Chapter 8   133

• **Exercise 7** •

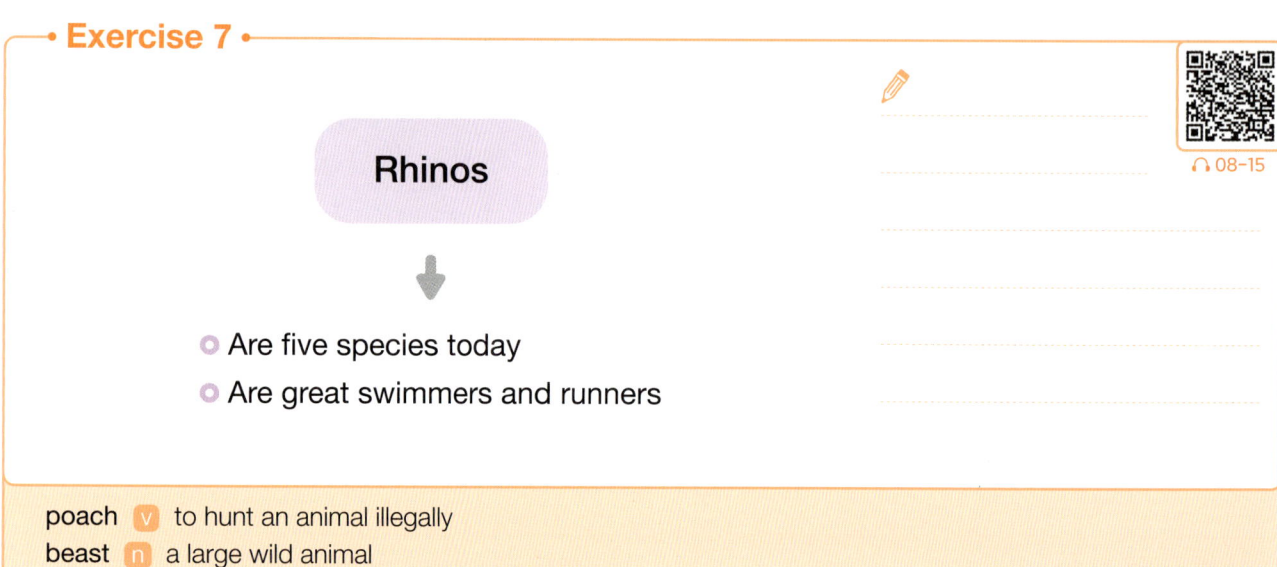

🎧 08-15

poach v to hunt an animal illegally
beast n a large wild animal

Q1 What does the professor imply about rhinos?
   Ⓐ The African rhino is the biggest.
   Ⓑ Some of them have three horns.
   Ⓒ They are losing their habitats.
   Ⓓ More of them lived on the Earth long ago.

Q2 What does the professor imply when he says this: "They are built like tanks."
   Ⓐ Rhinos are very fast.
   Ⓑ Rhinos are good swimmers.
   Ⓒ Rhinos are tough.
   Ⓓ Rhinos need protection.

Listening Skills Listening for Numbers

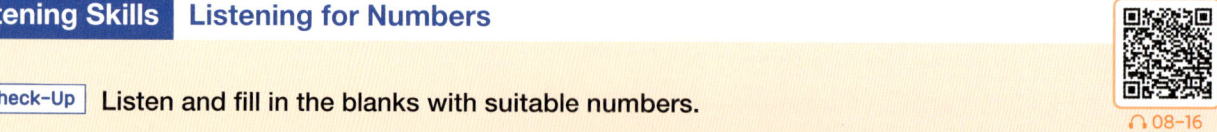

🎧 08-16

✓ **Check-Up** Listen and fill in the blanks with suitable numbers.
  1 Experts estimate there are around _____ rhinos left on the Earth.
  2 Most rhinos can run around _____ miles per hour.
  3 In captivity, there are more than _____.

• Exercise 8 •

Tigers
↓
- Are about 5,000 left in the wild
- Are caught and sold as pets

🎧 08-17

| trap | v | to catch |
| cub | n | a baby animal |

Q1 What can be inferred about tigers?
- Ⓐ They once lived everywhere in the world.
- Ⓑ They only hunt meat in their habitats.
- Ⓒ Hunters prefer to trap them.
- Ⓓ There are species of them smaller than the Siberian tiger.

Q2 What does the professor imply about tiger hunters?
- Ⓐ They are good people.
- Ⓑ They make a lot of money.
- Ⓒ They often go to jail.
- Ⓓ They are cruel.

Listening Skills Listening for Numbers

🎧 08-18

✔ **Check-Up** Listen and fill in the blanks with suitable numbers.

1 It can weigh more than _____ pounds.
2 There were more than _____ tigers _____ years ago.
3 Experts think there are only about _____ tigers left in the wild now.

Chapter ❽ 135

Vocabulary Review

A Circle the words that best complete the sentences.

1 Sadly, many animal species are now (**extinct** / growing).
2 The boss (**threatened** / believed) to fire me this morning.
3 Many students (leave / **imagine**) they will have bright futures.
4 That bird's (feather / **habitat**) is in danger.
5 Some snakes are (**aggressive** / endangered) and attack people.

B Choose the best words to complete the sentences.

1 The desert is a very _____ place.
   A cold
   B easy
   C harsh
   D polluted

2 The animal has _____ jaws.
   A lazy
   B based
   C best
   D powerful

3 When the _____ is complete, a big lake will form behind it.
   A river
   B ship
   C dam
   D pond

4 A(n) _____ is a warm-blooded animal that breathes air and has hair.
   A mammal
   B insect
   C reptile
   D fish

5 Most bears are _____ animals.
   A cut
   B furry
   C illegal
   D double

C Choose the words with the closest meanings to the highlighted words.

1 Some animals can reach the age of 100.
   - Ⓐ beware
   - Ⓑ get to
   - Ⓒ live in
   - Ⓓ fly to

2 A lion's cubs look similar to housecats.
   - Ⓐ fur
   - Ⓑ eyes
   - Ⓒ habitat
   - Ⓓ babies

3 Some wild beasts are dangerous to humans.
   - Ⓐ animals
   - Ⓑ preys
   - Ⓒ fish
   - Ⓓ people

4 There are many different species of sharks in the oceans.
   - Ⓐ teeth
   - Ⓑ males
   - Ⓒ kinds
   - Ⓓ attractions

5 Hunters often trap animals to sell them later.
   - Ⓐ catch
   - Ⓑ shoot
   - Ⓒ push
   - Ⓓ find

D Complete the sentences by filling in the blanks with the best words from the list. Change the forms of the words if necessary. Use each word only once.

> comeback   wingspan   protected   polluted   paws

1 The tiger has very large _____.
2 The _____ of an eagle is sometimes more than seven feet.
3 Fortunately, some species are making a _____.
4 It is so _____ here that it is hard to breathe.
5 Many kinds of animals are _____ by the government.

Practice Test

1-4 Listen to part of a lecture in a biology class.

08-19

Biology

1   What does the professor think of bears?

    Ⓐ He thinks they are lazy.
    Ⓑ He thinks they are too fat.
    Ⓒ He thinks they are amazing.
    Ⓓ He thinks they sleep too long.

2   Do the following sentences refer to the bears or other hibernating animals?
    Click in the correct box for each sentence.

	Bears	Other Hibernating Animals
1 They can sleep for three months.		
2 They do not eat during hibernation.		
3 They wake during hibernation.		
4 They get up every couple of days.		

3   According to the lecture, where do animals often hibernate?

    Ⓐ In nests
    Ⓑ In dens
    Ⓒ In tunnels
    Ⓓ In holes

4   What does the professor imply when he says this: "Other hibernating animals like raccoons must wake often to eat stored food or, um, to relieve themselves."

    Ⓐ Raccoons drink a lot of water.
    Ⓑ The professor must take a break.
    Ⓒ Raccoons must wake from hibernation.
    Ⓓ Raccoons are light sleepers.

Actual Test

Actual Test 1

Questions 1-3 Listen to part of a conversation between a student and a professor.

1. What problem does the student have?
    Ⓐ She did badly on a test.
    Ⓑ She cannot attend class.
    Ⓒ She is very sick right now.
    Ⓓ She has not finished a report yet.

2. What does the student want to do?
    Ⓐ Get an extension
    Ⓑ Borrow a book
    Ⓒ Take a test again
    Ⓓ Copy some class notes

3. What will the professor probably do next?
    Ⓐ Go to his next class
    Ⓑ Show the student her current grade
    Ⓒ Ask the student some more questions
    Ⓓ Tell the student about an assignment

Questions 4-7 Listen to part of a lecture in a meteorology class.

4 What is the lecture mainly about?
- Ⓐ How weather and climate are different
- Ⓑ How weather affects climate
- Ⓒ How climate can change weather
- Ⓓ How climate is more important than weather

5 What can be inferred about the professor?
- Ⓐ He is teaching the first class of the semester.
- Ⓑ He will give the students a test soon.
- Ⓒ He wants the students to answer his questions.
- Ⓓ He believes the Earth is getting colder.

6 How is the lecture organized?
- Ⓐ The professor asks questions and then answers them.
- Ⓑ The professor discusses weather and then covers climate.
- Ⓒ The professor covers material by reading from the textbook.
- Ⓓ The professor shows a video and then explains it.

7 Do the following refer to weather or climate?
Click in the correct box for each sentence.

	Weather	Climate
1 Refers to long-term events		
2 Refers to short-term events		
3 Covers average conditions		
4 Describes specific conditions		

Actual Test 2

Questions 1-3 Listen to part of a conversation between a student and a librarian.

09-03

1. Why does the student visit the librarian?
    - Ⓐ To look for a book
    - Ⓑ To inquire about a job
    - Ⓒ To get a library card
    - Ⓓ To talk about a library fine

2. Why does the student mention his local library?
    - Ⓐ To describe his work experience
    - Ⓑ To say how many books it has
    - Ⓒ To state its location
    - Ⓓ To talk about the librarian there

3. What is the purpose of the woman's response: "Come with me then."
    - Ⓐ To indicate that the student is hired
    - Ⓑ To ask the student for more information
    - Ⓒ To tell the student where to go
    - Ⓓ To advise the student to return later

Actual Test 2

Questions 4–7 Listen to part of a lecture in an education class.

Education

4 What is the lecture mainly about?
- Ⓐ A history of teaching methods
- Ⓑ The Montessori Method
- Ⓒ Rote learning
- Ⓓ The life of Maria Montessori

5 What is rote learning?
- Ⓐ Learning at a fast pace
- Ⓑ Using memorization to learn
- Ⓒ Learning by playing
- Ⓓ Doing practical activities to learn

6 Why does the professor discuss hands-on learning?
- Ⓐ To explain how students do it
- Ⓑ To argue that it does not help students
- Ⓒ To show how some students learn
- Ⓓ To give some examples of it

7 What will the professor probably do next?
- Ⓐ Let the students go home for the day
- Ⓑ Have the students watch a video
- Ⓒ Give the students a demonstration
- Ⓓ Wait for a student to answer her question

Actual Test 3

Questions 1-3 Listen to part of a conversation between a student and a professor.

09-05

1. What are the speakers mainly discussing?
   Ⓐ The student's class schedule
   Ⓑ A seminar the student is taking
   Ⓒ A class the professor will teach
   Ⓓ The student's grade in a class

2. What is the professor's attitude toward the student?
   Ⓐ She is impressed with his hard work.
   Ⓑ She is displeased with his comments.
   Ⓒ She is understanding of his problem.
   Ⓓ She is sympathetic toward him.

3. What does the student imply about next year?
   Ⓐ He will find a part-time job.
   Ⓑ He will change his major.
   Ⓒ He will apply for an internship.
   Ⓓ He will take the professor's class.

Actual Test 3

Questions 4-7 Listen to part of a lecture in a history of music class.

History of Music

4   What aspect of Handel does the professor mainly discuss?

   Ⓐ His life
   Ⓑ His performances
   Ⓒ His works
   Ⓓ His reputation

5   What is the professor's opinion of Handel?

   Ⓐ She considers him a great composer.
   Ⓑ She thinks only his oratories were good.
   Ⓒ She believes he is the best composer in history.
   Ⓓ She thinks that Bach was better than him.

6   Why does the professor mention Bach?

   Ⓐ To name some of his works
   Ⓑ To call him a Baroque composer
   Ⓒ To say when he was born
   Ⓓ To compare his works with Handel's

7   What is the most famous work by Handel?

   Ⓐ *Water Music*
   Ⓑ *Messiah*
   Ⓒ *Music for the Royal Fireworks*
   Ⓓ *Orlando*

Appendix

Dictation Exercise

Dictation Exercises

Chapter 1

Sample Question

M Professor: Most thunderstorms _____ when the _____ is very, um, moist and _____. _____ and _____ are _____ during thunderstorms. So is very heavy rain. Clouds _____ thunderstorms are _____ dark. They may _____ be black. Thunderstorms can _____ very _____ and be quite _____. You _____ always _____ when a thunderstorm is _____.

Exercise 1

M Professor: There are many _____ of precipitation, class. Rain is _____. Of course, it is very _____. Another type, _____ hail, is _____ uncommon. _____ in cloud _____ in _____ winds. Drops of rain _____ around in cloud. As they do this, they _____ more and more _____. This moisture also _____ very quickly. The drops _____ heavier and _____ as they get bigger. Finally, the hail falls to the _____. Some hail can be the _____ of a golf ball.

Exercise 2

W Professor: Cold _____ move toward the _____. Well, they _____ the south and the _____. They usually _____ with _____ air. So along the _____ front line, there is often _____ weather. This _____ be in the form of rain or snow. It _____ the season and the area. But soon, the cold front _____ the bad weather. The weather then _____ dry and cool. This _____ because high _____ follows the cold front.

Exercise 3

M Professor: Okay. Let's _____ the tornado's _____ relative: the _____. First, _____ tornadoes, waterspouts _____ on water. They _____ form over large lakes and oceans. They are also not nearly as _____ as tornadoes. _____ are _____ than tornadoes, too. Oh, there's another _____ between the two. Waterspouts form on the _____ of the water and then _____ in the air _____ clouds. Tornadoes, however, typically _____ in clouds and then move _____.

Exercise 4

M Professor: No rain for a week or two does not make a _____. Droughts _____ only after a long period of time _____ regular rainfall. It may rain _____ that time. However, it doesn't rain _____. _____, a long period of time means months or years. The _____ of a drought can spell _____ for an area. Let's see . . . Lakes begin to dry up. _____ takes a big hit. And then there are small plants and _____. Fires _____ lots of _____ that is _____ alive.

Exercise 5

W Professor: There are many _____ of clouds in the sky. Usually, we _____ them by their _____ and _____. Let me give you an example. _____ the highest clouds are _____ clouds. They look like a horse's tail in the sky. You can usually see them on a clear day.

A _____ mid-level cloud is the _____ cloud. It looks _____ small cotton balls in the sky. This type of cloud is also _____ white. But it _____ also have _____ of gray. This means that rain is probably on the way.

Then there are _____ cumulonimbus clouds. They're the _____ ones in the sky. These can be white or dark gray. They come with high winds and form very quickly. Be careful of these, class. _____ thunderstorms _____ in these kinds of clouds.

Exercise 6

M Professor: That was a lot of _____ we had this _____. Well, what is fog? It's _____ clouds close to the _____. So fog can cause _____ problems for people. I _____, it's hard to see _____ clouds, isn't it? _____ does fog form? Let me _____ you. First, you need _____ 100% _____. So there _____ be lots of water _____ in the air. Next, the water vapor _____, so it _____ from a _____ state to a liquid one. The water _____ then join with dust or _____ to _____ fog. Uh, that's why cities _____ get fog. You know, uh, they usually _____ lots of pollution. And fog is quite _____ near _____ of water such as lakes, oceans, and seas.

Exercise 7

M Professor: Scientists _____ to learn about the weather. This _____ them _____ it better. It also tells them what _____ of weather is _____. Let me tell you about some of their _____. First, of course, is the _____. It tells the _____. The _____ is another important instrument. It _____ air pressure. Usually, _____ air pressure means _____ weather. When the air pressure is falling, there will be _____ or _____ weather. Those are the two _____ tools. But there are others. _____ tell which _____ the wind is _____. Rain _____ are very useful. They measure the _____ of rain that falls during a storm. _____ make use of rain _____. They need to know _____ much water their _____ are _____.

Exercise 8

W Professor: There are two _____ types of _____. The first _____ when there is _____ in an area. Bodies of water _____ as

lakes and rivers cannot _____ all of the water that _____ flows into them. As a _____, they _____. This is a _____ flood. A flash flood can have dire effects on a region. How _____ it is _____ on the amount and _____ of the rainfall. _____ rain can _____ everything. Then, the ground is _____. Trees and cars _____ _____ away. Houses and other buildings are _____. Flash _____ can be _____ _____.

_____ _____ the other type of flood? This is a river flood. _____ rain, hurricanes, and _____ snow can cause river floods. This type of flood usually _____ in places with _____ climates.

Practice Test

M Professor: Ocean _____ are like rivers of _____ water in the ocean. One of the best-known _____ is the Gulf Stream. It _____ in the Gulf of Mexico. It then _____ into the Atlantic Ocean and heads up the _____ coast of the United States. It then _____ west _____ the Atlantic and _____ up in _____ Europe.

Something _____ about ocean _____ is that they can affect the weather. The Gulf Stream is a warm-water current. It _____ part of the eastern _____ of the U.S. It also _____ Northwest Europe a _____ deal. How so? Well, it makes the _____ in those two places warmer than they _____ be. For _____, England is at a _____ high _____. So it _____ be a very cold place. However, the Gulf Stream _____ near the country. So it _____ make the _____ in England warmer. There are some other _____ that _____ the weather in _____ places. _____ me tell you _____ one that's _____ South America . . .

🎧 01-19

Chapter 2

Sample Question

M Professor: Good afternoon, Lisa. _____ are you _____ today?

W Student: I _____ a _____. I want to talk about our _____ assignment.

M: Sure. Did you already _____ it?

W: _____, I have not _____. I don't _____ it.

M: Okay. Let me _____ to _____ it for you.

W: _____? Can you _____ that?

M: Of _____. It's _____ at all.

Exercise 1

M1 Student: Professor Stephens, are you _____?

M2 Professor: Not _____. I have a _____ minutes. What can I _____ for you?

M1: I, um, _____ to _____ on my _____ for next semester. You're my advisor. So I thought you could _____ me.

M2: Sure. Do you _____ any _____?

M1: Well, I have _____ most of my _____. But I _____ one more _____.

M2: Why don't you _____ my _____? You could _____ that with no _____.

M1: You're _____ one? I didn't know that.

M2: I just _____ to do it.

Exercise 2

W Librarian: Can I _____ you?

M Student: Yes, I don't know _____ to find any books.

W: It's really _____. You _____ to _____ the library's _____ system.

M: Right. But _____ do I _____?

W: First, _____ in the _____ or _____ of the book. Or _____ the _____ of the book.

M: Great. What's _____?

W: Next, _____ on the _____ you _____. Then, you can _____ the book's _____.

M: The call number?

W: Yes, the call number _____ the book's _____. There's the call number. So now you can _____ the _____.

M: Wow. That's _____.

Exercise 3

W1 Student: Professor Duncan, you _____ to see me?

W2 Professor: Yes, Melissa. I'd _____ to _____ about your _____ _____.

W1: Oh, you _____ it, didn't you? I'm so _____.

W2: Melissa, please. Let me _____. Actually, I _____ it was _____ _____.

W1: Really?

W2: Yes. I really _____ you had some _____. In fact, I firmly _____ you ought to _____ to _____ your report in a _____ or journal.

W1: Wow. I had _____.

W2: Of course, you can _____ some of your _____. But I can _____ you with that.

Dictation Exercises   161

Exercise 4

W Student: I'm _____ in _____ in another _____ .

M Study Abroad Employee: Great. Which _____ are you _____ of?

W: Well, I can _____ and some _____ .

M: Hmm . . . _____ would be a _____ . Or maybe you could _____ to _____ America.

W: South America? That _____ .

M: Would you like some more _____ ?

W: Sure. First, I'd _____ to _____ I can go. I'd also like to _____ the _____ of going to each _____ . I don't have that much _____ .

M: No problem. Here, _____ these _____ and _____ at them.

Exercise 5

W Professor: Do you _____ I want to _____ with you?

M Student: Um, not _____ .

W: It's about your _____ assignments.

M: _____ homework _____ ?

W: You have had _____ homework assignments this _____ . But you have _____ of them.

M: I _____ about _____ homework assignments.

W: They are on your _____ .

M: Oh, I _____ that on the _____ day of class.

W: Well, you have to _____ your _____ . It's _____ percent of your _____ . And right now, you have a great big _____ .

M: That is _____ , is it?

W: No. But there are still _____ more homework assignments _____ . I _____ you _____ them all. That way, you'll only _____ on your _____ grade.

M: Yes, ma'am. I'll _____ my _____ from now on.

Exercise 6

M Student: Hello, Professor Maddux. You _____ to _____ me?

W Professor: That's right, Eric. _____ sit down here? I have something _____ to _____ with you.

M: Okay. What's _____ on?

W: Remember how you _____ to take a class in _____ Greek? You _____ that to me two weeks ago.

M: Ah, yes. That _____ be great. Is the school going to _____ a class?

W: No, we _____ be _____ that. However . . .

M: Yes?

W: There will be a class on _____ Greek at Central University next semester. Our schools have an _____. Students here are _____ to take classes at Central University.

M: I had no idea. The school is only about fifteen minutes _____ from here, so it's not far.

W: One of my friends is the _____. I'm sure you'll _____ it.

M: That _____ perfect. If it _____ my schedule, I'll be sure to _____ up for it. Thanks so much.

W: You're welcome.

Exercise 7

W Student: Hello, Professor Sanders. May I _____ you a _____?

M Professor: Of course, Emily. _____ do you _____?

W: Well . . . it's about my _____ exam _____. It's _____ than I _____.

M: Ah, you _____ a B–, right?

W: Yes, sir. That's the _____ grade I've ever _____.

M: You _____ be too _____. I am a very _____ grader. Actually, your _____ was the fourth _____ in the class.

W: Wow, I didn't know that.

M: But I can _____ why you _____ that grade.

W: Yes, please. That would _____ me _____.

M: Okay. This was an essay test. But you didn't _____ an _____ essay. You need to _____ your point better. You made a few _____ mistakes, too.

W: I see. Thanks for the _____ .

Exercise 8

W Cafeteria Employee: Good morning. What can I _____ for _____ ?

M Student: I, uh, _____ a question. It's _____ my meal plan.

W: Sure. Go ahead.

M: Can I _____ it? I don't _____ here very _____ .

W: What meal plan _____ you _____ ?

M: The three-meals-a-day plan. You know, twenty-one a week.

W: Okay, you can _____ it to the fourteen- or ten-meal plan. There's also a seven-a-week plan, but most people don't _____ that.

M: Hmm . . . I'm not sure.

W: Well, with _____ meals a week, you can _____ a day. _____ students _____ breakfast. With ten a week, most students _____ every night and lunch _____ times a week.

M: Oh, right. Do you have the price for each? I want to _____ much they _____ .

W: Here you are.

Practice Test

M Student: Hi. Um, _____ I in the _____ place for student ID cards?

W Student Services Center Employee: Yes. A new student card or a _____ card?

M: I need a _____ ID card.

W: Oh, I see. Why do you need a _____ ?

M: Well, I _____ stuff a lot.

W: That's a _____ good idea. You're the first person to _____ for one.

M: Really. Well, _____ you _____ me one please?

W: Sure. _____ me _____ your student ID card.

164

M: _____ I just _____ you my student number?

W: Yes, but I also _____ to see some _____ of picture ID.

M: I understand. _____ my driver's license?

W: That's fine.

M: Here you are.

W: Uh-oh. This license _____ last month. _____ a university meal card?

M: I don't _____ meals on _____. Oh, how about my _____ membership ID?

W: That _____ work . . . Okay. That's _____. The _____ for a _____ ID card is ten dollars.

M: Really? I _____ it was five.

W: The school just _____ the price this semester.

Chapter 3

Sample Question

W Professor: You see, class, the _____ is not just one _____ _____. It is a _____ of instruments. It _____ the _____, the _____, and the _____. They are all _____ of _____. The _____ is the _____. But it is the most _____. It _____ a variety of _____ _____.

🎧 03-01

Exercise 1

M Professor: John Philip Sousa is one of the _____ names in _____ _____. He wasn't a singer _____. He was a _____. He _____ band music. His music _____ had a _____ _____. What _____ he compose? Well, he _____ *Semper Fidelis*, which is a Marine _____. He also _____ *The Stars and Stripes Forever*. You _____ not _____ the name, but you _____ know the

🎧 03-03

_____. Let's _____ to it now.

Exercise 2

W Professor: Miles Davis was _____ of the _____ jazz _____ ever. He was a _____ with the trumpet. _____, he helped _____ a new style of jazz. We _____ it cool jazz. It _____ about in the United States in the _____ 1940s. But that wasn't _____ for Miles Davis. In the 1970s, he _____ to _____ jazz with rock music. _____, class, that without Miles Davis, _____ genres of _____ music might not _____ _____.

🎧 03-05

Exercise 3

W Professor: There are _____ musical _____ to Korea. The *gayageum* is the _____ of them. It is a _____ instrument. Let me see. It _____ has only twelve _____. But some of them _____ _____ twenty-one strings. The _____ of the *gayageum* is _____ _____ wood. Inside, it is _____. The musician _____ the strings. This produces a _____ sound that is _____ and relaxed. Most often, the *gayageum* is _____ for traditional Korean _____ music.

🎧 03-07

Exercise 4

W Professor: _____ did you _____ that music, class? _____, isn't it? You _____ some Gregorian chants. They _____ first _____ in the ninth or tenth century. This was _____ the Middle Ages _____ Europe. Gregorian chants _____ church music. As you _____, there were no musical _____. It was just a group of _____ all _____ in unison. They were _____ in Latin by the way. So I guess _____ the words, right?

🎧 03-09

166

Exercise 5

M Professor: The harmonica is _____ of the _____ instruments. It _____ a slim _____ with hole in it. Some people also _____ it the _____, the mouth harp, or the French _____. _____ _____, doesn't it? The harmonica is a _____ instrument. A musician _____ into its tiny holes to _____ sound. A musician can also _____ in _____ for different tones. _____, metal _____ or pipes _____. That _____ the different sounds. _____, musicians _____ the harmonica for country or folk music. _____, you'll also _____ it in jazz, rock, and pop music. It's _____ of the _____ popular instruments. For example, my son _____ _____ and hip-hop music. These days, he's _____ playing songs. In one song, I _____ a harmonica being _____.

Exercise 6

W Professor: The Beatles _____ in the late 1950s. The Beatles _____ of _____ members: John Lennon, Paul McCartney, George Harrison, and Ringo Starr. Lennon and McCartney usually _____ the songs. They first _____ together in _____ clubs _____ Liverpool, England. _____ of their major _____ was Elvis Presley. _____ long, England _____ big _____ for the Beatles. So they _____ they'd _____ the United States. In 1964, the Beatles _____ the British _____ of the U.S. They _____ the U.S. _____ storm. Americans hadn't _____ anything _____ the Beatles. Radio stations _____ their every _____. Thousands of _____ fans, especially _____ teenagers, _____ outside their hotels. Their fans just couldn't _____ enough. They _____ a _____ of the four boys from England.

Exercise 7

W Professor: Let's _____ a _____ at singer Luciano Pavarotti. He was _____ of the _____ opera singers _____. Now, uh, there are _____ basic _____ of singers: baritone, tenor, and alto. Pavarotti was a tenor. His voice was _____ and _____ of emotion. His _____ in the opera world is _____. His _____ performance in the United States _____ by _____. He was a young singer with an opera group in Miami. This was in 1965, I _____. Well, the lead singer _____. He didn't _____. Another singer _____ Pavarotti for the _____ role. Pavarotti _____ in and _____ like a pro. He didn't _____ any _____. The audience was very _____ with the young Pavarotti. That was the beginning of a new _____ in opera.

Exercise 8

M Professor: Most people _____ jazz _____ in New Orleans, Louisiana. It's an original _____ of American music. _____, it's African-American. Black musicians _____ performing _____ in the city. That's right. The roots of jazz _____ African-American. Now, the _____ in jazz are usually _____. The trumpet, the violin, and the coronet are the _____ instruments. However, other _____ are _____. Today, jazz musicians _____ a _____ of instruments. For _____, musicians _____ the drums and the piano. Of _____, the saxophone's a _____ instrument in a lot of jazz music. So _____ jazz from other _____ of music is _____. Musicians _____ the music in different directions. I _____ that they improvise—or change—the original song during a performance. That's what makes jazz _____ and _____ to many people.

Practice Test

W Professor: There are many different _____ of classical music. _____ is the Baroque Period. I consider it _____ of the greatest _____ in history. So much _____ music was made then. Let me tell you a bit _____ it. It _____ around the year 1600. And it _____ in 1750. Concertos _____ popular compositions then. But, of _____, many other types of music _____ _____ then. There was a lot of hymnal music _____ that time. The organ _____ in Baroque music. So was the harpsichord. Composers also often _____ music for the violin and the cello. _____ Baroque composers? Well, _____ of the greatest in history _____ during this time. Who were some? Johann Sebastian Bach was one. George Friderich Handel was another. Handel _____ to be my personal _____. We're _____ to _____ to parts of his *Water Music* in a moment. Antonio Vivaldi was a Baroque _____. He _____ *The Four Seasons*. I'm _____ you all know it. Okay, let's _____ to some music. Try to _____ the different instruments you _____.

Chapter 4

Sample Question

M Professor: Hi, Emily. _____ can I _____ you?
W Student: I'm _____ my essay.
M: What _____ of _____?
W: I _____ on a topic.
M: Well, _____ _____ you _____ a topic you _____ _____ in?
W: That's a great idea. I think I'll _____ dolphin communication.
M: See. That wasn't _____.
W: Thanks, Professor. See you later.

Dictation Exercises 169

Exercise 1

W Student Services Center Employee: Can I _____ you?

M Student: Yes. I _____ a new student ID card.

W: Okay. Please _____ me your student number.

M: It's 233-7-510.

W: I also _____ to see another _____ of photo ID.

M: Is a driver's license okay?

W: Sure. That's fine.

M: Here you are.

W: Okay. _____ you _____ to _____ your old picture?

M: Um, I _____ _____ in that one. Can you _____ a new one?

W: No problem. Just _____ _____ here.

M: Is there an _____ _____ ?

W: No, it is _____.

M: Great. Thanks _____ your _____.

Exercise 2

W1 Student: Professor Clark, _____ you _____ a minute?

W2 Professor: Sure. Please _____ in.

W1: Oh, thank you. I _____ to _____ you about the study-abroad program.

W2: Sure.

W1: _____ can I _____ for it?

W2: Well, you _____ to _____ at least a B+ _____.

W1: Okay. Anything else?

W2: _____ year _____ you?

W1: I'm a sophomore.

W2: Where are you _____ ?

W1: London is my first _____.

W2: _____ that program is _____, what is your _____ _____ ?

W1: Probably Paris.

W2: Here is an application. _____ it _____ tomorrow.

W1: Great, Thank, Professor Clark.

Exercise 3

W Student Housing Office Employee: Welcome to the student housing office. _____ can I _____ you?

M Student: Hi. I have a problem with my _____ room.

W: Sure. What's _____ with it?

M: The heater is _____.

W: _____ is it broken?

M: Uh, it just _____ work. No heat _____ out when I _____ it on. So my room is _____ cold.

W: Okay. We can _____ someone to _____ it soon.

M: How soon? It's _____ to _____ really cold tonight.

W: Hopefully, somebody _____ your room this afternoon.

M: That's great.

W: Okay. I _____ some information. _____ your name, and _____ is your _____?

M: I'm Jason Howard, and I _____ in room 202 in Deacon Hall.

Exercise 4

W Student: Oh, hello, Professor Foreman. Do you _____ a minute?

M Professor: Yes, but I _____ to _____ soon. I have _____ in a bit.

W: I need some advice.

M: Okay.

W: I _____ what to _____ in, writing or literature.

M: I think you _____ in literature.

W: Really? Why?

M: You _____ to be a teacher, right?

W: That's correct.

M: I think the literature _____ _____ students better for teaching.

W: But I love writing.

M: You _____ do a lot of _____ as a literature major.

W: I didn't _____ that.

Exercise 5

M1 Financial Aid Department Employee: Next!

M2 Student: Yes, um, hi. I _____ to apply _____ financial aid.

M1: Okay. Did you _____ out the _____?

M2: No, not yet.

M1: Well, the deadline is in one week. So you _____.

M2: One week?

M1: Yes. Here are the _____.

M2: Okay. Which _____ I _____ first?

M1: First, _____ the pink one. Then, the blue one. Last, you _____ the white one.

M2: Okay.

M1: As soon as you _____, _____ them to me.

M2: Sure. Um, when _____ I _____ if I _____?

M1: You will _____ a _____ two weeks.

M2: Really? That fast?

M1: Yes. But try to _____ the _____ to me soon.

M2: Okay. Thank you _____ your _____.

M1: Your welcome. Next!

Exercise 6

M Professor: _____ can I _____ for you today, Jennifer?

W Student: Well, I didn't do _____ _____ on the midterm exam.

M: Yes, I remember. _____ did _____ study for it?

W: I _____ the chapter _____ in the book.

M: That was a good _____. But it was not _____.

W: Really?

M: I _____ the _____ of the questions from the _____ _____.

W: I see. That's _____ I did so _____.

M: Probably. Be sure to _____ notes in class.

W: Okay.

M: In addition, _____ the notes _____ night.

W: All right.

M: That _____ you do much _____ on the _____ _____.

W: Thanks so much _____ your _____, sir.

M: You are welcome.

Exercise 7

M Student Services Center Employee: Hello. _____ can I _____ you?

W Student: I _____ to get a student parking _____.

M: _____ would you like?

W: There's more than one?

M: Yes. There are _____: bronze, silver, and gold.

W: What is the _____?

M: The bronze _____ is twenty dollars. You can only park in the parking lots _____ bronze.

W: I see.

M: The silver one is forty dollars. You _____ in bronze and silver parking areas.

W: Okay. And the _____ one is sixty dollars. You can park _____, right?

M: That's _____. So which one do you _____?

W: I _____ the bronze permit. The lot next to my department is bronze.

M: Good choice. You _____ always _____ later.

Dictation Exercises   173

W: Oh, okay.

M: Great. Now I _____ your license plate number and student ID.

Exercise 8

W Professor: Seth, I _____ to _____ to you about something.

M Student: Did I do _____ _____ ?

W: Oh, no. _____ at _____ .

M: That's a _____ .

W: I want to _____ your _____ for summer.

M: I'm _____ summer school. I'll be _____ one course.

W: That's great, Seth. I'll be _____ on my new book all summer. I _____ some help.

M: What _____ I _____ to do?

W: Oh, just _____ _____ books at the library for me. _____ do some _____ . Things like that.

M: What _____ the pay?

W: We _____ _____ _____ that later. Are you _____ ?

M: Of course.

W: Great. _____ in tomorrow _____ lunch. We'll _____ _____ then.

M: Okay. See you then.

04-17

Practice Test

W Professor: Oh, hey, Hunter. Come on in.

M Student: Hi, Professor Jackson. You _____ to see me?

W: Yes, it's about your class _____ . You _____ every class last week.

M: I had a _____ cold.

W: Yes, I _____ a bad bug was _____ around. I'm glad you're feeling better.

M: Thanks. _____ , I want to ask you for a _____ .

W: Sure. What is it?

04-19

174

M: I _____ a letter of _____ for a part-time job.

W: _____ _____ of job?

M: Well, you _____ I want to go to law school. A local law _____ needs a clerk.

W: That's great, Hunter.

M: Well, I didn't _____ the _____, ma'am.

W: I know. Of _____ I'll write a letter of recommendation for you.

M: That's great. Thanks so much. Oh, there's one more thing. I _____ it by tomorrow morning. My _____ is at 9:00.

W: 9:00 AM? I can _____ that. Just _____ by my office on your way there.

M: Okay. I've got class. See you tomorrow.

Chapter 5

Sample Question

M Student: Hi. I _____ to _____ for the scuba diving class.

W Registrar's Office Employee: Okay. Please _____ this _____. There is also a fee of fifty dollars.

M: Wow, fifty, huh . . . ? Do you _____ ?

W: Sure. Is it _____ a local bank?

M: Yes. _____ is the first class?

W: _____ at the student union pool at 2 PM.

🎧 05-01

Exercise 1

M Professor: Sarah, can I _____ to you for a _____ ?

W Student: Sure.

M: _____ did you _____ class last week?

W: I _____ you _____ it.

M: No. We had class.

W: I'm sorry, Professor Green. My classmate said there was no class.

M: That's okay. We just _____ a film.

🎧 05-03

W: Oh, that's good.

M: But I also _____ a homework assignment.

W: Really? _____ you _____ _____ in, please?

Exercise 2

M Student Services Center Employee: You want to _____ for a scholarship, right?

W Student: That's right. _____ _____ I do that?

M: Well, it's _____ easy. I just _____ your name _____ the computer.

W: And then?

M: The computer will _____ your _____ with the scholarships.

W: What _____ that _____?

M: That _____ it automatically _____ for you.

W: Wow. That's great!

M: Yes. You will _____ an email _____ later. It will give you _____ information about any scholarship you _____.

🎧 05-05

Exercise 3

W Student: Hello, Professor Kimball. You _____ to _____ me after class?

M Professor: Yes. Hello, Lisa. I have something to tell you.

W: Is it _____ news or _____ news?

M: Good news. Very good news.

W: Okay . . .

M: Your _____ won _____ prize in the _____ contest.

W: Really? _____ do you _____?

M: I was one of the _____.

W: Oh, that's _____.

M: Congratulations. We will _____ it in the university magazine, too.

W: I can't _____ it. I had almost _____ about the _____.

🎧 05-07

Exercise 4

W Librarian: Hello, Todd. You _____ to _____ with me about something?

M Student: Yes, ma'am. It's about my shift this weekend.

W: Do you _____ the shift you work on Saturday evening?

M: Yes, that's correct.

W: So . . . _____ _____ it?

M: I _____ to _____ my home this weekend, so I can't do the _____.

W: All right. I _____ I'll have to _____ someone to work it.

M: Um . . . actually . . .

W: Yes?

M: Actually, I _____ with Wendy. She said she could do it.

W: That's _____. Thank you for finding a substitute.

M: You're welcome. I'll _____ her that you're _____ with her working then. Thanks, Ms. Roper.

Exercise 5

W Professor: Come in!

M Student: Do you _____ a second, Professor Arnold?

W: Sure, Adam. What is going on?

M: Did you _____ to look at my paper?

W: Yes, I did.

M: What _____ you _____?

W: It is _____ than the last one.

M: Really? I'm so glad!

W: I'm _____. It _____ you _____ a lot of time on it.

M: I did a lot of _____ in the library.

W: Good for you. I _____ you _____ do it.

M: By the way, what _____ did I get?

W: Let me see. I have it right here . . . Yes, an A–.

Dictation Exercises 177

M: An A–! Are you sure?

W: Yes, why? What did you _____?

M: Not an A. Actually, that's _____ _____ A in college.

Exercise 6

W Student: Hello. This is the student _____ office, isn't it?

M Student Activities Office Employee: That's _____. Is there something I can _____ you _____?

W: I hope so. I'm here about a club.

M: Great. There _____ many clubs on _____ that you _____ _____.

W: Oh, no. I want to _____ my _____ club.

M: I see. What _____ of club?

W: I want to _____ a hiking club.

M: Interesting. We _____ had a hiking club here in years.

W: Really? That's too bad. It's a great way to _____ shape. It's fun, too.

M: I _____. Okay, you need to _____ some _____. Take these.

W: Thank you.

M: And you need to _____ up _____ ten people. All _____ need that number of members.

Exercise 7

M Student: Excuse me, Professor Lansing. _____ I _____ with you?

W Professor: Sure, I have a minute or two.

M: I was hoping I _____ _____ your history class.

W: Are you a _____?

M: No. I'm a biology major.

W: I see. Well, it is an _____ class.

M: I know. But I _____ it to _____.

W: Really? Okay. Come to our first class tomorrow.

M: I'm in?

W: I'll _____ what I can do. The _____ _____ very good.

M: I really _____ to _____ now, ma'am.

W: Well, let me see. The class is _____ now. But I usually _____ one or two more students.

M: Is there a _____ _____?

W: You're the first one on it. So _____ up tomorrow, and you'll _____ _____. Okay?

M: Thanks so much. I really _____ it.

Exercise 8

M Student: Is there _____ _____ I can see the doctor now?

W Nurse: You _____ to _____ like everyone else.

M: _____ _____ will _____ take?

W: Right now, it's about a two-hour wait.

M: I have a test in one hour. I _____ _____ it.

W: _____ _____ come back after the exam?

M: I feel _____. I was _____ to get some medicine before the test.

W: Do you _____ a _____?

M: No. Just a bad _____.

W: Here is some aspirin. That _____ _____.

M: Thank you.

W: But _____ _____ to the health center _____ your test.

M: Okay.

W: You _____ the doctor _____ at you.

M: Okay. Thanks. I'll _____ _____ in a couple of hours.

Practice Test

W Student: Hi. I need to _____ a parking _____.

M Student Services Center Employee: Okay. Do you _____ the _____ with you?

W: No.

M: Then _____ you give me your license plate number?

W: It's FDR-O2Z.

M: O2Z. Okay . . . Just a _____. Hmm . . . That's interesting . . .

W: What? Is there something _____?

M: Well, yes. The computer _____ you _____ _____ for, um, eight tickets.

W: That many, huh. I didn't _____ . . .

M: The computer doesn't _____. It's eight.

W: Oh, my gosh! What is the total?

M: A lot. It's 364.91 dollars.

W: Oh, no! Do you take _____?

M: Is it from a _____ _____?

W: Yes, it is.

M: Then that's _____.

W: Okay. Here you go.

M: Thanks. You know, you're _____ _____.

W: I am? I _____ _____ so lucky.

M: Usually, when you _____ that _____ tickets, your car _____ _____.

W: Oh, I didn't _____ of that. You're right.

M: Then you have to _____ another hundred dollars to get your car back.

W: Another hundred? You're right. I am _____.

Chapter 6

Sample Question

M Professor: Let's talk about _____. One of the _____ _____ is called rote learning. That's R-O-T-E. What is _____ learning? Basically, it _____ through memorization. Students _____ something _____ times so that they can _____ it. Remember when you _____ the alphabet? You said it again and again, right? Well, that is an example of rote learning.

Exercise 1

W Professor: Language _____ is very important in Europe. Students _____ from a very young _____. In _____, in the U.S., this is _____. Students there first study a _____ language in high school. _____, in many schools in America it is not _____. I mean, they don't have to _____ it _____ they don't want to. _____, in Europe, languages like English and French _____ courses through high school.

Exercise 2

W Professor: Homeschooling is _____ these days, _____ in the U.S. Parents educate their kids _____ teachers. And there are a couple of _____. They _____ it is better. In addition, they _____ their children learn more. But some _____ it isn't all good. Homeschooled kids do not _____ others _____ much. They also can't _____ school activities like clubs or sports. The debate _____ about homeschooling.

Exercise 3

M Professor: Now, I'd _____ to _____ you some _____ of _____ arts classes. They _____ art, music, and dance. They are important in education. For example, they help _____ students' _____. They can also be very fun. Fine arts classes _____ students. By that, I _____ that students _____ well-rounded individuals. _____ only English, history, or science is not _____. Students _____ also study the fine arts. They can also _____ some students _____ their true _____. Some students may even _____ professional _____ one day.

Exercise 4

W Professor: _____, children _____ _____ five years old _____ kindergarten. It is _____ of an introduction to school. More than _____, in kindergarten, students _____ with one another. They do a lot of _____ and painting, too. It _____ students _____ from home life to school life. Most of all, of course, students _____ lots of new friends. _____ you can see, kindergarten is a _____ for children to _____ their educations.

Exercise 5

W Professor: _____ the Internet, online learning is _____ these days. Now, uh, _____ me _____ it with traditional classes so that you can understand it.
In traditional learning, students _____ classes at school. The teacher lectures, and the students learn _____ reading, listening, writing, and doing _____ other activities.
In online learning, the students and the teacher are in _____. The learning _____ over the computer.
There are _____ types of online programs. Sometimes the teacher does a live lecture, and students _____ to a website to see it. Other times, the teacher's lecture

is _____. Then, students _____ _____ it anytime. Some online learning programs _____ _____ lectures. Students get class material they _____ read. Then, they do _____ assignments and _____ them.

Exercise 6

M Professor: I'd _____ _____ _____ about early education. Many _____ _____ the education of children _____ before _____. That's right. It _____ before mothers give birth. This is _____ _____ education. Basically, the mother and the father _____ to the baby in the mothers' belly. They _____ books to the baby. People _____ babies _____ to _____ like this. It _____ their brains going. Here are some other _____. Many parents play music for their _____ babies. And some mothers _____ to their babies. This is their first _____ of communication. As a _____, songs _____ _____ trust _____ the mother and her baby. Songs also _____ the baby. Remember that hearing is the first sense babies _____. So music and songs _____ _____ the first _____ to _____ them. _____ amazing, isn't it?

Exercise 7

W Professor: Many people are _____. They _____ _____ physical disabilities. Two of the _____ common are _____ and _____. There are two _____ why this happens. Some people are _____ that way. Other times, people _____ blind or deaf _____ or through a _____.

They need to _____ _____ their disabilities. For example, blind students must _____ to read. They mostly learn _____. This is a language for the blind. It _____ _____ small, _____. They _____ letters and words. Braille _____ blind people read special books. They _____ their fingers _____ the dots to read.

_____ the deaf? They also have their _____ language. It's called _____ language. _____ it, people _____ words with their fingers and hands. They also use gestures. _____ deaf _____ blind people _____ special schools to _____ these languages.

Exercise 8

M Professor: Our school _____ many buildings with lots of classrooms. But did you know that in the _____, one-room schools _____? One-room schools _____ in _____ in places in the United States, Canada, and Europe. What were they? Well, there was just one teacher. And all the students _____ in the same room. It _____ how old the students _____. Some students were five or six _____ others _____ fifteen or sixteen. _____ did these schools work? Let me tell you . . . The teacher _____ basic _____ math, reading, and writing. The teacher _____ one group of students and _____ a lesson. Then, those students _____ an assignment, and the teacher _____ a different group. In addition, older students were _____ help younger ones. This system _____ worked _____ well.

🎧 06-17

Practice Test

M Professor: Homework is an _____ of your _____. It is _____. Of course, it helps _____ the lessons you learn. It also helps _____ you for future lessons. Doing homework _____ you _____ information. But, class, homework _____ much, much _____ than that. First, it _____ self-discipline. You will be _____, um, responsible. It also _____ you to be independent. Now, um, I'm not _____ you _____ do your homework by yourself. Actually, it's good if your parents _____ you _____ a little. But the _____ here are "a little." They

🎧 06-19

184

_____ _____ do all of your homework. Homework _____ you to _____ things _____ for yourself. That's _____ independent. Now, I don't _____ teachers should _____ lots of homework every night. Not at all. This can cause students to get _____ _____. Their _____ won't be _____ for the next day of lessons. But a bit each night is _____ healthy. It is also important for developing _____ in young people, not just _____.

Chapter 7

Sample Question

W Professor: Vitamins are very _____ to our _____. We feel _____ and _____ if our bodies don't have _____ _____. We can _____ very _____. One _____ vitamin is vitamin C. We can _____ it _____ fruits like oranges and tangerines. Another is vitamin A. We _____ it _____ green vegetables. It _____ us have good _____.

🎧 07-01

Exercise 1

M Professor: Junk food is a _____ problem for people today. _____ like pizza and hamburgers are good _____ of junk food. They have little _____. I know. I know . . . They _____ good. But they _____ _____ your bodies. They can make you fat. Another word _____ fat is _____. Being obese can _____ many health problems. Please _____ to _____ from junk food. You'll _____ me _____ it.

🎧 07-03

Exercise 2

W Professor: Everyone _____ for their bodies. It is _____ for everybody's _____. It _____ the body's _____. It gives people energy. And it helps _____ people _____. Young people _____ than adults. They are _____ growing, so their bodies need protein more than adults' bodies do. Foods like meat, eggs, and tofu are _____ _____ of protein. So is cheese. You need to be sure to _____ protein in _____ on a _____.

Exercise 3

W Professor: _____ nutrition is _____ for people _____ sports. _____ need fuel _____ _____ perform well. Carbohydrates are _____ of the best _____ of energy. _____ a _____, athletes need to _____ up on _____ before a game. _____ me give you an example. _____ like spaghetti and potatoes are _____ in carbs. Rice, bread, and oatmeal also give athletes _____ energy and power. _____ you _____ see athletes _____ those foods before games. _____ carbohydrates, they won't _____ energy.

Exercise 4

M Professor: Let's _____ for a bit. Bananas are a _____ source of this _____ nutrient. So try to eat a lot of them. Potassium _____ the body— _____ a person's life—in balance. Potassium, um, also _____ with _____. Oh, there's something else. It _____ the muscles _____ work _____ they can. And just _____ you don't like bananas . . . Most vegetables and meats _____ it, too. So you can _____ them _____ potassium as well.

Exercise 5

W Professor: Nowadays, many people _____ _____. They _____ lots of fast food. They eat junk food and drink sodas. As a result, they don't get their _____ _____ of vitamins and minerals.

_____, people can _____ supplements. These _____ people with the _____ amount of vitamins and _____. Now, uh, there are all _____ of _____. Some people _____ multivitamins, which _____ several different vitamins their bodies need. Others just _____ vitamin C, zinc, or calcium, for example.

What are the _____? There are many. Supplements can make people _____. They can help people _____ their weight. Some can _____ such as cancer. Of course, some people _____ _____ many supplements, which can _____ their bodies. But _____ you _____ supplements in _____, you'll be _____.

Exercise 6

M Professor: I _____ a list of _____ foods. We _____ to eat these foods as _____ as _____. The first is _____. Maybe many of you don't _____ its _____. Still, it is good for the muscles.

Next is yogurt. It _____ cancer. Another is tomatoes. They _____ the body fight _____. What else . . . ? Oh, carrots. They also fight cancer and are _____ _____. Next are blueberries and blackberries. These _____ brain activity. They _____ memory, too.

Of course, I _____ not _____ out beans. Beans are _____ _____ many things, _____ the heart. What _____ walnuts? I love walnuts. They are _____ in protein. They have just _____ protein as steak and chicken. And last on my list is oats. They are _____ in _____ and _____ the heart.

Exercise 7

W Professor: Vegetarians do not _____ meat. Some don't _____ fish. There _____ and _____ to _____ a vegetarian. Let me see . . . One _____ advantage is that vegetarians experience _____ in general. Meat _____ have a higher _____ of _____ heart disease and cancer, to name _____. Vegetarians also have _____ cholesterol in their bodies. Their _____ are _____ in _____ vitamins and minerals, too. Of course, they are rarely fat like people _____, well, fast foods. But there are some _____, too. Vegetarian _____ are usually low in _____, calcium, and iron. These are _____ for _____ bones and healthy muscles. Sometimes vegetarians must take extra vitamins. These _____ them get _____ every day. Lots of vegetarians eat plenty of _____, too. Tofu is _____ in protein.

Exercise 8

M Professor: There are many different _____ of cooking _____. But you need to _____ that the _____ you cook food _____ its nutritional _____.

Let's _____ with frying. Fried food is _____ in oil. Most of the time, frying _____ plenty of oil. Well, fried food _____ delicious, but it's not good for your body. All that oil in the food can make you _____ weight. It can _____ heart _____ and other problems, too. I _____ cutting back on fried food. Instead, I _____ steaming food. Steaming _____ the steam from _____ water to cook foods _____ vegetables. This is one of the healthiest cooking _____. Steamed foods _____ their _____. The _____ in vegetables get _____, too, so they are easier for the body to _____. Steamed foods taste _____ as well.

Practice Test

M Professor: The fact is that people _____ caffeine every day. _____ the soft drinks and coffee we drink. One reason is that we _____ the taste, uh, you know, the _____. But another _____ is the caffeine. Caffeine gives us a boost. It _____ us _____ and alert. I read _____ that said that over ninety percent of Americans _____ caffeine every single day. Now, um, caffeine is a natural _____. This means it _____ in the nervous system. Of course, um, there are some side effects. For example, Mr. Smith _____ three or four cups of coffee every day. However, he _____ to cut back on his coffee. So he _____ side effects such as _____ and _____. Now, um, another _____ of caffeine can be _____ problems. For example, a student drinks six colas _____ a prime-time movie. That night, she _____ asleep. The reason is that the caffeine in her system is still _____. So it's keeping her from sleeping. In addition, _____ much caffeine makes people _____ or _____.

Chapter 8

Sample Question

W Professor: The gray wolf is a _____. It is _____ three feet _____ and four feet _____. One _____ is a _____ more _____ thirty centimeters. Hunters _____ made it _____ in the 1900s. Today, the gray wolf is _____. Still, it _____ a _____ life. It sometimes _____ to find food. It fights with other wolves and _____. Most gray wolves _____ in the _____ for only about six to eight years.

Exercise 1

M Professor: The third-largest land animal is the hippopotamus. It _____ more than 7,000 pounds. It can also be _____ ten feet _____. And it can _____ up to five feet _____ at the shoulder. Hippos _____ to _____ in the water. These _____ animals can be _____. They are _____, can run fast, and will attack people and _____ boats _____ their territory.

Exercise 2

M Professor: The bald eagle is a _____ bird. Its white _____ and brown feathers make it look _____ nice. It's too bad that hunters _____ them all. But they are making a _____ today. Let me talk about its size. This is a big bird. _____ are often twenty-five percent _____ than _____. For example, the _____ female's wingspan is seven feet. That's about 213 centimeters. The average female's weight is _____ thirteen pounds. That's _____ 5.8 kilograms. A male, however, _____ around nine pounds.

Exercise 3

W Professor: The blue whale is the _____ animal _____ to live. This _____ the dinosaurs. Some of these animals _____ _____ 100 feet in _____. Their average _____ is about seventy feet. And listen to this . . . Most adult blue whales _____ about ninety tons. It's _____ that whale hunting _____ made them _____. However, in 1966, they _____ a _____ species. So their numbers _____ to increase. Still, _____ there are only around 10,000 in the world's oceans.

Exercise 4

M Professor: The grizzly bear _____ in the mountains of North America. It is a _____ species. This _____ that the grizzly bear's numbers are at _____ low levels. But they are _____ beginning to increase. Still, it is _____ to hunt them in Alaska and Canada.

Grizzlies are big, powerful bears. When they are _____, they can be about 2.4 meters in _____. Males weigh two times _____ females. Adult males _____ about 272 kilograms in _____.

Exercise 5

W Professor: You probably _____ that dolphins only _____ in salt water, right? Well, if you do, you're wrong. The pink river dolphin, or boto, _____ in _____ water. This dolphin can be _____ mainly in the Amazon and Orinoco rivers in South America. The pink river dolphin is the _____ river dolphin _____ in the world. It _____ to be around 8.2 meters in length. Males can _____ more than 180 kilograms. That's a big mammal, huh? Some of them _____ also _____ in the _____ for _____ thirty years.

There are a _____ of these dolphins in the wild. However, they are _____ a _____ species. The problem is that the _____ in some places they live is _____. In addition, dams are _____ with the _____ where many of these animals live.

Exercise 6

M Professor: Pandas are _____ the _____ loved animals on the planet. They are _____ the most popular _____ at zoos. Adults can _____ around 117 kilograms.

They are one of the most _____, too. These cute, _____, _____ bears could become _____ soon. Today, you can only find them in the wild in China. In 2005, there were 1,596 pandas in the wild. There, _____

Dictation Exercises 191

them for their _____ and paws. They once lived in Burma and Vietnam. But they became _____ in those areas because of hunters.

Pandas are also _____ their _____. And get this . . . They _____ about fourteen hours a day _____ bamboo. Most wild pandas can live to be about fifteen years old. They can _____ to be _____ thirty in zoos _____.

Exercise 7

M Professor: Rhinos _____ on the _____ of _____ species. A long time ago, there were more than twenty _____ of rhinos. Today, there are only five _____. Experts _____ there are around 30,000 rhinos left on the Earth. In _____, there are more than 7,500. The two main _____ are the African and Asian rhino.

The main _____ to rhinos _____ from poaching and the _____ of habitat. Poachers _____ hunt and kill rhinos for their horns. The African rhino has two horns. The Asian rhino has one. Many projects to save rhinos are _____. Still, rhinos need more _____.

Some of you might _____ that rhinos are really _____. Well, they are. They are _____ like tanks. They are also _____ swimmers and runners. Most rhinos can run around forty miles _____ hour. That's very _____ for such a big _____.

Exercise 8

W Professor: The Siberian tiger is the _____ tiger. It can _____ more than 670 pounds. However, the tiger has a _____ story. Just _____ 100 years ago, there were tigers _____ in Asia. They _____ in Nepal, China, India, Southeast Asia, and _____ places. But today, in many of these countries, the tiger is extinct.

_____ think there are only _____ 5,000 tigers _____ in the wild now. There were more than 100,000 tigers 100 years ago. _____ shocking! But it is a very sad _____. Hunters _____ and _____ them to sell their fur. But that's not all. Hunters sell the tiger meat, bones, and other _____, too. They _____ tiger cubs to sell as pets. I _____ people _____ buy tiger cubs. _____ terrible!

Practice Test

M Professor: Animals _____ to _____ fat _____. Many animals _____ a long time _____ the year. We call this _____.
_____ animals _____ themselves up to _____. Why? Well, in winter, food can _____, so it's hard to find. So animals eat as much as they can before winter _____. They eat and _____ it as fat in their bodies. _____ also _____ animals _____ energy.
Now, please _____ closely. During hibernation, the animal's body _____ drops. This _____ the animal _____ less energy even while it sleeps. We all know that bears _____ during winter. In fact, _____ of bears hibernate. They go into a _____, which is usually a cave or _____ an old tree trunk, and then sleep _____ winter. Many bears can spend more than three months hibernating. They do not _____, _____, or _____ about during this time. Isn't that amazing? Other hibernating animals like raccoons _____ _____ to eat stored food or, um, to _____ themselves. Bears, however, do not.

Actual Test 1

Actual Test 1 Conversation

W Student: Hello, Professor Madison. _____ I _____ with you for a _____?

M Professor: Sure, Wendy. What's on your _____?

W: It's the _____ exam.

M: Ah, yeah. You didn't _____ too _____ on it, did you?

W: Not at all. I was _____ really _____ last week.

M: I'm sorry. Are you _____ now?

W: Yes, I'm okay. So, uh . . . I _____ if . . .

M: Yes?

W: Could I _____ the test? I _____, uh, I was sick.

M: I'm really sorry, but I _____ do that.

W: Are you sure?

M: Yes. It's a school rule. _____ are not _____. But . . .

W: But what?

M: I can give you a _____. Are you _____ in that?

W: _____. That would _____ _____.

Actual Test 1 Lecture

M Professor: We need to _____ something _____. You will _____ two words in my class this _____. The words are _____ and _____. Most people _____ they're the _____. However, that isn't _____. Let me _____ the difference. Weather _____ to specific _____ in the _____. For _____, it _____ be sunny on a hot day. Or it could be snowy on a cold and cloudy day. Weather _____ events that _____ in just a few hours. It could also _____ to events that _____ in a few days or even weeks. Weather _____ refers to short-term _____.

194

What about climate? Well, climate refers to the _____ weather conditions over a long _____ of time. How long? _____, it's at _____ thirty years. It could be longer _____. For example, we can talk _____ the _____ climate _____ the time of the dinosaurs. That period covers millions of years.

Why is it important to know the _____? Hmm . . . _____ is one reason. During summer, the weather _____ very hot for a few days. Then, many people start claiming the Earth is _____. Sorry, but you can't tell that from just a few days of _____. You have to look at long-term data _____. You know, the _____. Try to remember this _____ all semester long. Okay?

Actual Test 2

Actual Test 2 Conversation

W Librarian: Good morning. _____ can I _____ you?

M Student: Hello. I'm _____ Ms. Julie Samuels.

W: That's me. And you are . . .?

M: My name is David Thompson. I called you yesterday.

W: Ah, yes, Mr. Thompson. We _____ a job, right?

M: That's right. I _____ you have a position _____ here.

W: You are _____. Do you have any _____ working in a library?

M: Actually, yes. I _____ volunteer at my local library.

W: What _____ you do there?

M: I _____ books. I helped people find material. I checked out books, too.

W: That's _____ what you _____ do here.

M: Great. Um . . . does that mean I'm _____?

W: It _____. There are two work _____. One is one Monday afternoon. The _____ is on Friday evening.

M: I'm free both days.

W: _____ me then. You need to _____ some paperwork.

M: Sounds good. Thanks a lot, Ms. Samuels.

Actual Test 2 Lecture

W Professor: In the past, many teachers _____ _____ rote learning. In fact, many _____ _____ it today. Rote learning _____ memorization. Students _____ information again and again. This _____ them memorize it. Rote learning is very effective. But it's _____ the only learning _____. It's also not the _____ method for some students.

One woman _____ her own learning _____. Her name was Maria Montessori. She _____ up with the Montessori Method. Montessori believed children _____ to _____ at different paces. Some were fast learners. Others were slow learners. In _____ classrooms, this was a problem. Why? Well, teachers went _____ _____ for the best students. And teachers went too fast for the _____ students. Montessori _____ students to _____ at their own _____. She wanted them to _____ on _____ their own natural _____, too. The students who learned with her method were given a lot of _____. Montessori _____ play was important. In fact, she said, "Play is work." She also liked _____ learning. Her classrooms had toys and other materials. Teachers _____ students to use them. That way, students could learn. Teachers also had students do _____ activities, such as _____ and cleaning.

This method is not for all students. But it has been _____ for many. I wonder . . . Did any of you _____ with the Montessori Method?

Actual Test 3

Actual Test 3 Conversation

W Professor: Good afternoon, Matt. _____ can I _____ you?

M Student: Hello, Professor Arnold. I just _____ the class list for next semester.

W: Oh? _____ are you going to _____?

M: I'd _____ _____ take your _____ on medieval _____.

W: You're a junior, right?

M: That's _____. Is that a problem?

W: Well, seniors usually _____ all the _____ in seminars.

M: How many students can _____ for it?

W: Only fifteen. And those spots _____ very fast.

M: So I probably won't _____ for it, right?

W: That's _____. Sorry about that.

M: That's a _____. I was really _____ it.

W: Don't worry too much. I have some _____ for you.

M: What's that?

W: I'm _____ to teach _____ seminar next year, too.

M: That's wonderful _____. I'm really _____ forward _____.

Actual Test 3 Lecture

W Professor: That _____ of music _____ from one of my favorite _____. Does anyone know it . . .? No . . .? That's too bad. It was from a _____ of orchestral music called *Water Music*. The _____ was George Frideric Handel. Handel _____ in 1685. That was _____ year Johann Sebastian Bach was born. _____, the two great _____ never _____. Handel died in 1759. He lived during the Baroque Period. He was _____ of that period's best _____.

Most people know Handel for his oratorios. An oratorio is a long musical work which usually has a _____. It _____ an orchestra. It also has solo singers _____ a chorus. Handel's most _____ work was the *Messiah*, an oratorio. It tells the story of Jesus Christ. _____, Handel _____ the _____ oratorio in just twenty-four days. The *Messiah* _____ an _____ hit. The "Hallelujah Chorus" is the best-known piece of music in it. _____ to stories, King George II of England was very _____ by the performance. So he stood up _____ the "Hallelujah Chorus." _____ then, _____ around the world have done the same.

Handel did not just _____ oratorios _____. He _____ operas, too. In fact, he _____ more than forty of them. One _____ opera of his was *Orlando*. *Music for the Royal Fireworks* was another _____ work of Handel's.

Publisher Kyudo Chung
Editors Minhyuck Kim, Sangik Cho
Author William Link
Designers Minji Kim, Kyuok Jeong

First published in December 2007 by Happy House
Second edition first published in June 2023 by Darakwon, Inc.
Darakwon Bldg., 211, Munbal-ro, Paju-si, Gyeonggi-do 10881
Republic of Korea
Tel: 82-2-736-2031 (Ext. 250)
Fax: 82-2-732-2037

Copyright © 2007 Happy House, 2023 Darakwon

All rights reserved. No part of this publication may be reproduced, stored in a retrieval system, or transmitted in any form or by any means, electronic, mechanical, photocopying or otherwise, without the prior consent of the copyright owner. Refund after purchase is possible only according to the company regulations. Contact the above telephone number for any inquiries. Consumer damages caused by loss, damage, etc. can be compensated according to the consumer dispute resolution standards announced by the Korea Fair Trade Commission. An incorrectly collated book will be exchanged.

ISBN 978-89-277-8058-8 14740
        978-89-277-8056-4 14740 (set)

www.darakwon.co.kr

Photo Credits
Shutterstock.com

Components Main Book / Answer Key
8 7 6 5 4 3 2   24 25 26 27 28

High Score iBT TOEFL LISTENING For Junior

2nd Edition

Beginner

Answer Key

DARAKWON

CHAPTER 1 Weather

Understanding TOEFL Question Types & Listening Skills p.14

1 Question Types ▶ Sample Question
Ⓓ

스크립트 🎧 01-01

M Professor: Most thunderstorms occur when the atmosphere is very, um, moist and unstable. Lightning and thunder are common during thunderstorms. So is very heavy rain. Clouds during thunderstorms are usually dark. They may even be black. Thunderstorms can develop very quickly and be quite dangerous. You should always seek shelter when a thunderstorm is approaching.

해석

M Professor: 대부분의 뇌우(雷雨)는 대기가 매우 습하고 불안정할 때 발생합니다. 뇌우는 보통 번개와 천둥을 동반하죠. 그래서 비도 매우 많이 옵니다. 뇌우 발생시 보통 먹구름이 낍니다. 검은 색을 띨 수도 있죠. 뇌우는 매우 빠르게 발달해서 상당히 위험할 수도 있어요. 뇌우가 다가오면 항상 대피할 곳을 찾아야 합니다.

2 Listening Skills ▶ Check-Up

1 Lightning and thunder are common during thunderstorms.
2 Clouds during thunderstorms are usually dark.
3 They may even be black.

• Exercise 1 • p.16

정답 Ⓑ

스크립트 🎧 01-03

M Professor: There are many types of precipitation, class. Rain is one. Of course, it is very common. Another type, called hail, is more uncommon. Hail forms in cloud layers in swirling winds. Drops of rain spin around in cloud. As they do this, they collect more and more moisture. This moisture also freezes very quickly. The drops become heavier and heavier as they get bigger. Finally, the hail falls to the ground. Some hail can be the size of a golf ball.

해석

M Professor: 학생 여러분, 강우에는 여러 종류가 있습니다. 그 중 하나가 비죠. 물론 비가 가장 일반적입니다. 또 다른 종류인 우박은 그리 흔하지 않습니다. 우박은 소용돌이치는 바람에 의해 구름층에서 형성됩니다. 빗방울이 구름 속에서 빙빙 돌다가 점차 습기를 모으게 됩니다. 이 습기는 또한 급속히 냉각됩니다. 물방울은 커질 수록 더 무거워집니다. 마침내 우박이 땅으로 떨어집니다. 일부 우박은 크기가 골프공만 할 수도 있습니다.

Listening Skills

1 It is very common.
2 Hail forms in cloud layers in swirling winds.
3 Some hail can be the size of a golf ball.

• Exercise 2 • p.17

정답 Ⓐ

스크립트 🎧 01-05

W Professor: Cold fronts move toward the south. Well, they move to the south and the east. They usually clash with warmer air. So along the actual front line, there is often unstable weather. This could be in the form of rain or snow. It depends on the season and the area. But soon, the cold front pushes away the bad weather. The weather then becomes dry and cool. This happens because high pressure follows the cold front.

해석

W Professor: 한랭전선은 남쪽으로 이동합니다. 음, 남쪽과 동쪽으로 이동을 하죠. 한랭전선은 보통 따뜻한 공기와 충돌합니다. 그래서 실제 전선 주변의 날씨는 종종 불안정합니다. 비나 눈이 내릴 수도 있습니다. 계절과 지역에 따라 다르지만요. 그러나 곧 한랭전선이 궂은 날씨를 몰아냅니다. 그런 다음에는 날씨가 건조하고 추워집니다. 이는 고기압이 한랭전선을 따라다니기 때문입니다.

Listening Skills

1 It depends on the season and the area.
2 The weather then becomes dry and cool.
3 This happens because high pressure follows the cold front.

• Exercise 3 • p.18

정답 Ⓓ

스크립트 🎧 01-07

M Professor: Okay. Let's discuss the tornado's close relative: the waterspout. First, unlike tornadoes, waterspouts form on water. They normally form over large lakes and oceans. They are also not nearly as strong as tornadoes. Waterspouts are usually smaller than tornadoes, too. Oh, there's another difference between the two. Waterspouts form on the surface of the water and then rise in the air toward clouds. Tornadoes, however, typically develop in clouds and then move downward.

해석

M Professor: 좋아요. 토네이도와 아주 유사한 물기둥에 대해 논의해 봅시다. 먼저 물기둥은 물에서 발생하는데, 토네이도와는 달리 주로 큰 호수나 대양에서 발생합니다. 물기둥은 육지의 토네이도만큼 강력하지는 않습니다. 또한 물기둥은 토네이도보다 보통 작습니다. 그리고 둘 사이에는 또 다른 차이점이 있습니다. 물기둥은 수면 위에서 형성되어 구름 쪽으로 올라갑니다. 하지만 토네이도는 일반적으로 구름에서 발생해서 아래로 내려오죠.

Listening Skills

1 Waterspouts form on water.
2 Waterspouts form on the surface of the water.
3 There's another difference between the two.

• Exercise 4 • p.19

정답 Ⓐ

스크립트 🎧 01-09

M Professor: No rain for a week or two does not make a drought. Droughts occur only after a long period of time without regular rainfall. It may rain during that time. However, it doesn't rain much. By the way, a long period of time means months or years. The effects of a drought can spell disaster for an area. Let's see . . . Lakes begin to dry up. Agriculture takes a big hit. And then there are small plants and bushes. Fires destroy lots of vegetation that is still alive.

해석

M Professor: 한두 주 동안 비가 오지 않는다고 해서 가뭄이 일어나는 것은 아닙니다. 가뭄은 장기간 동안 일정량의 비가 내리지 않아야만 발생합니다. 이러한 기간 동안 비가 내릴 수도 있습니다. 하지만 충분하지가 않죠. 그건 그렇고, 장기간은 몇 개월이나 몇 년을 의미합니다. 가뭄의 결과로 일정 지역에 지해가 발생할 수도 있습니다. 그러니까… 호수가 마르기 시작합니다. 농사는 꽤 큰 타격을 입습니다. 그리고 작은 식물과 관목들이 있습니다. 화재로 인해 살아남았던 많은 식물들이 사라집니다.

Listening Skills

1 It may rain during that time.
2 Lakes begin to dry up.
3 Agriculture takes a big hit.

• Exercise 5 • p.20

정답 Q1 Ⓒ Q2 Ⓒ

스크립트 🎧 01-11

W Professor: There are many types of clouds in the sky. Usually, we classify them by their altitude and formation. Let me give you an example. Among the highest clouds are cirrus clouds. They look like a horse's tail in the sky. You can usually see them on a clear day.
A common mid-level cloud is the altocumulus cloud. It looks like small cotton balls in the sky. This type of cloud is also mostly white. But it might also have shades of gray. This means that rain is probably on the way.
Then there are huge cumulonimbus clouds. They're the largest ones in the sky. These can be white or dark gray. They come with high winds and form very quickly. Be careful of these, class. Powerful thunderstorms develop in these kinds of clouds.

해석

W Professor: 하늘에는 아주 많은 종류의 구름이 있습니다. 우리는 주로 고도와 형태에 따라 구름을 분류합니다. 예를 들어보죠. 가장 높은 곳에 있는 구름은 권운입니다. 권운은 하늘에서 말의 꼬리처럼 보입니다. 주로 맑은 날 볼 수 있죠.
중간 높이에 있는 구름은 보통 고적운입니다. 하늘에서 작은 솜뭉치처럼 보이죠. 이들도 보통 하얗습니다. 그러나 때때로 회색 빛깔을 띠기도 해요. 이는 곧 비가 내릴 수 있다는 의미일 수도 있습니다.
그리고 크기가 거대한 적란운이 있습니다. 하늘에서 가장 큰 구름이죠. 흰색이나 어두운 회색을 띨 수 있습니다. 높은 바람을 동반하며 아주 빠르게 형성됩니다. 여러분, 이 구름은 조심해야 합니다. 이러한 구름에서 강력한 뇌우가 발생합니다.

Listening Skills

1 Among the highest clouds are cirrus clouds.
2 You can usually see them on a clear day.
3 This means that rain is probably on the way.

• Exercise 6 • p.21

정답 Q1 Ⓓ Q2 Ⓐ

스크립트 🎧 01-13

M Professor: That was a lot of fog we had this morning. Well, what is fog? It's basically clouds close to the ground. So fog can cause visibility problems for people. I mean, it's hard to see through clouds, isn't it?
How does fog form? Let me tell you. First, you need nearly 100% humidity. So there should be lots of water vapor in the air. Next, the water vapor condenses, so it changes from a gaseous state to a liquid one. The water droplets then join with dust or pollution to create fog. Uh, that's why cities often get fog. You know, uh, they usually have lots of pollution. And fog is quite common near bodies of water such as lakes, oceans, and seas.

해석

M Professor: 오늘 아침 안개가 많이 끼었더군요. 자, 안개란 무엇일까요? 기본적으로 지면 가까이에 있는 구름입니다. 그래서 안개는 사람들에게 시야 문제를 일으킬 수 있습니다. 구름 사이로 보는 것은 어렵다는 뜻이에요, 그렇지 않나요?
안개는 어떻게 만들어지는 걸까요? 말씀을 드리죠. 첫째, 거의 100%의 습도가 필요합니다. 따라서 공기 중에 많은 수증기가 있어야 해요. 다음으로, 수증기가 응축되어 기체 상태에서 액체 상태로 변하게 됩니다. 그러면 물방울들이 먼지나 오염 물질과 결합해서 안개가 만들어지죠. 어, 이것이 바로 도시에 안개가 자주 끼는 이유입니다. 아시다시피, 어, 도시에는 보통 오염 물질들이 많으니까요. 그리고 안개는 호수, 바다, 그리고 바다와 같은 수역 근처에서도 상당히 흔히 발생합니다.

Listening Skills

1 So fog can cause visibility problems for people.
2 First, you need nearly 100% humidity.
3 The water droplets then join with dust or pollution to create fog.

• Exercise 7 • p.22

정답 Q1 Ⓐ Q2 Ⓓ

스크립트 🎧 01-15

M Professor: Scientists try to learn about the weather. This helps them forecast it better. It also tells them what kind of weather is happening. Let me tell you about some of their tools.
First, of course, is the thermometer. It tells the temperature. The barometer is another important instrument. It measures air pressure. Usually, rising air pressure means pleasant weather. When the air pressure is falling, there will be rainy or snowy weather.
Those are the two primary tools. But there are others. Windsocks tell which direction the wind is blowing. Rain gauges are very useful. They measure the amount of rain that falls during a storm. Farmers make use of rain gauges. They need to know how much water their crops are getting.

해석

M Professor: 과학자들은 날씨를 알기 위해 노력합니다. 그러면 날씨를 더 잘 예측할 수가 있죠. 또한 어떤 날씨가 나타날 것인지도 알려줍니다. 그들의 도구 중 몇 가지를 말씀드리죠.
첫째는 당연하게도 온도계입니다. 온도를 알려주죠. 또 다른 중요한 도구는 기압계입니다. 기압을 측정하죠. 보통, 기압이 상승하면 쾌적한 날씨가 이어집니다. 기압이 떨어질 때에는 비나 눈이 내리게 되죠.
이들은 두 가지 중요한 도구입니다. 하지만 다른 도구들도 있어요. 바람자루는 바람이 어느 방향으로 불고 있는지를 말해줍니다. 우량계도 매우 유용해요. 우량계는 폭풍 동안 내리는 비의 양을 측정합니다. 농부들이 유량계를 사용합니다. 자신의 농작물에 얼마나 많은 물이 유입되는지 알아야 하거든요.

Listening Skills

1 Scientists try to learn about the weather.
2 The barometer is another important instrument.
3 They measure the amount of rain that falls during a storm.

• Exercise 8 • p.23

정답 Q1 Ⓐ Q2 Ⓒ

스크립트 🎧 01-17

W Professor: There are two main types of floods. The first happens when there is heavy rainfall in an area. Bodies of water such as lakes and rivers cannot hold all of the water that suddenly flows into them. As a result, they overflow. This is a flash flood. A flash flood can have dire effects on a region. How dangerous it is depends on the amount and duration of the rainfall. Nonstop rain can flood everything. Then, the ground is completely covered. Trees and cars are washed away. Houses and other buildings are damaged. Flash floods can be quite harmful.
What about the other type of flood? This is a river flood. Long-lasting rain, hurricanes, and melting snow can cause river floods. This type of flood usually happens in places with wet climates.

해석

W Professor: 크게 두 가지 유형의 홍수가 있습니다. 첫 번째는 한 지역에 폭우가 내릴 때 발생하죠. 호수나 강과 같은 수역이 갑자기 유입된 물을 감당할 수 없게 됩니다. 결국 물이 넘쳐납니다. 이는 갑작스러운 홍수입니다. 갑작스러운 홍수는 한 지역에 심각한 영향을 미칠 수 있어요. 얼마나 위험한지는 강우량 및 강우 시간에 달려 있습니다. 쉬지 않고 비가 내리면 모든 것이 범람할 수 있습니다. 그렇게 되면 지면이 완전히 잠깁니다. 나무와 차들이 떠내려가죠. 주택과 기타 건물들도 손상됩니다. 갑작스러운 홍수는 꽤 해로울 수 있어요.
다른 유형의 홍수는 어떨까요? 바로 강 홍수입니다. 장기간의 비, 허리케인, 그리고 녹는 눈으로 인해 강 홍수가 일어날 수 있습니다. 이러한 유형의 홍수는 보통 기후가 습한 지역에서 발생합니다.

Listening Skills

1 There are two main types of floods.
2 A flash flood can have dire effects on a region.
3 Long-lasting rain, hurricanes, and melting snow can cause river floods.

Vocabulary Review p.24

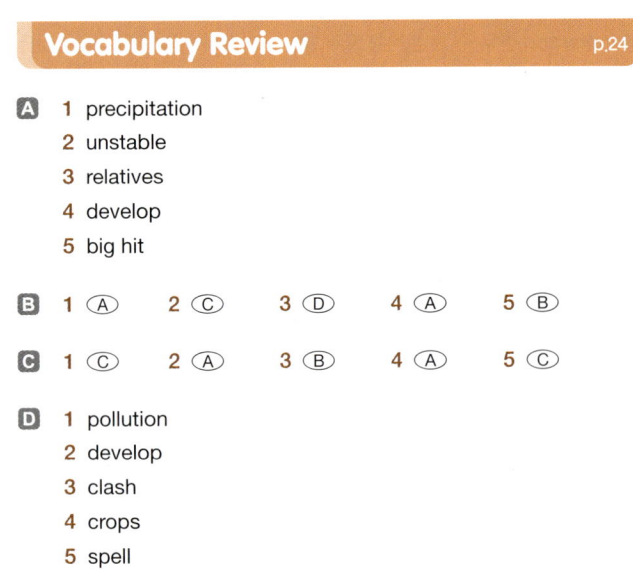

A 1 precipitation
   2 unstable
   3 relatives
   4 develop
   5 big hit

B 1 Ⓐ 2 Ⓒ 3 Ⓓ 4 Ⓐ 5 Ⓑ

C 1 Ⓒ 2 Ⓐ 3 Ⓑ 4 Ⓐ 5 Ⓒ

D 1 pollution
   2 develop
   3 clash
   4 crops
   5 spell

Practice Test p.26

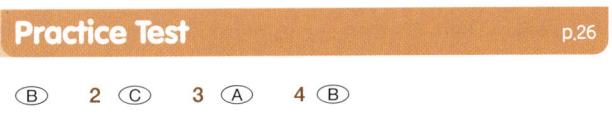

1 Ⓑ 2 Ⓒ 3 Ⓐ 4 Ⓑ

스크립트 🎧 01-19

M Professor: Ocean currents are like rivers of moving water in the ocean. One of the best-known currents is the Gulf Stream. It begins in the Gulf of Mexico. It then goes into the Atlantic Ocean and heads up the eastern coast of the United States. It then heads west across the Atlantic and winds up in northern Europe.
Something interesting about ocean currents is that they can affect the weather. The Gulf Stream is a warm-water current. It influences part of the eastern coast of the U.S. It also affects Northwest Europe a great deal. How so? Well, it makes the climates in those two places warmer than they should be. For

instance, England is at a fairly high latitude. So it should be a very cold place. However, the Gulf Stream flows near the country. So it helps make the temperature in England warmer. There are some other currents that affect the weather in different places. Let me tell you about one that's near South America . . .

해석

M Professor: 해류는 바다에서 흐르는 강물과 같습니다. 가장 잘 알려진 해류 중 하나는 걸프 스트림입니다. 이는 멕시코 만에서 시작되죠. 그리고 나서 대서양으로 흘러 미국의 동쪽 해안으로 향합니다. 그 다음에는 대서양을 가로질러 서쪽으로 흘러가서 북유럽에서 끝나게 됩니다.

해류의 흥미로운 점은 해류가 날씨에 영향을 미칠 수 있다는 것입니다. 걸프 스트림은 따뜻한 해류입니다. 이는 미국 동부의 일부 해안가에 영향을 미칩니다. 또한 북서 유럽에도 많은 영향을 미치죠. 어떻게요? 음, 이 두 지역의 기후를 원래보다 더 따뜻하게 만듭니다. 예를 들어 영국은 꽤 높은 위도에 위치해 있어요. 그래서 매우 추운 곳이어야 합니다. 하지만 걸프 스트림이 영국 주변을 흐릅니다. 그래서 영국의 기온을 더 따뜻하게 만들어주는 것이죠.

여러 지역의 날씨에 영향을 미치는 또 다른 해류들도 있습니다. 남미 근처에 있는 해류에 대해 말씀을 드리면…

CHAPTER 2 Office Hour & Service Encounters

Understanding TOEFL Question Types & Listening Skills

p.30

1 Question Types ▶ Sample Question

B

스크립트 🎧 02-01

M Professor: Good afternoon, Lisa. Why are you here today?
W Student: I have a problem. I want to talk about our homework assignment.
M: Sure. Did you already complete it?
W: No, I have not begun yet. I don't understand it.
M: Okay. Let me try to clarify it for you.
W: Really? Can you do that?
M: Of course. It's no problem at all.

해석

M Professor: 안녕하세요, 리사. 여기엔 무슨 일이죠?
W Student: 문제가 좀 있어서요. 과제에 대해 이야기를 나누고 싶어요.
M: 좋아요. 이미 다 했나요?
W: 아뇨. 아직 시작도 못 했어요. 이해가 가지 않아서요.
M: 알겠어요. 내가 다시 설명해 주도록 하죠.
W: 정말인가요? 그렇게 해 주실 수 있으세요?
M: 물론이죠. 전혀 문제될 것이 없어요.

2 Listening Skills ▶ Check-Up

1 complete it
2 clarify it
3 have not begun
4 at all

• Exercise 1 •

p.32

정답

스크립트 🎧 02-03

M1 Student: Professor Stephens, are you busy?
M2 Professor: Not really. I have a few minutes. What can I do for you?
M1: I, um, need to decide on my schedule for next semester. You're my advisor. So I thought you could assist me.
M2: Sure. Do you have any problems?
M1: Well, I have decided on most of my schedule. But I need one more literature class.
M2: Why don't you take my seminar? You could join that with no problem.
M1: You're teaching one? I didn't know that.
M2: I just recently decided to do it.

해석

M1 Student: 스티븐스 교수님, 바쁘신가요?

M2 Professor: 글쎄요, 몇 분 정도는 시간이 있어요. 무슨 일이죠?
M1: 어, 제가 다음 학기 스케줄을 짜야 하는데요. 제 지도교수님이시잖아요. 그래서 저를 도와주실 거라고 생각했어요.
M2: 물론이죠, 물론이고 말고요. 어떤 문제가 있나요?
M1: 대부분의 스케줄은 짰는데, 문학 강의를 하나 더 들을까 해요.
M2: 내 세미나 수업을 듣는 건 어때요? 수업에 들어와도 괜찮아요.
M1: 교수님께서 강의를 하신다구요? 제가 몰랐군요.
M2: 최근에 그렇게 하기로 결정을 했죠.

Listening Skills

1 most of
2 my advisor
3 you could assist me
4 have decided on

• Exercise 2 • p.33

정답 Ⓐ

스크립트 02-05

W Librarian: Can I help you?
M Student: Yes, I don't know how to find any books.
W: It's really easy. You need to use the library's computer system.
M: Right. But what do I do?
W: First, type in the author or title of the book. Or type the subject of the book.
M: Great. What's next?
W: Next, click on the book you want. Then, you can find the book's call number.
M: The call number?
W: Yes, the call number shows the book's location. There's the call number. So now you can find the book.
M: Wow. That's easy.

해석

W Librarian: 도와드릴까요?
M Student: 네, 제가 책을 찾는 방법을 몰라서요.
W: 아주 쉬워요. 도서관 컴퓨터 시스템을 이용하면 돼요.
M: 그렇죠. 그런데 어떻게 해야 하나요?
W: 먼저 책의 저자나 제목을 입력해요. 아니면 책의 주제를 입력하세요.
M: 좋아요. 다음엔요?
W: 그리고 나서는 원하는 책을 클릭하세요. 그러면 책의 도서정리번호가 나올 거예요.
M: 도서정리번호요?
W: 네, 도서정리번호가 책의 위치를 알려주죠. 여기 도서정리번호가 있네요. 이제 책을 찾을 수 있을 거예요.
M: 와, 쉽네요.

Listening Skills

1 find any books
2 It is really easy.
3 subject of
4 That's easy.

• Exercise 3 • p.34

정답 Ⓐ

스크립트 02-07

W1 Student: Professor Duncan, you wanted to see me?
W2 Professor: Yes, Melissa. I'd like to speak about your recent report.
W1: Oh, you hated it, didn't you? I'm so sorry.
W2: Melissa, please. Let me finish. Actually, I thought it was quite fascinating.
W1: Really?
W2: Yes. I really think you had some great ideas. In fact, I firmly believe you ought to try to publish your report in a magazine or journal.
W1: Wow. I had no idea.
W2: Of course, you can improve on some of your ideas. But I can help you with that.

해석

W1 Student: 던컨 교수님, 부르셨어요?
W2 Professor: 네, 멜리사. 최근에 제출한 보고서에 대해 이야기를 좀 하고 싶어요.
W1: 오, 맘에 안 드셨군요. 죄송합니다.
W2: 멜리사, 잠깐만요. 끝까지 들어야죠. 실은 아주 잘 썼다고 생각했어요.
W1: 정말인가요?
W2: 그래요. 실제로 학생이 아주 멋진 아이디어를 가지고 있다고 생각했어요. 사실, 멜리사가 잡지나 간행물에 보고서를 발표해야 한다고 생각하고 있어요.
W1: 와, 전혀 몰랐어요.
W2: 물론 아이디어를 좀 더 발전시킬 수 있을 거예요. 그 점에 대해서는 제가 도와줄 수 있어요.

Listening Skills

1 you hated it
2 I am so sorry.
3 great ideas
4 But I can help you with that.

• Exercise 4 • p.35

정답 Ⓓ

스크립트 02-09

W Student: I'm interested in studying in another country.
M Study Abroad Employee: Great. Which country are you thinking of?
W: Well, I can speak Spanish and some Italian.
M: Hmm . . . Europe would be a good choice. Or maybe you could go to South America.
W: South America? That sounds intriguing.
M: Would you like some more information?
W: Sure. First, I'd like to know where I can go. I'd also like to

know the price of going to each country. I don't have that much money.
M: No problem. Here, take these brochures and look at them.

해석

W Student: 저는 해외 유학에 관심이 있어요.
M Study Abroad Employee: 좋아요. 어떤 나라를 생각하고 있나요?
W: 음, 제가 스페인어와 이태리어를 좀 할 수 있어요.
M: 음… 유럽은 좋은 선택이 될 수 있죠. 아니면 남미로 갈 수도 있을 것이고요.
W: 남미요? 흥미롭게 들리는군요.
M: 그에 대한 정보를 더 드릴까요?
W: 물론이죠. 먼저 제가 어디를 갈 수 있는지 알고 싶어요. 또 각각의 나라에 가는 비용도 알고 싶고요. 돈이 그렇게 많지는 않아서요.
M: 문제 없어요. 여기, 이 안내책자를 보세요.

Listening Skills

1 interested in
2 Spanish and some Italian
3 be a good choice
4 the price of going to each country

• Exercise 5 • p.36

정답 Q1 ⒟ Q2 Ⓑ
스크립트 🎧 02-11
W Professor: Do you know why I want to speak with you?
M Student: Um, not really.
W: It's about your homework assignments.
M: What homework assignments?
W: You have had five homework assignments this semester. But you have submitted none of them.
M: I didn't know about any homework assignments.
W: They are on your syllabus.
M: Oh, I lost that on the first day of class.
W: Well, you have to do your homework. It's worth twenty percent of your grade. And right now, you have a great big zero.
M: That is not good, is it?
W: No. But there are still four more homework assignments remaining. I hope you do them all. That way, you'll only lose ten points on your final grade.
M: Yes, ma'am. I'll do my best from now on.

해석

W Professor: 왜 학생을 불렀는지 알고 있나요?
M Student: 음, 사실 모르겠습니다.
W: 학생의 과제 때문이에요.
M: 무슨 과제인가요?
W: 이번 학기 과제가 5개잖아요. 그런데 학생은 그 중 하나도 제출하지 않았어요.
M. 과제가 있는지 몰랐어요.
W: 강의 계획서에 나와 있어요.
M: 오, 제가 수업 첫날에 그걸 잃어버렸어요.

W: 음, 학생은 과제를 해야만 해요. 학점의 20%를 차지하죠. 그리고 지금으로서는 학생의 점수가 0점이에요.
M: 좋지 않네요, 그렇죠?
W: 맞아요. 하지만 아직 4개의 과제가 남아 있어요. 그건 다 하길 바라요. 그러면 최종 점수에서 10점만 깎이게 될 테니까요.
M: 네, 교수님. 지금부터 최선을 다하도록 하겠습니다.

Listening Skills

1 percent of your grade
2 is it
3 why I want
4 that is not good

• Exercise 6 • p.37

정답 Q1 Ⓓ Q2 Ⓒ
스크립트 🎧 02-13
M Student: Hello, Professor Maddux. You wanted to see me?
W Professor: That's right, Eric. Why don't you sit down here? I have something important to discuss with you.
M: Okay. What's going on?
W: Remember how you wanted to take a class in ancient Greek? You mentioned that to me two weeks ago.
M: Ah, yes. That would be great. Is the school going to offer a class?
W: No, we won't be doing that. However . . .
M: Yes?
W: There will be a class on ancient Greek at Central University next semester. Our schools have an agreement. Students here are permitted to take classes at Central University.
M: I had no idea. The school is only about fifteen minutes away from here, so it's not far.
W: One of my friends is the instructor. I'm sure you'll enjoy it.
M: That sounds perfect. If it fits my schedule, I'll be sure to sign up for it. Thanks so much.
W: You're welcome.

해석

M Student: 안녕하세요, 매덕스 교수님, 저를 보고자 하셨죠?
W Professor: 맞아요, 에릭. 여기 앉지 그래요? 의논해야 할 중요한 일이 있어서요.
M: 네, 무슨 일인가요?
W: 학생이 고대 그리스어 수업을 듣고 싶어했던 점을 기억하나요? 2주 전에 제게 말을 했잖아요.
M: 아, 네. 그러면 좋을 것 같아요. 학교측이 수업을 개설할 건가요?
W: 아니요, 그렇지는 않아요. 하지만…
M: 네?
W: 다음 학기에 센트럴 대학에서 고대 그리스어 수업이 있을거에요. 우리 학교들은 협정을 맺고 있죠. 이곳 학생들이 센트럴 대학에서 수업을 듣는 것도 가능해요.
M: 전혀 몰랐어요. 그 학교는 여기서 불과 15분 정도 거리에 있기 때문에 멀지 않아요.

W: 내 친구 중 한 명이 교수예요. 분명 재미있을 거예요.
M: 완벽하군요. 제 스케줄과 맞으면 꼭 등록하도록 할게요. 정말 감사합니다.
W: 천만에요.

Listening Skills

1 why don't you
2 remember how you wanted
3 we won't be doing that
4 fifteen minutes away

• Exercise 7 • p.38

정답 Q1 ⓒ   Q2 Ⓐ
스크립트 🎧 02-15

W Student: Hello, Professor Sanders. May I ask you a question?
M Professor: Of course, Emily. What do you need?
W: Well . . . it's about my midterm exam grade. It's lower than I expected.
M: Ah, you got a B–, right?
W: Yes, sir. That's the lowest grade I've ever received.
M: You shouldn't be too disappointed. I am a very tough grader. Actually, your test was the fourth highest in the class.
W: Wow, I didn't know that.
M: But I can explain why you got that grade.
W: Yes, please. That would make me happy.
M: Okay. This was an essay test. But you didn't write an effective essay. You need to argue your point better. You made a few factual mistakes, too.
W: I see. Thanks for the explanation.

해석

W Student: 안녕하세요, 샌더스 교수님, 질문을 하나 드려도 될까요?
M Professor: 물론이죠, 에밀리. 무엇인가요?
W: 그러니까… 제 중간고사 점수에 대한 건데요. 제가 기대했던 것보다 낮아서요.
M: 아, B–였죠, 맞나요?
W: 네, 교수님. 그건 제가 지금까지 받았던 것 중에서 가장 낮은 점수예요.
M: 너무 실망할 필요는 없어요. 원래 내가 점수를 좀 짜게 주죠. 실제로 학생 점수는 반에서 네 번째로 높은 거예요.
W: 와, 전 몰랐어요.
M: 하지만 학생이 왜 그 점수를 받았는지 설명해 줄 수 있어요.
W: 네, 부탁드려요. 그러면 마음이 편해질 것 같아요.
M: 좋아요. 이게 에세이 테스트였죠. 하지만 학생은 효과적인 에세이를 쓰지 못했어요. 자신의 논점을 보다 잘 제시해야 해요. 또 사실 관계에서도 몇 가지 잘못된 부분이 있었고요.
W: 알겠습니다. 설명해 주셔서 감사해요.

Listening Skills

1 it's about my midterm exam grade
2 got a B–
3 I am a very tough grader.

4 you made a

• Exercise 8 • p.39

정답 Q1 ⓒ   Q2 Ⓑ
스크립트 02-17

W Cafeteria Employee: Good morning. What can I do for you?
M Student: I, uh, have a question. It's about my meal plan.
W: Sure. Go ahead.
M: Can I change it? I don't eat here very often.
W: What meal plan are you on?
M: The three-meals-a-day plan. You know, twenty-one a week.
W: Okay, you can change it to the fourteen- or ten-meal plan. There's also a seven-a-week plan, but most people don't purchase that.
M: Hmm . . . I'm not sure.
W: Well, with fourteen meals a week, you can eat twice a day. Most students skip breakfast. With ten a week, most students have dinner every night and lunch three times a week.
M: Oh, right. Do you have the price for each? I want to see how much they cost.
W: Here you are.

해석

W Cafeteria Employee: 안녕하세요. 무엇을 도와드릴까요?
M Student: 어, 질문이 하나 있는데요. 식사계획에 대한 거예요.
W: 네, 말씀해 보세요.
M: 바꿀 수 있나요? 이곳에서 그다지 자주 식사를 하지는 않아서요.
W: 현재 어떤 식사계획을 이용 중이죠?
M: 1일 3식, 그러니까 주당 21식이에요.
W: 그렇군요. 그러면 주당 14식, 또는 10식으로 바꿀 수 있어요. 주당 7식도 있죠. 대부분의 학생들이 구입하는 것은 아니지만요.
M: 음… 잘 모르겠네요.
W: 그러니까 주당 14식은 하루에 두 끼를 먹는 거예요. 대부분 학생들이 아침 식사를 거르고 있죠. 주당 10식에서는 대부분의 학생들이 매일 저녁을 먹고 점심은 일주일에 3번 먹어요.
M: 오, 그렇군요. 각각의 가격표가 있나요? 가격이 얼마나 되는지 알고 싶어요.
W: 여기 있어요.

Listening Skills

1 I don't eat here
2 there's also
3 twice a day
4 the price for each

Vocabulary Review p.40

Ⓐ 1 semester
   2 skipped
   3 expected

4 syllabus
5 meal plan

B 1 Ⓐ   2 Ⓒ   3 Ⓐ   4 Ⓑ   5 Ⓐ

C 1 Ⓓ   2 Ⓑ   3 Ⓓ   4 Ⓒ   5 Ⓑ

D 1 purchase
   2 fit
   3 submit
   4 tough
   5 instructor

Practice Test   p.42

1 Ⓐ   2 Ⓓ   3 Ⓐ

스크립트 02-19

M Student: Hi. Um, <u>am</u> I in the <u>right</u> place for student ID cards?
W Student Services Center Employee: Yes. A new student card or a <u>replacement</u> card?
M: I need a <u>duplicate</u> ID card.
W: Oh, I see. Why do you need a <u>duplicate</u>?
M: Well, I <u>lose</u> stuff a lot.
W: That's a <u>pretty</u> good idea. You're the first person to <u>ask</u> for one.
M: Really? Well, <u>can</u> you <u>give</u> me one please?
W: Sure. <u>Let</u> me <u>see</u> your student ID card.
M: <u>Can</u> I just <u>give</u> you my student number?
W: Yes, but I also <u>need</u> to see some <u>form</u> of picture ID.
M: I understand. <u>How about</u> my driver's license?
W: That's fine.
M: Here you are.
W: Uh-oh. This license <u>expired</u> last month. <u>How about</u> a university meal card?
M: I don't <u>eat</u> meals on <u>campus</u>. Oh, how about my <u>gym</u> membership ID?
W: That <u>will</u> work . . . Okay. That's <u>fine</u>. The <u>fee</u> for a <u>duplicate</u> ID card is ten dollars.
M: Really? I <u>thought</u> it was five.
W: The school just <u>increased</u> the price this semester.

해석

M Student: 안녕하세요. 음, 여기가 학생증을 담당하는 곳이 맞나요?
W Student Services Center Employee: 네. 신규 발급인가요, 아니면 재발급인가요?
M: 저는 학생증 사본이 필요해요.
W: 아, 알겠어요. 왜 사본이 필요한 거죠?
M: 음, 물건을 너무 자주 잃어버려서요.
W: 좋은 생각이네요. 학생증 사본을 요청한 것은 학생이 처음이에요.
M: 그런가요? 음, 사본을 주시겠어요?
W: 물론이죠. 학생증을 보여주세요.
M: 학번만 말씀드려도 되나요?
W: 네, 하지만 사진이 들어 있는 다른 신분증이 필요해요.
M: 그렇군요. 운전면허증도 되나요?
W: 그래요.
M: 여기 있어요.
W: 이런. 이 면허증은 지난 달에 기한이 만료되었군요. 대학 식권 카드가 있나요?
M: 전 학교에서 식사를 하지 않아요. 아, 체육관 멤버쉽 카드는 되나요?
W: 될 거예요… 좋아요, 되었어요. 학생증 사본에 대한 요금은 10달러예요.
M: 정말인가요? 전 5달러라고 알고 있었는데요.
W: 이번 학기부터 가격이 인상되었어요.

CHAPTER 3 Music

Understanding TOEFL Question Types & Listening Skills
p.46

1 Question Types ▶ Sample Question

D

스크립트 🎧 03-01

W Professor: You see, class, the violin is not just one musical instrument. It is a family of instruments. It includes the violin, the viola, and the cello. They are all made of wood. The violin is the smallest. But it is the most important. It produces a variety of brilliant sounds.

해석

W Professor: 여러분, 알다시피 바이올린족은 한 개의 악기가 아닙니다. 악기 종류이죠. 바이올린족에는 바이올린, 비올라, 그리고 첼로가 포함됩니다. 이들은 모두 나무로 만들어져 있어요. 바이올린이 가장 작습니다. 하지만 가장 중요하죠. 바이올린은 다채롭고 화려한 음색을 냅니다.

2 Listening Skills ▶ Check-Up

1 It is a family of instruments.
2 They are all made of wood.
3 The violin is the smallest.
4 It produces a variety of brilliant sounds.

• Exercise 1 •
p.48

정답 D

스크립트 🎧 03-03

M Professor: John Philip Sousa is one of the biggest names in American music. He wasn't a singer though. He was a composer. He composed band music. His music often had a military nature. What did he compose? Well, he wrote Semper Fidelis, which is a Marine tune. He also composed The Stars and Stripes Forever. You may not know the name, but you surely know the music. Let's listen to it now.

해석

M Professor: 존 필립 수자는 미국 음악에서 가장 중요한 이름 중 하나입니다. 하지만 그는 가수가 아니었어요. 작곡가였죠. 그는 밴드 음악을 작곡했습니다. 그의 음악은 종종 군가의 성격을 띠었습니다. 그가 무엇을 작곡했을까요? 음, 그는 해병대 군가인 충성 행진곡을 작곡했습니다. 또한 성조기여 영원하라도 작곡했죠. 여러분들도 그 이름은 몰라도 음악은 확실히 알고 있을 거예요. 지금 들어봅시다.

Listening Skills

1 He wasn't a singer though.
2 He was a composer.
3 He also composed The Stars and Stripes Forever.
4 Let's listen to it now.

• Exercise 2 •
p.49

정답 C

스크립트 🎧 03-05

W Professor: Miles Davis was one of the coolest jazz musicians ever. He was a genius with the trumpet. Actually, he helped develop a new style of jazz. We call it cool jazz. It came about in the United States in the late 1940s. But that wasn't enough for Miles Davis. In the 1970s, he started to mix jazz with rock music. Remember, class, that without Miles Davis, several genres of modern music might not even exist.

해석

W Professor: 마일즈 데이비스는 가장 멋진 재즈 뮤지션 중 한 사람이었습니다. 트럼펫에 천부적인 재능을 가지고 있었죠. 실제로 그는 새로운 스타일의 재즈를 발전시키는데 일조를 했습니다. 우리는 이를 쿨재즈라고 부르죠. 쿨재즈는 1940년대 후반 미국에서 시작되었습니다. 하지만 이는 마일즈 데이비스에게 충분하지 않았습니다. 1970년대에 그는 재즈와 록 음악을 결합시켰습니다. 여러분, 마일즈 데이비스가 없었다면 몇몇 현대 음악 장르는 존재할 수 없었을 것이라는 점을 기억하세요.

Listening Skills

1 Miles Davis was one of the coolest jazz musicians ever.
2 Actually, he helped develop a new style of jazz.
3 He was a genius with the trumpet.
4 He started to mix jazz with rock music.

• Exercise 3 •
p.50

정답 A

스크립트 🎧 03-07

W Professor: There are many musical instruments native to Korea. The *gayageum* is the best known of them. It is a string instrument. Let me see. It usually has only twelve strings. But some of them may have twenty-one strings. The body of the *gayageum* is made of wood. Inside, it is hollow. The musician plucks the strings. This produces a unique sound that is slow and relaxed. Most often, the *gayageum* is used for traditional Korean folk music.

해석

W Professor: 한국에는 많은 전통 악기가 있습니다. 그 중에서 *가야금*이 가장 잘 알려져 있죠. 이는 현악기입니다. 보세요. 보통은 현이 12개뿐입니다. 하지만 21개의 현을 가지고 있는 것도 있죠. *가야금*의 몸통은 나무로 되어 있습니다. 그 속은 비어있습니다. 연주자는 현을 잡아 뜯습니다. 그러면 느리면서도 편안한, 독특한 음색이 만들어집니다. 일반적으로 *가야금*은 한국의 전통 음악에서 사용됩니다

Listening Skills

1 It is a string instrument.

2 The body of the *gayageum* is made of wood.
3 The musician plucks the strings.
4 The *gayageum* is used for traditional Korean folk music.

• Exercise 4 • p.51

정답 B

스크립트 🎧 03-09

W Professor: How did you enjoy that music, class? Interesting, isn't it? You heard some Gregorian chants. They were first sung in the ninth or tenth century. This was during the Middle Ages in Europe. Gregorian chants were church music. As you heard, there were no musical instruments. It was just a group of men all singing in unison. They were singing in Latin by the way. So I guess nobody understood the words, right?

해석

W Professor: 음악이 마음에 드셨나요, 여러분? 흥미로웠죠, 그렇지 않나요? 여러분들은 그레고리오 성가를 들었습니다. 그레고리오 성가는 9세기나 10세기에 처음 불려졌습니다. 유럽의 중세 시대 때였죠. 그레고리오 성가는 교회 음악이었어요. 들으신 것처럼 악기는 없었습니다. 그저 한 무리의 남자들이 함께 노래를 불렀습니다. 그나저나 노래는 라틴어로 불려졌습니다. 그래서 아무도 가사를 이해하지 못했을 것으로 생각하는데, 그렇죠?

Listening Skills

1 They were first sung in the ninth or tenth century.
2 This was during the Middle Ages in Europe.
3 As you heard, there were no musical instruments.
4 So I guess nobody understood the words, right?

• Exercise 5 • p.52

정답 Q1 B Q2 C

스크립트 🎧 03-11

M Professor: The harmonica is one of the simplest musical instruments. It looks like a slim metal block with holes in it. Some people also call it the mouth organ, the mouth harp, or the French harp. Makes sense, doesn't it?
The harmonica is a wind instrument. A musician blows air into its tiny holes to create sound. A musician can also draw in air for different tones. Inside, metal reeds or pipes vibrate. That produces the different sounds. Typically, musicians use the harmonica for country or folk music. However, you'll also hear it in jazz, rock, and pop music. It's one of the most popular instruments. For example, my son enjoys rap and hip-hop music. These days, he's always playing songs. In one song, I heard a harmonica being played.

해석

M Professor: 하모니카는 가장 간단한 악기 중 하나입니다. 구멍이 있는 얇은 금속 블록처럼 보이죠. 어떤 사람들은 하모니카를 마우스 오르간 혹은 마우스 하프라고도 부르고, 이를 프렌치 하프라고 부르는 사람들도 있습니다. 말이 되긴 합니다, 그렇죠?
하모니카는 관악기입니다. 연주자들은 소리를 내기 위해 작은 구멍으로 공기를 불어 넣습니다. 또한 공기를 들이 마셔서 다른 음을 낼 수도 있어요. 내부에서는 금속으로 된 리드나 파이프가 진동합니다. 이로써 다양한 사운드가 만들어지죠. 일반적으로 연주자들은 컨트리 음악이나 포크 음악에서 하모니카를 사용합니다. 하지만 재즈, 록, 그리고 팝 음악에서도 하모니카 소리를 들을 수 있습니다. 하모니카는 가장 인기 있는 악기 중 하나입니다. 예를 들어 우리 아들은 랩과 힙합 음악을 좋아합니다. 요즘에는 항상 노래를 부르고 다니죠. 한 노래에서, 저는 하모니카 소리를 들은 적이 있습니다.

Listening Skills

1 he's .... He's always playing songs.
2 doesn't it .... Makes sense, doesn't it?
3 you'll .... You'll also hear it in jazz, rock, and pop music.
4 it's .... It's one of the most popular instruments.

• Exercise 6 • p.53

정답 Q1 D Q2 B

스크립트 🎧 03-13

W Professor: The Beatles formed in the late 1950s. The Beatles consisted of four members: John Lennon, Paul McCartney, George Harrison, and Ringo Starr. Lennon and McCartney usually wrote the songs. They first started playing together in small clubs in Liverpool, England. One of their major influences was Elvis Presley.
Before long, England wasn't big enough for the Beatles. So they decided they'd tour the United States. In 1964, the Beatles led the British Invasion of the U.S. They hit the U.S. by storm. Americans hadn't experienced anything like the Beatles. Radio stations documented their every move. Thousands of screaming fans, especially female teenagers, waited outside their hotels. Their fans just couldn't get enough. They wanted a glimpse of the four boys from England.

해석

W Professor: 비틀즈는 50년대 후반에 결성되었습니다. 비틀즈는 4명의 멤버, 즉 존 레논, 폴 메카트니, 조지 해리슨, 그리고 링고 스타로 구성되었습니다. 존 레논과 폴 메카트니가 주로 노래를 작곡했어요. 그들은 영국 리버풀의 한 작은 클럽에서 처음으로 함께 연주를 시작했습니다. 그들에게 영향을 끼친 주요 인물 중 한 명은 엘비스 프레슬리였습니다.
얼마 후 영국은 비틀즈에게는 충분히 넓은 곳이 아니었습니다. 그래서 그들은 미국으로 건너가기로 결정을 했어요. 1964년 비틀즈는 미국에 대한 영국의 공습을 이끌었습니다. 그들은 미국을 강타했어요. 미국은 이제껏 비틀즈 같은 그룹을 경험해 본 일이 없었죠. 라디오 방송국은 그들의 움직임 하나하나를 기록했습니다. 수천 명의 팬들은, 특히 10대 여성들이 소리를 지르면서 호텔 밖에서 그들을 기다렸어요. 팬들은 정말로 원했습니다. 영국에서 온 4명의 남자들을 잠깐이라도 보고 싶어했던 것이었죠.

Listening Skills

1 wasn't .... England wasn't big enough for the Beatles.
2 couldn't .... Their fans just couldn't get enough.

3 hadn't .... Americans hadn't experienced anything like the Beatles.
4 they'd .... So they decided they'd tour the United States.

• Exercise 7 •   p.54

정답 Q1 Ⓒ   Q2 Ⓐ
스크립트 🎧 03-15

W Professor: Let's take a look at singer Luciano Pavarotti. He was one of the most famous opera singers ever. Now, uh, there are three basic types of singers: baritone, tenor, and alto. Pavarotti was a tenor. His voice was powerful and full of emotion.
His rise in the opera world is interesting. His first performance in the United States took place by accident. He was a young singer with an opera group in Miami. This was in 1965, I believe. Well, the lead singer couldn't perform. He didn't feel well. Another singer recommended Pavarotti for the lead role. Pavarotti stepped in and sang like a pro. He didn't show any nervousness. The audience was very impressed with the young Pavarotti. That was the beginning of a new star in opera.

해석

W Professor: 성악가 파바로티에 대해 살펴봅시다. 그는 역사상 가장 유명했던 유명한 오페라 가수 중 한 명이었어요 자, 어, 기본적으로 세 가지의 성악가 유형이, 즉 바리톤, 테너, 그리고 알토가 있습니다. 파바로티는 테너였어요. 그의 목소리에는 힘이 있었고 감정이 풍부했습니다.
오페라 세계에서 그가 유명해진 것은 흥미로운 일입니다. 그의 첫 미국 공연은 우연히 이루어졌어요. 그는 마이애미의 오페라단의 젊은 성악가였습니다. 이때가 1965년이었다고 생각됩니다. 음, 리드싱어가 공연을 할 수 없게 되었어요. 몸이 좋지 않았습니다. 다른 성악가가 리드싱어로 파바로티를 추천했어요. 파바로티는 무대에 올라 프로처럼 노래를 했습니다. 전혀 긴장감을 나타내지 않았어요. 청중들은 젊은 파바로티에게 큰 감명을 받았습니다. 이로써 새로운 오페라 스타가 탄생하게 되었습니다.

Listening Skills

1 let's .... Let's take a look at singer Luciano Pavarotti.
2 couldn't .... The lead singer couldn't perform.
3 didn't .... He didn't feel well.
4 didn't .... He didn't show any nervousness.

• Exercise 8 •   p.55

정답 Q1 Ⓒ   Q2 Ⓑ
스크립트 🎧 03-17

M Professor: Most people believe jazz started in New Orleans, Louisiana. It's an original form of American music. Actually, it's African-American. Black musicians began performing complex rhythms in the city. That's right. The roots of jazz are African-American.
Now, the notes in jazz are usually strong. The trumpet, the violin, and the coronet are the main instruments. However, other instruments are used. Today, jazz musicians play a variety of instruments. For example, musicians play the drums and the piano. Of course, the saxophone's a major instrument in a lot of jazz music.
So what separates jazz from other types of music is adaptation. Musicians take the music in different directions. I mean that they improvise—or change—the original song during a performance. That's what makes jazz exciting and appealing to many people.

해석

M Professor: 대부분의 사람들은 재즈가 미국 루이지애나 뉴올리언스에서 시작되었다고 알고 있어요. 재즈는 독창적인 형태의 미국 음악입니다. 실제로는 미 흑인들의 음악이죠. 흑인 뮤지션들이 시내에서 복잡한 리듬을 연주하기 시작했어요. 맞아요. 재즈의 뿌리는 미 흑인에서 찾을 수 있습니다.
자, 재즈의 선율은 보통 강렬합니다. 트럼펫, 바이올린, 그리고 코로넷이 메인 악기들입니다. 하지만 다른 악기들도 사용됩니다. 오늘날에는 재즈 뮤지션들이 다양한 악기들을 사용하고 있어요. 예컨대 뮤지션들은 드럼과 피아노를 연주합니다. 물론 색소폰도 여러 재즈 음악에서 메인 악기로 사용되고 있어요.
따라서 재즈가 다른 음악과 구별되는 점은 리메이크라고 할 수 있어요. 뮤지션들은 각기 다른 방식으로 음악을 받아들입니다. 제 말은 그들이 연주를 할 때 즉흥적으로 노래를 부르거나 원곡을 바꾼다는 뜻입니다. 바로 이러한 점 때문에 많은 사람들이 재즈에 흥분하고 매력을 느끼는 것이죠.

Listening Skills

1 that's .... That's right.
2 saxophone's .... The saxophone's a major instrument in a lot.
3 it's .... Actually, it's African-American.
4 that's .... That's what makes jazz exciting and appealing to many people.

Vocabulary Review   p.56

Ⓐ 1 brilliant
    2 major
    3 rise
    4 club
    5 glimpse

Ⓑ 1 Ⓑ   2 Ⓓ   3 Ⓑ   4 Ⓐ   5 Ⓓ

Ⓒ 1 Ⓑ   2 Ⓐ   3 Ⓓ   4 Ⓑ   5 Ⓒ

Ⓓ 1 document
    2 hollow
    3 unison
    4 adaptation
    5 slim

Practice Test   p.58

1 Ⓑ   2 Ⓓ   3 Ⓒ   4 Ⓒ

스크립트 03-19

W Professor: There are many different periods of classical music. One is the Baroque Period. I consider it one of the greatest periods in history. So much incredible music was made then. Let me tell you a bit about it. It started around the year 1600. And it ended in 1750. Concertos were popular compositions then. But, of course, many other types of music were made then. There was a lot of hymnal music during that time. The organ was common in Baroque music. So was the harpsichord. Composers also often wrote music for the violin and the cello.
What about Baroque composers? Well, several of the greatest in history lived during this time. Who were some? Johann Sebastian Bach was one. George Friderich Handel was another. Handel happens to be my personal favorite. We're going to listen to parts of his *Water Music* in a moment. Antonio Vivaldi was a Baroque composer. He wrote *The Four Seasons*. I'm sure you all know it. Okay, let's listen to some music. Try to identify the different instruments you hear.

해석

W Professor: 클래식 음악의 경우 매우 다양한 시대가 존재합니다. 하나가 바로크 시대죠. 저는 이때가 역사상 가장 위대한 시대 중 하나라고 생각해요. 당시 엄청난 음악들이 만들어졌죠. 그에 대해서 조금 말씀을 드릴게요. 바로크 시대는 1600년경에 시작되었어요. 그리고 1750년에 끝이 났죠. 이때에는 협주곡이 많이 작곡되었습니다. 하지만 물론 다른 종류의 음악들도 많이 만들어졌어요. 이 시기에 찬송가들도 많았습니다. 바로크 음악에서는 오르간이 일반적으로 사용되었어요. 하프시코드도 마찬가지였고요. 또한 작곡가들은 바이올린과 첼로를 위한 곡들도 종종 썼습니다.
바로크 시대의 작곡가들은 어땠을까요? 음, 역사상 가장 위대한 인물들 중 일부가 이 시기에 살았습니다. 누가 있었을까요? 요한 세바스찬 바흐도 그 중 한 명이었습니다. 게오르크 프리드리히 헨델도 있었고요. 헨델은 제가 개인적으로 가장 좋아하는 작곡가입니다. 잠시 후에 그의 수상음악 일부를 들을 예정이에요. 안토니오 비발디 역시 바로크 시대의 작곡가입니다. *사계*를 작곡했죠. 분명 다 아실 거예요. 좋아요, 음악을 들어보죠. 소리가 들리는 여러 악기들이 무엇인지 생각해 보세요.

CHAPTER 4 Office Hours & Service Encounters

Understanding TOEFL Question Types & Listening Skills

p.62

1 Question Types ▶ Sample Question

스크립트 04-01

M Professor: Hi, Emily. How can I help you?
W Student: I'm having trouble with my essay.
M: What kind of trouble?
W: I cannot decide on a topic.
M: Well, why don't you choose a topic you are interested in?
W: That's a great idea. I think I'll write about dolphin communication.
M: See. That wasn't hard.
W: Thanks, Professor. See you later.

해석

M Professor: 안녕하세요, 에밀리. 어떻게 도와줄까요?
W Student: 에세이와 관련해서 문제를 겪고 있어요.
M: 어떤 문제인가요?
W: 주제를 정할 수가 없어요.
M: 음, 관심을 가지고 있는 주제를 선택하는 것이 어떨까요?
W: 좋은 생각이군요. 돌고래의 커뮤니케이션에 대한 글을 쓰면 될 것 같아요.
M: 보세요. 어렵지 않잖아요.
W: 고맙습니다, 교수님. 또 뵙겠습니다.

2 Listening Skills ▶ Check-Up

1 I'm having trouble / with my essay.
2 I cannot decide on / a topic.
3 I think / I'll write about / dolphin communication.
4 Well, / why don't you choose / a topic / you are interested in?

• Exercise 1 • ——————————————— p.64

정답

스크립트 04-03

W Student Services Center Employee: Can I help you?
M Student: Yes. I need a new student ID card.
W: Okay. Please tell me your student number.
M: It's 233-7-510.
W: I also need to see another form of photo ID.
M: Is a driver's license okay?
W: Sure. That's fine.
M: Here you are.
W: Okay. Would you like to use your old picture?
M: Um, I look terrible in that one. Can you take a new one?
W: No problem. Just step over here.

M: Is there an extra charge?
W: No, it is free.
M: Great. Thanks for your help.

해석
W Student Services Center Employee: 도와 드릴까요?
M Student: 네. 학생증이 새로 필요해서요.
W: 알겠어요. 학번을 말씀해 주세요.
M: 233-7-510입니다.
W: 사진이 들어 있는 다른 신분증도 필요해요.
M: 운전면허증이면 되나요?
W: 물론이에요. 괜찮죠.
M: 여기 있습니다.
W: 좋아요. 예전 사진을 사용하시겠어요?
M: 음, 그 사진에서는 제가 이상하게 나왔어요. 새로 찍어 주실 수 있나요?
W: 물론이죠. 이쪽에 서 보세요.
M: 추가 비용이 있나요?
W: 아니요. 무료에요.
M: 잘 되었군요. 도와주셔서 고맙습니다.

Listening Skills
1 I need / a new student ID card.
2 I also need / to see another form of photo ID.
3 Would you like to use / your old picture?
4 Um, / I look terrible / in that one. Can you take / a new one?

• **Exercise 2** • p.65

정답 B
스크립트 04-05

W1 Student: Professor Clark, do you have a minute?
W2 Professor: Sure. Please come in.
W1: Oh, thank you. I want to ask you about the study-abroad program.
W2: Sure.
W1: How can I qualify for it?
W2: Well, you need to have at least a B+ average.
W1: Okay. Anything else?
W2: What year are you?
W1: I'm a sophomore.
W2: Where are you interested in studying?
W1: London is my first choice.
W2: If that program is full, what is your next choice?
W1: Probably Paris.
W2: Here is an application. Bring it back tomorrow.
W1: Great. Thank you, Professor Clark.

해석
W1 Student: 클라크 교수님, 잠깐 시간이 되시나요?
W2 Professor: 물론이죠. 들어와요.
W1: 오, 고맙습니다. 해외 유학 프로그램에 대해 여쭤볼 것이 있어서요.
W2: 그래요.
W1: 자격이 어떻게 되나요?
W2: 음, 평균 학점이 최소 B+이어야 해요.
W1: 그렇군요. 그리고요?
W2: 몇 학년이죠?
W1: 2학년입니다.
W2: 어디에서 공부하고 싶나요?
W1: 1순위는 런던이에요.
W2: 프로그램의 인원이 다 찬 경우, 그 다음으로 선택하고 싶은 곳은요?
W1: 아마도 파리요.
W2: 여기 신청서예요. 내일 다시 가지고 오세요.
W1: 잘 되었군요. 고맙습니다, 클라크 교수님.

Listening Skills
1 I want to ask you / about the study-abroad program.
2 Well, / you need to have / at least a B+ average.
3 If that program is full, / what is your next choice?
4 Bring it back / tomorrow.

• **Exercise 3** • p.66

정답 B
스크립트 04-07

W Student Housing Office Employee: Welcome to the student housing office. How can I help you?
M Student: Hi. I have a problem with my dorm room.
W: Sure. What's wrong with it?
M: The heater is broken.
W: How exactly is it broken?
M: Uh, it just won't work. No heat comes out when I turn it on. So my room is pretty cold.
W: Okay. We can send someone to fix it soon.
M: How soon? It's going to get really cold tonight.
W: Hopefully, somebody can visit your room this afternoon.
M: That's great.
W: Okay. I need some information. What's your name, and where is your dorm?
M: I'm Jason Howard, and I live in room 202 in Deacon Hall.

해석
W Student Housing Office Employee: 학생 기숙사 사무실에 오신 것을 환영합니다. 무엇을 도와드릴까요?
M Student: 안녕하세요. 제 기숙사 방에 문제가 있어서요.
W: 그렇군요. 무엇인 문제인가요?
M: 히터가 고장났어요.
W: 정확하게 어디가 고장이 났나요?
M: 어, 작동이 되지 않아요. 전원을 켜도 전혀 열이 나오지 않아요. 그래서 방이 너무 추워요.
W: 알겠어요. 곧 수리할 사람을 보낼 수 있어요.
M: 얼마나 빨리요? 오늘밤에 정말로 추워질 것 같아요.
W: 아마 오늘 오후에는 방문을 할 수 있을 거예요.
M: 잘 되었군요.
W: 좋아요. 몇가지 정보가 필요해요. 학생 이름과 방 위치가 어떻게 되죠?

M: 저는 제이슨 하워드이고, 디콘홀 202호에서 살아요.

Listening Skills

1 I have / a problem / with my dorm room.
2 The heater / is broken.
3 We can send / someone to fix it / soon.
4 Hopefully, / somebody can visit / your room / this afternoon.

• Exercise 4 • ───────────────────── p.67

정답 ⓑ

스크립트 04-09

W Student: Oh, hello, Professor Foreman. Do you have a minute?
M Professor: Yes, but I need to run soon. I have class in a bit.
W: I need some advice.
M: Okay.
W: I cannot decide what to major in, writing or literature.
M: I think you should major in literature.
W: Really? Why?
M: You want to be a teacher, right?
W: That's correct.
M: I think the literature major prepares students better for teaching.
W: But I love writing.
M: You will do a lot of writing as a literature major.
W: I didn't know that.

해석

W Student: 오, 안녕하세요. 포먼 교수님. 시간이 있으신가요?
M Professor: 네, 하지만 곧 나가야 해요. 잠시 후에 수업이 있거든요.
W: 제게 조언이 필요해요.
M: 그래요.
W: 작문과 문학 중 어떤 것을 전공해야 할지 결정을 못 내리겠어요.
M: 저는 학생이 문학을 전공해야 한다고 생각해요.
W: 정말인가요? 왜죠?
M: 교사가 되고 싶죠, 그렇죠?
W: 맞아요.
M: 문학을 전공하면 학생들을 가르치는데 더 도움이 될 것으로 생각해요.
W: 하지만 저는 작문을 좋아해요.
M: 학생은 문학 전공자로서 많은 글을 쓰게 될 거예요.
W: 그 점은 제가 몰랐네요.

Listening Skills

1 I cannot decide / what to major in, / writing / or literature.
2 You / want to be a teacher, / right?
3 You will do / a lot of writing / as a literature major.
4 I think / the literature major / prepares students better / for teaching.

• Exercise 5 • ───────────────────── p.68

정답 Q1 ⓑ Q2 ⓒ
스크립트 04-11

M1 Financial Aid Department Employee: Next!
M2 Student: Yes, um, hi. I want to apply for financial aid.
M1: Okay. Did you fill out the forms?
M2: No, not yet.
M1: Well, the deadline is in one week. So you must hurry.
M2: One week?
M1: Yes. Here are the forms.
M2: Okay. Which should I do first?
M1: First, fill out the pink one. Then, the blue one. Last, you should complete the white one.
M2: Okay.
M1: As soon as you finish, bring them to me.
M2: Sure. Um, when will I know if I qualify?
M1: You will receive a response within two weeks.
M2: Really? That fast?
M1: Yes. But try to get the forms to me soon.
M2: Okay. Thank you for your help.
M1: Your welcome. Next!

해석

M1 Financial Aid Department Employee: 다음 분이요!
M2 Student: 네, 음, 안녕하세요. 학자금 지원을 신청하고자 해요.
M1: 그렇군요. 서류는 작성했나요?
M2: 아니요, 아직이요.
M1: 음, 마감이 일주일 남았어요. 그러니 서둘러야 해요.
M2: 일주일이요?
M1: 네. 여기 양식이 있어요.
M2: 알겠습니다. 먼저 무엇을 해야 하나요?
M1: 먼저 분홍색 신청서를 작성하세요. 그런 다음에는 파란색을요. 마지막으로 하얀색 신청서를 작성하셔야 해요.
M2: 좋아요.
M1: 끝내자마자 저에게 가져다 주시고요.
M2: 그럴게요. 음, 제가 자격이 되는지는 언제쯤 알 수 있나요?
M1: 2주 안에 연락이 갈 거예요.
M2: 그래요? 그렇게 빨리요?
M1: 네. 하지만 빨리 저에게 양식을 주도록 하세요.
M2: 알겠습니다. 도와주셔서 감사해요.
M1: 천만에요. 다음 분!

Listening Skills

1 I want to apply / for financial aid.
2 Last, / you should complete / the white one.
3 As soon as you finish, / bring them / to me.
4 You will receive / a response / within two weeks.

• Exercise 6 • —————————————————— p.69

정답 Q1 Ⓐ Q2 Ⓒ
스크립트 🎧 04-13

M Professor: What can I do for you today, Jennifer?
W Student: Well, I didn't do too well on the midterm exam.
M: Yes, I remember. How did you study for it?
W: I studied the chapter reviews in the book.
M: That was a good start. But it was not enough.
W: Really?
M: I take the bulk of the questions from the class lectures.
W: I see. That's why I did so badly.
M: Probably. Be sure to take good notes in class.
W: Okay.
M: In addition, read over the notes each night.
W: All right.
M: That should help you do much better on the final exam.
W: Thanks so much for your help, sir.
M: You are welcome.

해석

M Professor: 무엇을 도와드릴까요, 제니퍼?
W Student: 음, 제가 중간 고사를 그다지 잘 보지 못해서요.
M: 그래요, 기억이 나는군요. 어떻게 시험 공부를 했나요?
W: 책에 있는 챕터 리뷰를 공부했어요.
M: 시작이 좋았군요. 하지만 그것만으로는 충분하지 않았어요.
W: 정말인가요?
M: 저는 강의에서 다룬 내용에서 문제를 많이 내는 편이에요.
W: 그렇군요. 제가 시험을 못 본 이유가 거기에 있었네요.
M: 아마도요. 잊지 말고 수업 시간에 필기를 잘 하도록 하세요.
W: 그럴게요.
M: 또한 밤마다 노트를 읽도록 해요.
W: 좋아요.
M: 그렇게 하면 기말 시험에서는 훨씬 좋은 점수를 받게 될 거예요.
W: 도와주셔서 감사합니다, 교수님.
M: 천만에요.

Listening Skills

1 In addition, / read over the notes / each night.
2 I take / the bulk of the questions / from the class lectures.
3 Well, / I didn't do too well / on the midterm exam.
4 That should help you do / much better / on the final exam.

• Exercise 7 • —————————————————— p.70

정답 Q1 Ⓑ Q2 Ⓓ
스크립트 🎧 04-15

M Student Services Center Employee: Hello. How can I help you?
W Student: I would like to get a student parking permit.
M: Which kind would you like?
W: There's more than one?
M: Yes. There are three types: bronze, silver, and gold.
W: What is the difference?

M: The bronze one is twenty dollars. You can only park in the parking lots marked bronze.
W: I see.
M: The silver one is forty dollars. You may park in bronze and silver parking areas.
W: Okay. And the expensive one is sixty dollars. You can park anywhere, right?
M: That's correct. So which one do you want?
W: I would like the bronze permit. The lot next to my department is bronze.
M: Good choice. You can always upgrade later.
W: Oh, okay.
M: Great. Now I need your license plate number and student ID.

해석

M Student Services Center Employee: 안녕하세요. 어떻게 도와드릴까요?
W Student: 학생용 주차권을 받고 싶어요.
M: 어떤 종류를 원하시나요?
W: 하나가 아니라 여러 개가 있나요?
M: 그래요. 골드, 실버, 브론즈, 세 종류가 있죠.
W: 어떻게 다른가요?
M: 브론즈 주차권은 20달러예요. 브론즈라고 표시된 주차 공간에만 주차할 수 있죠.
W: 알겠어요.
M: 실버는 40달러예요. 브론즈와 실버로 표시된 주차 구역에 주차가 가능하죠.
W: 알겠어요. 그리고 비싼 건 60달러겠네요. 아무데나 주차할 수 있죠, 그렇죠?
M: 맞아요. 그러면 어떤 것을 원하시나요?
W: 브론즈 주차권으로 할게요. 제 학과 옆 주차장이 브론즈거든요.
M: 좋은 선택이네요. 나중에 언제라도 업그레이드를 할 수 있어요.
W: 오, 그렇군요.
M: 좋아요. 이제 자동차 번호판 번호와 학번을 말씀해주세요.

Listening Skills

1 I would like to get / a student parking permit.
2 There are three types: / bronze, / silver, / and gold.
3 You may park / in bronze / and silver parking areas.
4 Now / I need / your license plate number / and student ID.

• Exercise 8 • —————————————————— p.71

정답 Q1 Ⓑ Q2 Ⓒ
스크립트 🎧 04-17

W Professor: Seth, I want to talk to you about something.
M Student: Did I do something wrong?
W: Oh, no. Not at all.
M: That's a relief.
W: I want to know your plans for summer.
M: I'm attending summer school. I'll be taking one course.
W: That's great, Seth. I'll be working on my new book all

summer. I need some help.
M: What would I have to do?
W: Oh, just pick up books at the library for me. Maybe do some typing. Things like that.
M: What about the pay?
W: We can talk about that later. Are you interested?
M: Of course.
W: Great. Come in tomorrow during lunch. We'll talk more then.
M: Okay. See you then.

해석

W Professor: 세스, 학생과 이야기하고 싶은 것이 있어요.
M Student: 제가 잘못한 것이 있나요?
W: 오, 아니에요. 전혀 아니에요.
M: 다행이네요.
W: 학생의 여름 방학 계획을 알고 싶어요.
M: 여름 계절 학기를 들을 거예요. 수업을 하나 들을 예정이죠.
W: 잘 되었네요. 세스. 저는 여름 내내 새로 책을 쓸 예정이에요. 도움이 좀 필요해요.
M: 제가 무엇을 해야 하나요?
W: 오, 도서관에서 책을 찾아서 제게 가져다주기만 하면 돼요. 타이핑을 좀 해야 할 수도 있고요. 그런 일들이에요.
M: 보수는요?
W: 그건 나중에 이야기 하도록 하죠. 관심이 있나요?
M: 물론이에요.
W: 좋아요. 내일 점심 시간에 들러주세요. 그때 더 이야기해요.
M: 알겠습니다. 그때 뵐게요.

Listening Skills

1 I want to know / your plans / for summer.
2 I'll be working / on my new book / all summer.
3 Oh, / just pick up books / at the library / for me.
4 I'm attending / summer school.

Vocabulary Review   p.72

A 1 trouble
   2 extra
   3 majored in
   4 prepare
   5 permit

B 1 Ⓓ   2 Ⓐ   3 Ⓒ   4 Ⓐ   5 Ⓒ

C 1 Ⓐ   2 Ⓑ   3 Ⓓ   4 Ⓒ   5 Ⓑ

D 1 bulk
   2 turn on
   3 heater
   4 deadline
   5 abroad

Practice Test   p.74

1 Ⓒ   2 Ⓓ   3 Ⓑ

스크립트  04-19

W Professor: Oh, hey, Hunter. Come on in.
M Student: Hi, Professor Jackson. You wanted to see me?
W: Yes, it's about your class attendance. You missed every class last week.
M: I had a terrible cold.
W: Yes, I heard a bad bug was going around. I'm glad you're feeling better.
M: Thanks. Actually, I want to ask you for a favor.
W: Sure. What is it?
M: I need a letter of recommendation for a part-time job.
W: What kind of job?
M: Well, you know I want to go to law school. A local law firm needs a clerk.
W: That's great, Hunter.
M: Well, I didn't get the job yet, ma'am.
W: I know. Of course I'll write a letter of recommendation for you.
M: That's great. Thanks so much. Oh, there's one more thing. I need it by tomorrow morning. My interview is at 9:00.
W: 9:00 AM? I can manage that. Just drop by my office on your way there.
M: Okay. I've got class. See you tomorrow.

해석

W Professor: 오, 왔군요. 헌터. 들어오세요.
M Student: 안녕하세요. 잭슨 교수님. 저를 보고 싶다고 하셨죠?
W: 네, 학생의 수업 출석과 관련된 일 때문이에요. 지난주 모든 수업에 출석을 하지 않았잖아요.
M: 제가 지독한 감기에 걸렸거든요.
W: 네, 독감이 유행이라고 듣기는 했어요. 나아지고 있는 것 같아 다행이에요.
M: 고맙습니다. 사실, 교수님께 부탁드리고 싶은 것이 있어요.
W: 그래요. 무엇인가요?
M: 아르바이트를 위한 추천서가 필요합니다.
W: 어떤 일인데요?
M: 음, 아시다시피 저는 로스쿨에 가고자 해요. 지역 로펌에서 직원을 필요로 하더군요.
W: 잘 됐네요, 헌터.
M: 음, 아직 일자리를 구한 것은 아니에요, 교수님.
W: 알아요. 당연히 추천서를 써줄게요.
M: 잘 되었군요. 정말 감사합니다. 아, 한 가지 더 있어요. 내일 아침까지 필요해요. 9시에 면접이 있거든요.
W: 오전 9시요? 가능해요. 가는 길에 제 사무실에 들르세요.
M: 알겠습니다. 저는 수업이 있어서요. 내일 뵙겠습니다.

CHAPTER 5 Office Hours & Service Encounters

Understanding TOEFL Question Types & Listening Skills
p.78

1 Question Types ▶ Sample Question

스크립트 🎧 05-01

M Student: Hi. I would like to register for the scuba diving class.
W Registrar's Office Employee: Okay. Please fill out this form. There is also a fee of fifty dollars.
M: Wow, fifty, huh . . . ? Do you take checks?
W: Sure. Is it from a local bank?
M: Yes. When is the first class?
W: Next Wednesday at the student union pool at 2 PM.

해석

M Student: 안녕하세요. 스쿠버다이빙 수업을 예약하고 싶어요.
W Registrar's Office Employee: 그래요. 이 양식을 완성해 주시면 돼요. 비용은 50달러입니다.
M: 와, 50이요…? 수표도 되나요?
W: 물론이죠. 지역 은행에서 발행한 것인가요?
M: 네. 첫 수업은 언제인가요?
W: 다음 주 수요일 오후 2시 학생 회관 수영장에서 있어요.

2 Listening Skills ▶ Check-Up

Student: Do you take checks?
Employee: Sure. Is it from a local bank?
Student: Yes. When is the first class?
Employee: Next Wednesday at the student union pool at 2 PM.

• Exercise 1 •
p.80

정답

스크립트 🎧 05-03

M Professor: Sarah, can I speak to you for a moment?
W Student: Sure.
M: Why did you miss class last week?
W: I thought you canceled it.
M: No. We had class.
W: I'm sorry, Professor Green. My classmate said there was no class.
M: That's okay. We just watched a film.
W: Oh, that's good.
M: But I also gave a homework assignment.
W: Really? Could you fill me in, please?

해석

M Professor: 사라, 잠시 이야기할 수 있을까요?
W Student: 물론이죠.
M: 왜 지난 주 수업에 오지 않았나요?
W: 전 수업이 취소되었다고 생각했는데요.
M: 아니에요. 수업을 했어요.
W: 죄송합니다. 그린 교수님. 제 친구가 수업이 없다고 말했거든요.
M: 괜찮아요. 영화를 봤을 뿐이었어요.
W: 오, 다행이네요.
M: 하지만 과제를 내줬어요.
W: 정말인가요? 제게도 알려주실 수 있나요?

Listening Skills

Professor: Why did you miss class last week?
Student: I thought you canceled it.
Professor: No. We had class.
Student: I'm sorry, Professor Green.

• Exercise 2 •
p.81

정답 B

스크립트 🎧 05-05

M Student Services Center Employee: You want to apply for a scholarship, right?
W Student: That's right. How can I do that?
M: Well, it's pretty easy. I just input your name into the computer.
W: And then?
M: The computer will match your records with the scholarships.
W: What does that mean?
M: That means it automatically applies for you.
W: Wow. That's great!
M: Yes. You will receive an email notification later. It will give you specific information about any scholarship you receive.

해석

M Student Services Center Employee: 장학금을 신청하고자 하는 것이죠, 그렇죠?
W Student: 맞아요. 어떻게 하면 되나요?
M: 음, 아주 쉬워요. 컴퓨터에 학생 이름을 입력하기만 하면 되죠.
W: 그 다음에는요?
M: 컴퓨터가 학생의 성적에 맞는 장학금을 찾아 줄 거에요.
W: 그게 무슨 뜻인가요?
M: 자동으로 신청이 된다는 말이에요.
W: 와, 대단하군요.
M: 그래요. 학생은 나중에 이메일로 공지를 받게 될 거에요. 거기에 학생이 받을 장학금에 대한 상세한 내용이 들어 있을 것이고요.

Listening Skills

Employee: The computer will match your records with the scholarships.
Student: What does that mean?
Employee: That means it automatically applies for you.
Student: Wow. That's great!

• Exercise 3 •   p.82

정답 Ⓐ

스크립트 🎧 05-07

W Student: Hello, Professor Kimball. You <u>asked</u> to <u>see</u> me after class?
M Professor: Yes, Lisa. I have something to tell you.
W: Is it <u>good</u> news or <u>bad</u> news?
M: Good news. Very good news.
W: Okay . . .
M: Your <u>poem</u> won <u>first</u> prize in the <u>poetry</u> contest.
W: Really? <u>How</u> did you <u>know</u>?
M: I was one of the <u>judges</u>.
W: Oh, that's <u>wonderful</u>.
M: Congratulations. We will <u>publish</u> it in the university magazine, too.
W: I can't <u>believe</u> it. I had almost <u>forgotten</u> about the <u>competition</u>.

해석

W Student: 킴벌 교수님, 안녕하세요. 수업 후에 저를 보자고 하셨죠?
M Professor: 그래요. 리사. 할 얘기가 있어요.
W: 좋은 소식인가요, 나쁜 소식인가요?
M: 좋은 소식이에요. 아주 좋은 소식이죠.
W: 알겠어요…
M: 학생의 시가 공모전에서 1등을 했어요.
W: 정말인가요? 어떻게 아셨어요?
M: 제가 심사위원 중 한 명이었거든요.
W: 오, 잘 되었군요.
M: 축하해요. 대학 잡지에도 시를 실을 예정이에요.
W: 정말 믿기지가 않아요. 공모전에 대해서는 거의 잊고 있었어요.

Listening Skills

Student: <u>Really</u>? How do you <u>know</u>?
Professor: I was one of the <u>judges</u>.
Student: Oh, that's <u>wonderful</u>.
Professor: <u>Congratulations</u>. We will <u>publish</u> it in the <u>university magazine</u>, too.

• Exercise 4 •   p.83

정답 Ⓒ

스크립트 🎧 05-09

W Librarian: Hello, Todd. You <u>need</u> to <u>speak</u> with me about something?
M Student: Yes, ma'am. It's about my shift this weekend.
W: Do you <u>mean</u> the shift you work on Saturday evening?
M: Yes, that's correct.
W: So . . . <u>what</u> <u>about</u> it?
M: I <u>need</u> to <u>visit</u> my home this weekend, so I can't do the <u>shift</u>.
W: All right. I <u>guess</u> I'll have to <u>find</u> someone to work it.
M: Um . . . actually . . .
W: Yes?

M: Actually, I <u>already</u> <u>spoke</u> with Wendy. She said she could do it.
W: That's <u>wonderful</u>. Thank you for finding a substitute.
M: You're welcome. I'll <u>tell</u> her that you're <u>fine</u> with her working then. Thanks, Ms. Roper.

해석

W Librarian: 안녕하세요, 토드. 저와 할 말이 있다고요?
M Student: 네, 선생님. 제 이번 주말 근무 때문에요.
W: 토요일 저녁 근무를 말하는 건가요?
M: 네, 맞아요.
W: 그러면… 무슨 일인가요?
M: 제가 주말에 집에 좀 가봐야 해서 그 시간에 근무가 어려울 것 같아요.
W: 좋아요. 다른 사람을 찾아야 할 것 같군요.
M: 음… 실은…
W: 네?
M: 사실, 제가 이미 웬디에게 이야기를 했어요. 그 애가 할 수 있다고 하더라구요.
W: 잘 되었군요. 대신 근무할 사람을 찾아줘서 고마워요.
M: 천만에요. 선생님께서 괜찮다고 하셨다고 그 애에게 이야기할게요. 로퍼 선생님, 고맙습니다.

Listening Skills

Student: <u>Yes</u>, ma'am. It's about my <u>shift</u> this <u>weekend</u>.
Librarian: Do you <u>mean</u> the shift you work on <u>Saturday</u> <u>evening</u>?
Student: <u>Yes</u>, that's <u>correct</u>.
Librarian: So . . . <u>what</u> about it?

• Exercise 5 •   p.84

정답 Q1 Ⓒ Q2 Ⓐ

스크립트 🎧 05-11

W Professor: Come in!
M Student: Do you <u>have</u> a second, Professor Arnold?
W: Sure, Adam. What is going on?
M: Did you <u>get</u> a <u>chance</u> to look at my paper?
W: Yes, I did.
M: What <u>did</u> you <u>think</u>?
W: It is <u>much</u> <u>better</u> than the last one.
M: Really? I'm so glad!
W: I'm <u>serious</u>. It <u>looks</u> <u>like</u> you <u>spent</u> a lot of time on it.
M: I did a lot of <u>research</u> in the library.
W: Good for you. I <u>knew</u> you <u>could</u> do it.
M: By the way, what <u>grade</u> did I get?
W: Let me see. I have it right here . . . Yes, an A–.
M: An A–! Are you sure?
W: Yes. Why? What did you <u>expect</u>?
M: Not an A. Actually, that's <u>my</u> <u>first</u> A in college.

해석

W Professor: 들어오세요!
M Student: 아놀드 교수님, 시간 좀 있으세요?
W: 물론이죠, 아담. 무슨 일이죠?

M: 혹시 제 보고서를 보셨나요?
W: 네, 봤어요.
M: 어떻게 생각하셨나요?
W: 지난 번보다 훨씬 좋더군요.
M: 정말이죠? 정말 기쁘네요!
W: 진심이에요. 시간을 많이 들인 것 같아요.
M: 도서관에서 조사를 많이 했거든요.
W: 잘 했어요. 학생이 해낼 수 있을 거라고 생각했어요.
M: 그건 그렇고, 성적은 어떻게 되었나요?
W: 봅시다. 여기에 있어요… 네, A–이군요.
M: A–라니! 정말인가요?
W: 그래요. 왜요? 무엇을 기대했나요?
M: A는 기대도 안 했거든요. 사실 대학 와서 처음 A를 받은 거예요.

Listening Skills

Student: By the way, what grade did I get?
Professor: Let me see. I have it right here . . . Yes, an A–.
Student: An A–! Are you sure?
Professor: Yes. Why? What did you expect?

• **Exercise 6** • ─────────── p.85

정답 Q1 Ⓐ   Q2 Ⓑ
스크립트 ∩ 05-13

W Student: Hello. This is the student activities office, isn't it?
M Student Activities Office Employee: That's correct. Is there something I can assist you with?
W: I hope so. I'm here about a club.
M: Okay. There are many clubs on campus that you can join.
W: Oh, no. I want to start my own club.
M: I see. What kind of club?
W: I want to start a hiking club.
M: Interesting. We haven't had a hiking club here in years.
W: Really? That's too bad. It's a great way to get in shape. It's fun, too.
M: I agree. Okay, you need to fill out some forms. Take these.
W: Thank you.
M: And you need to sign up at least ten people. All clubs need that number of members.

해석

W Student: 안녕하세요. 여기가 학생 활동 센터죠, 아닌가요?
M Student Activities Office Employee: 맞아요. 제가 도울 일이 있을까요?
W: 네. 저는 동아리 때문에 왔어요.
M: 그래요. 학생이 가입할 수 있는 동아리들이 교내에 많이 있어요.
W: 오, 아니에요. 저는 동아리를 만들어 보고 싶어요.
M: 그렇군요. 어떤 종류의 동아리인가요?
W: 하이킹 동아리를 만들려고 해요.
M: 흥미롭네요. 수년간 하이킹 동아리는 없었거든요.
W: 정말인가요? 안타깝네요. 건강을 유지할 수 있는 멋진 방법인데요. 재미도 있고요.
M: 같은 생각이에요. 좋아요, 여기 양식을 채워주세요. 받으세요.
W: 고맙습니다.

M: 그리고 최소한 10명이 가입해야 해요. 모든 동아리에 그 정도의 회원들이 필요하거든요.

Listening Skills

Student: Oh, no. I want to start my own club.
Employee: I see. What kind of club?
Student: I want to start a hiking club.
Employee: Interesting. We haven't had a hiking club here in years.

• **Exercise 7** • ─────────── p.86

정답 Q1 Ⓐ   Q2 Ⓒ
스크립트 ∩ 05-15

M Student: Excuse me, Professor Lansing. Can I speak with you?
W Professor: Sure, I have a minute or two.
M: I was hoping I could join your history class.
W: Are you a history major?
M: No. I'm a biology major.
W: I see. Well, it is an advanced class.
M: I know. But I need it to graduate.
W: Really? Okay. Come to our first class tomorrow.
M: I'm in?
W: I'll see what I can do. The chances are very good.
M: I really need to know now, ma'am.
W: Well, let me see. The class is full now. But I usually take one or two more students.
M: Is there a waiting list?
W: You're the first one on it. So show up tomorrow, and you'll get in. Okay?
M: Thanks so much. I really appreciate it.

해석

M Student: 실례합니다, 랜싱 교수님. 이야기를 나눌 수 있을까요?
W Professor: 물론이죠. 일이분 정도 시간이 있어요.
M: 저는 교수님의 역사 수업을 듣고 싶었어요.
W: 역사 전공인가요?
M: 아니요. 생물학 전공이에요.
W: 그렇군요. 음, 그 수업은 고급 과정이에요.
M: 알고 있어요. 하지만 졸업을 하기 위해서는 그 수업을 들어야 해요.
W: 그런가요? 알겠어요. 내일 첫 수업에 오세요.
M: 제가 수업에 들어간건가요?
W: 제가 무엇을 할 수 있는지 알아볼게요. 가능성은 매우 높아요.
M: 교수님, 저는 정말로 지금 알아야 해요.
W: 음, 봅시다. 이미 수업은 꽉 차 있어요. 하지만 보통 한두 명을 더 받고 있어요.
M: 대기자 명단이 있나요?
W: 학생이 대기자 명단의 첫 번째 대기자예요. 그러니 내일 오면 수업을 듣게 될 거예요. 알겠죠?
M: 고맙습니다. 정말 감사드려요.

Listening Skills

Student: Excuse me, Professor Lansing. Can I speak with you?
Professor: Sure, I have a minute or two.
Student: I was hoping I could join your history class.
Professor: Are you a history major?

• **Exercise 8** • ──────────────── p.87

정답 Q1 Ⓐ   Q2 Ⓑ
스크립트  05-17

M Student: Is there any way I can see the doctor now?
W Nurse: You need to wait like everyone else.
M: How long will it take?
W: Right now, it's about a two-hour wait.
M: I have a test in one hour. I can't miss it.
W: Why not come back after the exam?
M: I feel terrible. I was hoping to get some medicine before the test.
W: Do you have a fever?
M: No. Just a bad headache.
W: Here is some aspirin. That should help.
M: Thank you.
W: But come back to the health center after your test.
M: Okay.
W: You should let the doctor look at you.
M: Okay. Thanks. I'll be back in a couple of hours.

해석

M Student: 지금 당장 의사 선생님을 뵐 수 있을까요?
W Nurse: 다른 사람들처럼 기다리셔야 해요.
M: 얼마나 걸릴까요?
W: 지금은 2시간 정도 기다리셔야 해요.
M: 한 시간 후에 시험이 있어서요. 시험을 놓칠 순 없어요.
W: 시험을 본 후에 오시는 것은 어떨까요?
M: 몸이 너무 안 좋아서요. 시험을 보기 전에 약을 좀 먹으면 좋겠어요.
W: 열이 있나요?
M: 아니요. 그냥 두통이 심할 뿐이에요.
W: 여기 아스피린을 드릴게요. 도움이 될 거예요.
M: 고맙습니다.
W: 하지만 시험이 끝나면 보건실로 다시 오세요.
M: 알겠습니다.
W: 의사 선생님께 진료를 받도록 하세요.
M: 그럴게요. 고맙습니다. 두 시간 후에 다시 올게요.

Listening Skills

Student: I feel terrible. I was hoping to get some medicine before the test.
Nurse: Do you have a fever?
Student: No. Just a bad headache.
Nurse: Here is some aspirin. That should help.

Vocabulary Review   p.88

A 1 shift
       2 sholarship
       3 fill in
       4 second
       5 grade

B 1 Ⓐ   2 Ⓓ   3 Ⓒ   4 Ⓐ   5 Ⓐ

C 1 Ⓐ   2 Ⓑ   3 Ⓐ   4 Ⓐ   5 Ⓑ

D 1 miss
       2 substitute
       3 automatically
       4 individual
       5 fill out

Practice Test   p.90

1 Ⓒ   2 Ⓑ   3 Ⓐ

스크립트 05-19

W Student: Hi. I need to pay a parking fine.
M Student Services Center Employee: Okay. Do you have the ticket with you?
W: No.
M: Then could you give me your license plate number?
W: It's FDR-O2Z.
M: O2Z. Okay . . . Just a moment. Hmm . . . That's interesting . . .
W: What? Is there something wrong?
M: Well, yes. The computer says you haven't paid for, um, eight tickets.
W: That many, huh. I didn't remember . . .
M: The computer doesn't lie. It's eight.
W: Oh, my gosh! What is the total?
M: A lot. It's 364.91 dollars.
W: Oh, no! Do you take checks?
M: Is it from a local bank?
W: Yes, it is.
M: Then that's fine.
W: Okay. Here you go.
M: Thanks. You know, you're pretty lucky.
W: I am? I don't feel so lucky.
M: Usually, when you have that many tickets, your car gets towed.
W: Oh, I didn't think of that. You're right.
M: Then you have to pay another hundred dollars to get your car back.
W: Another hundred? You're right. I am lucky.

해석

W Student: 안녕하세요. 주차 위반 벌금을 내야 해서요.
M Student Services Center Employee: 그래요. 주차 위반 딱지를 가지고

있나요?
W: 아니요.
M: 그럼 자동차 번호판 번호를 말씀해 주시겠어요?
W: FDR-O2Z예요.
M: O2Z요. 좋아요… 잠시만요… 흥미로운데…
W: 네? 무슨 문제라도 있나요?
M: 음, 그래요. 컴퓨터로 보니 학생이, 음, 8건의 주차 위반 벌금을 내지 않았다고 나오네요.
W: 그렇게나 많나요. 기억이 나지 않는데…
M: 컴퓨터는 거짓말을 하지 않죠. 8건이에요.
W: 오, 이런! 모두 합쳐 얼마인가요?
M: 많아요. 364.91달러예요.
W: 오, 세상에! 수표도 받으시나요?
M: 지역 은행의 수표인가요?
W: 네, 그래요.
M: 그럼 돼요.
W: 알겠습니다. 여기 있어요.
M: 고마워요. 아시겠지만 학생은 운이 꽤 좋은 편이에요.
W: 제가요? 전 운이 좋다고 생각하지 않는데요.
M: 보통, 그렇게 주차 위반 딱지를 많이 뗀 경우에는 차가 견인이 되어요.
W: 오, 그 생각은 못했군요. 선생님 말이 맞아요.
M: 그러면 차를 돌려받기 위해 또 100달러를 내야만 하죠.
W: 100달러를 더 낸다고요? 그렇군요. 제가 운이 좋은 편이네요.

CHAPTER 6 Education

Understanding TOEFL Question Types & Listening Skills   p.94

1 Question Types ▶ Sample Question

ⓑ

스크립트 🎧 06-01

M Professor: Let's talk about <u>learning</u> <u>methods</u>. One of the <u>most</u> <u>common</u> <u>methods</u> is called rote learning. That's R-O-T-E. What is <u>rote</u> learning? Basically, it <u>involves</u> <u>learning</u> through memorization. Students <u>repeat</u> something <u>enough</u> times so that they can <u>memorize</u> it. Remember when you <u>learned</u> the alphabet? You said it again and again, right? Well, that is an example of rote learning.

해석

M Professor: 학습 방법에 대해 이야기해 봅시다. 가장 일반적인 방법 중 하나는 암기 학습입니다. R-O-T-E에요. 암기 학습이란 무엇일까요? 기본적으로 외워서 익히는 방식입니다. 학생들은 외우기 위해 학습 내용을 충분히 반복을 합니다. 여러분이 알파벳을 배웠던 때를 기억하나요? 몇 번이고 반복해서 말을 했죠, 그렇죠? 음, 그것은 암기 학습의 한 가지 예입니다.

2 Listening Skills ▶ Check-Up

1 <u>Let's</u> <u>talk</u> <u>about</u> learning methods.
2 <u>Basically</u>, it involves learning through memorization.

• Exercise 1 •   p.96

정답 ⓑ

스크립트 🎧 06-03

W Professor: Language <u>education</u> is very important in Europe. Students <u>study</u> from a very young <u>age</u>. In <u>contrast</u>, in the U.S., this is <u>rare</u>. Students there first study a <u>foreign</u> language in high school. <u>Still</u>, in many schools in America it is not <u>mandatory</u>. I mean, they don't have to <u>take</u> it <u>if</u> they don't want to. <u>To</u> <u>sum</u> <u>up</u>, in Europe, languages like English and French <u>are</u> <u>required</u> courses through high school.

해석

W Professor: 유럽에서 언어 교육은 매우 중요해요. 학생들은 아주 어렸을 때부터 공부를 하죠. 그와는 대조적으로 미국에서는 이러한 경우가 드뭅니다. 미국의 학생들은 고등학교 때 처음으로 외국어를 배우죠. 이는 아직까지 미국의 많은 학교에서 필수 과목이 아닙니다. 제 말은, 학생들이 원하지 않는 경우, 반드시 들을 필요는 없다는 뜻이에요. 요약하자면, 유럽의 경우 영어와 프랑스어와 같은 언어 수업은 고등학교에서 필수 과목입니다.

Listening Skills

1 <u>In</u> <u>contrast</u>, in the U.S., this is rare.
2 <u>To</u> <u>sum</u> up, in Europe, languages like English and French are

required courses through high school.

• Exercise 2 • — p.97

정답 Ⓑ

스크립트 🎧 06-05

W Professor: Homeschooling is becoming popular these days, especially in the U.S. Parents educate their kids instead of teachers. And there are a couple of reasons why. They believe it is better. In addition, they think their children learn more. But some experts believe it isn't all good. Homeschooled kids do not interact with others as much. They also can't participate in school activities like clubs or sports. The debate continues about homeschooling.

해석

W Professor: 최근, 특히 미국에서, 홈스쿨링의 인기가 높아지고 있습니다. 부모들이 교사를 대신해서 아이들을 교육시키죠. 여기에는 두 가지 이유가 있습니다. 부모들이 홈스쿨링이 더 좋다고 생각을 합니다. 또한 더 많이 배운다고 생각을 하죠. 하지만 몇몇 전문가들은 홈스쿨링이 좋은 것만은 아니라고 생각해요. 홈스쿨링을 받는 아이들은 다른 아이들과 그다지 어울리지를 못합니다. 또한 동아리나 스포츠 활동과 같은 교내 활동에 참여할 수도 없죠. 홈스쿨링에 대한 논쟁은 계속되고 있습니다.

Listening Skills

1 In addition, they think their children learn more.
2 And there are a couple of reasons why.

• Exercise 3 • — p.98

정답 Ⓐ

스크립트 🎧 06-07

M Professor: Now, I'd like to give you some examples of fine arts classes. They include art, music, and dance. They are important in education. For example, they help develop students' imaginations. They can also be very fun. Fine arts classes complete students. By that, I mean that students become well-rounded individuals. Studying only English, history, or science is not enough. Students should also study the fine arts. They can also help some students discover their true passion. Some students may even become professional performers one day.

해석

M Professor: 이제 순수 예술 수업의 예를 들어보죠. 여기에는 미술, 음악 그리고 무용이 포함됩니다. 이들은 교육에서 중요합니다. 예를 들어 예술 수업은 학생들의 상상력을 발달시키는데 도움을 주죠. 매우 재미있을 수도 있습니다. 순수 예술 수업은 학생들을 완성시킵니다. 이 말은, 학생들이 균형 잡힌 인간이 된다는 뜻이에요. 영어, 역사, 혹은 과학만을 공부하는 것은 충분하지가 않습니다. 학생들은 순수 예술 또한 공부해야 해요. 이는 학생들이 참된 열정을 발견할 수 있도록 도움을 줄 수도 있습니다. 심지어 몇몇 학생들은 언제가 전문적인 예술가가 될 수도 있어요.

Listening Skills

1 For example, they help develop students' imaginations.
2 Now, I'd like to give you some examples of fine arts classes.

• Exercise 4 • — p.99

정답 Ⓑ

스크립트 🎧 06-09

W Professor: Usually, children who are five years old attend kindergarten. It is kind of an introduction to school. More than anything, in kindergarten, students interact with one another. They do a lot of drawing and painting, too. It helps students adjust from home life to school life. Most of all, of course, students make lots of new friends. As you can see, kindergarten is a great way for children to begin their educations.

해석

W Professor: 보통 5세인 아이들은 유치원에 다닙니다. 유치원은 일종의 초기 단계의 학교입니다. 무엇보다 유치원에서는 학생들이 서로 교류를 합니다. 그림도 많이 그리고요. 유치원은 학생들이 가정에서 나와 학교 생활에 적응하는데 도움을 줍니다. 무엇보다, 당연하게도, 학생들은 새로운 친구들을 많이 사귑니다. 아시겠지만, 유치원은 아이들의 교육을 시작하기에 좋은 곳입니다.

Listening Skills

1 Most of all, of course, students make lots of new friends.
2 As you can see, kindergarten is a great way for children to begin their educations.

• Exercise 5 • — p.100

정답 Q1 Ⓓ Q2 Ⓐ

스크립트 🎧 06-11

W Professor: Thanks to the Internet, online learning is popular these days. Now, uh, let me compare it with traditional classes so that you can understand it.
In traditional learning, students attend classes at school. The teacher lectures, and the students learn by reading, listening, writing, and doing various other activities. In online learning, the students and the teacher are in different locations. The learning happens over the computer.
There are several types of online programs. Sometimes the teacher does a live lecture, and students log on to a website to see it. Other times, the teacher's lecture is recorded. Then, students can watch it anytime. Some online learning programs have no lectures. Students get class material they must read. Then, they do various assignments and submit them.

해석

W Professor: 인터넷 덕분에 요즘 온라인 학습의 인기가 높습니다. 이제, 어, 여러분이 이해할 수 있도록, 이를 전통적인 수업과 비교해 보도록 할게요.
전통적인 학습에서는 학생들이 학교에서 수업을 듣습니다. 교사가 강의를 하면 학생들은 읽고, 듣고, 쓰고, 그리고 기타 다양한 활동들을 하면서 배웁니다.

온라인 학습에서는 학생들과 교사가 다른 곳에 있습니다. 학습은 컴퓨터를 통해 이루어지죠.

몇 가지 종류의 온라인 프로그램들이 있습니다. 때때로 교사가 라이브로 강의를 하면 학생들은 웹사이트에 접속해서 강의를 듣습니다. 어떨 때에는 교사의 강의가 녹화되기도 해요. 그러면 학생들은 언제라도 강의를 볼 수가 있습니다. 강의가 없는 온라인 학습 프로그램들도 있습니다. 학생들은 읽어야 할 자료들을 받습니다. 그리고 난 뒤 다양한 과제를 수행하고 이를 제출합니다.

Listening Skills

1 Now, uh, <u>let</u> <u>me</u> <u>compare</u> <u>it</u> <u>with</u> traditional classes so that you can understand it.
2 <u>Other</u> <u>times</u>, the teacher's lecture is recorded.
3 <u>Then</u>, they do various assignments and submit them.

• Exercise 6 • — p.101

정답 Q1 Ⓓ Q2 Ⓓ
스크립트 ∩ 06-13

M Professor: I'd <u>like</u> <u>to</u> <u>talk</u> about early education. Many <u>experts</u> <u>believe</u> the education of children <u>begins</u> before <u>birth</u>. That's right. It <u>happens</u> before mothers give birth. This is <u>called</u> <u>prenatal</u> education.
Basically, the mother and the father <u>talk</u> to the baby in the mothers' belly. They <u>read</u> books to the baby. People <u>believe</u> babies <u>begin</u> to <u>learn</u> like this. It <u>gets</u> their brains going. Here are some other <u>examples</u>. Many parents play music for their <u>unborn</u> babies. And some mothers <u>sing</u> to their babies. This is their first <u>form</u> of communication. As a <u>result</u>, songs <u>help</u> <u>develop</u> trust <u>between</u> the mother and her baby. Songs also <u>comfort</u> the baby. Remember that hearing is the first sense babies <u>develop</u>. So music and songs <u>are</u> <u>naturally</u> the first <u>way</u> to <u>educate</u> them. <u>Pretty</u> amazing, isn't it?

해석
M Professor: 조기 교육에 대한 이야기를 하고자 합니다. 많은 전문가들은 아이의 교육이 태어나기 전부터 시작된다고 생각을 해요. 맞습니다. 엄마 몸에서 나오기 부터 시작이 되죠. 이는 태교라고 불립니다.
기본적으로, 엄마와 아빠는 엄마의 뱃속에 있는 아기에게 말을 합니다. 아기에게 책도 읽어 주고요. 사람들은 아기들이 이런 식으로 배우기 시작한다고 생각합니다. 아기의 뇌가 발달하게 되는 것이죠. 다른 예도 있어요. 많은 부모들이 태아에게 음악을 들려줍니다. 그리고 몇몇 엄마들은 아기에게 노래도 들려주죠. 이것이 최초의 커뮤니케이션입니다. 따라서 노래는 엄마와 아기 간의 신뢰감을 증진시켜줍니다. 또한 노래는 아기를 편안하게 만듭니다. 청각이 가장 먼저 발달한다는 점을 기억하세요. 그래서 음악이나 노래는 자연스럽게 그들을 교육시키는 첫 번째 수단입니다. 꽤 놀랍습니다, 그렇지 않나요?

Listening Skills

1 <u>I'd</u> <u>like</u> <u>to</u> <u>talk</u> <u>about</u> early education.
2 <u>Here</u> <u>are</u> <u>some</u> <u>other</u> <u>examples</u>. Many parents play music for their unborn babies.
3 <u>As</u> <u>a</u> <u>result</u>, songs help develop trust between the mother and her baby.

• Exercise 7 • — p.102

정답 Q1 Ⓑ Q2 Ⓑ
스크립트 ∩ 06-15

W Professor: Many people are <u>disabled</u>. They <u>often</u> <u>have</u> physical disabilities. Two of the <u>most</u> common are <u>blindness</u> and <u>deafness</u>. There are two <u>reasons</u> why this happens. Some people are <u>born</u> that way. Other times, people <u>become</u> blind or deaf <u>by</u> <u>accident</u> or through a <u>sickness</u>.
They need to <u>deal</u> <u>with</u> their disabilities. For example, blind students must <u>learn</u> to read. They mostly learn <u>Braille</u>. This is a language for the blind. It <u>consists</u> <u>of</u> small, <u>raised</u> <u>dots</u>. They <u>form</u> letters and words. Braille <u>lets</u> blind people read special books. They <u>move</u> their fingers <u>over</u> the dots to read.
<u>What</u> <u>about</u> the deaf? They also have their <u>own</u> language. It's called <u>sign</u> language. <u>To use</u> it, people <u>form</u> words with their fingers and hands. They also use gestures. <u>Both</u> deaf <u>and</u> blind people <u>attend</u> special schools to <u>learn</u> these languages.

해석
W Professor: 많은 사람들이 장애를 가지고 있어요. 보통 신체적인 장애를 가지고 있죠. 가장 흔한 두 가지 장애는 시각 장애와 청각 장애입니다. 장애는 두 가지 이유로 발생합니다. 선천적으로 장애가 사람들도 있고요. 사고나 질병으로 시각이나 청각 장애를 얻게 되는 사람들도 있죠.
이들은 장애에 대처해야 합니다. 예를 들면, 시각 장애 학생들은 읽기를 배워야만 하죠. 주로 점자를 배웁니다. 점자는 시각 장애인들을 위한 언어예요. 작고 도드라진 점들로 이루어져 있습니다. 이들이 글자와 단어를 구성합니다. 점자 덕분에 시각 장애인들은 특별한 책을 읽을 수 있어요. 손가락을 점에 대면서 책을 읽습니다.
청각 장애인들은 어떨까요? 그들 역시 자신만의 언어를 가지고 있죠. 수화라는 것입니다. 수화를 하는 경우, 손가락과 손으로 단어를 만듭니다. 제스처도 사용하고요. 청각 장애인과 시각 장애인 모두 이러한 언어를 배우기 위해 특수 학교에 다닙니다.

Listening Skills

1 <u>There</u> <u>are</u> <u>two</u> <u>reasons</u> <u>why</u> this happens. Some people are born that way.
2 <u>What</u> <u>about</u> the deaf?
3 <u>To use</u> <u>it</u>, people form words with their fingers and hands.

• Exercise 8 • — p.103

정답 Q1 Ⓒ Q2 Ⓑ
스크립트 ∩ 06-17

M Professor: Our school <u>has</u> many buildings with lots of classrooms. But did you know that in the <u>past</u>, one-room schools <u>existed</u>?
One-room schools <u>mostly</u> <u>existed</u> in <u>rural</u> <u>areas</u> in places in the United States, Canada, and Europe. What were they? Well, there was just one teacher. And all the students <u>met</u> in the same room. It <u>didn't</u> <u>matter</u> how old the students <u>were</u>. Some students were five or six <u>while</u> others <u>were</u> fifteen or sixteen.
<u>How</u> did these schools work? Let me tell you . . . The teacher

taught basic subjects such as math, reading, and writing. The teacher focused on one group of students and taught a lesson. Then, those students did an assignment, and the teacher focused on a different group. In addition, older students were expected to help younger ones. This system actually worked quite well.

해석

M Professor: 우리 학교에는 많은 교실을 구비하고 있는 건물들이 많습니다. 하지만 과거에 원룸 학교가 존재했다는 것을 알고 있었나요?

원룸 학교는 대부분 미국, 캐나다, 그리고 유럽의 시골에 존재했어요. 어땠을까요? 음, 교사는 한 명 뿐이었어요. 그리고 모든 학생들이 같은 교실에 모였죠. 학생들의 나이는 중요하지 않았어요. 어떤 학생들은 대여섯 살이었고, 열다섯 살이나 열여섯 살인 학생들도 있었죠.

이들 학교는 어떻게 운영되었을까요? 말씀을 드리면… 교사가 수학, 읽기, 그리고 쓰기와 같은 기본 과목들을 가르쳤어요. 교사는 한 그룹의 학생들에게 집중해서 수업을 했습니다. 그리고 나면 이 학생들은 과제를 했고, 교사는 다른 그룹에 집중을 했죠. 또한 나이가 많은 학생들은 나이가 어린 학생들을 도우려고 했습니다. 이러한 시스템은 실제로 꽤 잘 작동했어요.

Listening Skills

1 But did you know that in the past, one-room schools existed?
2 Well, there was just one teacher.
3 In addition, older students were expected to help younger ones.

Vocabulary Review
p.104

A
1 participated
2 matter
3 expects
4 interact
5 well-rounded

B 1 Ⓑ 2 Ⓐ 3 Ⓑ 4 Ⓓ 5 Ⓐ

C 1 Ⓒ 2 Ⓓ 3 Ⓐ 4 Ⓐ 5 Ⓒ

D
1 traditional
2 adjust
3 form
4 Prenatal
5 gesture

Practice Test
p.106

1 Ⓑ 2 Ⓒ 3 Ⓑ 4 Advantage: ②, ④
Disadvantage: ①, ③

스크립트 🎧 06-19

W Professor: Homework is an important part of your education. It is necessary. Of course, it helps reinforce the lessons you learn. It also helps prepare you for future lessons. Doing homework helps you retain information.

But, class, homework does much, much more than that. First, it teaches self-discipline. You will be more, um, responsible. It also teaches you to be independent. Now, um, I'm not saying you must do your homework by yourself. Actually, it's good if your parents help you out a little. But the key words here are "a little." They should never do all of your homework. Homework allows you to figure things out for yourself. That's being independent.

Now, I don't believe teachers should give lots of homework every night. Not at all. This can cause students to get burned out. Their minds won't be fresh for the next day of lessons. But a bit each night is quite healthy. It is also important for developing character in young people, not just intelligence.

해석

W Professor: 숙제는 교육에 있어서 중요한 부분이에요. 필수적인 것이죠. 당연하게도, 숙제는 학습한 내용을 강화시켜 줍니다. 또한 이후에 배울 내용에 대비하도록 만들기도 하죠. 숙제를 하면 학습 내용을 기억하는데 도움이 됩니다.

그러나 여러분, 숙제는 그 이상의 것들을 해요. 첫째, 자기 관리를 가르칩니다. 보다, 음, 책임감을 기르게 해주죠. 또한 숙제는 독립성도 길러주어요. 자, 음, 여러분이 스스로 숙제를 해야 한다고 말하는 것이 아니에요. 사실 부모님이 숙제를 조금 도와주는 것은 좋습니다. 그러나 여기에서 키워드는 '조금'입니다. 부모가 모든 숙제를 다 해주어서는 안 되는 것이죠. 숙제는 여러분이 스스로 깨달을 수 있도록 만듭니다. 그래서 독립성이 길러집니다.

자, 저는 선생님들이 매일 밤 많은 숙제를 내주어야 한다고는 생각하지 않아요. 전혀 그렇게 생각하지 않죠. 그러면 학생들이 극도로 피곤할 수 있습니다. 다음 수업 때 정신이 맑지 않을 거예요. 하지만 매일 밤 약간의 숙제를 하는 것은 건강에 좋습니다. 또한 어른 학생들의 지능 발달 뿐만 아니라 인격 형성도 중요한 일입니다.

CHAPTER 7 Nutrition

Understanding TOEFL Question Types & Listening Skills p.110

1 Question Types ▶ Sample Question

Vitamin A: 2, 4   Vitamin C: 1, 3

스크립트 🎧 07-01

W Professor: Vitamins are very important to our health. We feel weak and tired if our bodies don't have enough vitamins. We can even get very sick. One important vitamin is vitamin C. We can get it from eating fruits like oranges and tangerines. Another is vitamin A. We get it from green vegetables. It helps us have good vision.

해석

W Professor: 비타민은 우리 건강에 매우 중요합니다. 체내에 비타민이 부족하면 힘이 빠지고 피곤함을 느끼게 되죠. 병에 걸릴 수도 있어요. 중요한 비타민 중 하나는 비타민C입니다. 이는 오렌지나 감귤과 같은 과일을 먹음으로써 섭취할 수 있어요. 또 다른 하나는 비타민A입니다. 이는 녹색 채소에서 얻을 수 있죠. 비타민A는 좋은 시력을 유지하는데 도움이 됩니다.

2 Listening Skills ▶ Check-Up

1 (very) - berry   2 peel - (feel)
3 (we) - vee   4 (will) - win

• Exercise 1 • p.112

정답 C

스크립트 🎧 07-03

M Professor: Junk food is a big problem for people today. Foods like pizza and hamburgers are good examples of junk food. They have little nutritional value. I know. I know . . . They taste good. But they are not good for your bodies. They can make you fat. Another word for being fat is obese. Being obese can cause many health problems. Please try to stay away from junk food. You'll thank me for it.

해석

M Professor: 오늘날 정크푸드가 큰 문제입니다. 피자와 햄버거와 같은 음식들이 정크푸드의 좋은 예입니다. 영양학적인 가치가 별로 없죠. 저도 알고 있습니다. 아는데… 맛이 좋아요. 그러나 몸에는 좋지가 않습니다. 살찌게 만들 수 있어요. 살이 찐다는 것은 비만을 의미합니다. 비만은 여러 가지 건강상의 문제를 야기할 수 있어요. 정크푸드는 멀리 하셔야 합니다. 저에게 고마워할 걸요.

Listening Skills

1 lot - (not)   2 (know) - low
3 (fat) - pat   4 tank - (thank)

• Exercise 2 • p.113

정답 High in Protein: 1, 3, 4

스크립트 🎧 07-05

W Professor: Everyone needs protein for their bodies. It is necessary for everybody's diet. It heals the body's tissues. It gives people energy. And it helps keep people active. Young people need more protein than adults. They are still growing, so their bodies need protein more than adults' bodies do. Foods like meat, eggs, and tofu are good sources of protein. So is cheese. You need to be sure to include protein in your diet on a daily basis.

해석

W Professor: 모든 사람들의 신체는 단백질을 필요로 해요. 단백질은 모든 사람들의 식단에서 필수적인 것입니다. 신체 조직을 치료해주죠. 그리고 사람들을 활동적으로 만듭니다. 어린이들은 성인보다 더 많은 단백질을 필요로 해요. 아직 성장 중이기 때문에 성인의 경우보다 더 많은 단백질을 필요로 합니다. 고기, 달걀, 그리고 두부 같은 음식에서 단백질을 얻을 수 있어요. 치즈도 마찬가지고요. 잊지 마시고 여러분의 식단에 매일 단백질이 포함되도록 하세요.

Listening Skills

1 (need) - lead   2 (food) - good
3 hear - (heal)   4 ten - (tell)

• Exercise 3 • p.114

정답 B

스크립트 🎧 07-07

W Professor: Proper nutrition is important for people who play sports. Athletes need fuel in order to perform well. Carbohydrates are one of the best sources of energy. As a result, athletes need to load up on carbs before a game. Let me give you an example. Foods like spaghetti and potatoes are high in carbs. Rice, bread, and oatmeal also give athletes extra energy and power. That's why you often see athletes eating those foods before games. Without carbohydrates, they won't have enough energy.

해석

W Professor: 운동을 하는 사람들에게는 적절한 영양섭취가 중요합니다. 운동선수들이 경기를 잘 하기 위해서는 연료가 필요하죠. 탄수화물은 최고의 에너지원 중 하나입니다. 따라서 운동선수들은 시합에 나가기 전에 탄수화물을 많이 섭취할 필요가 있습니다. 예를 들어 보죠. 스파게티와 감자와 같은 음식은 탄수화물 함량이 높습니다. 쌀, 빵, 그리고 오트밀 역시 운동선수들에게 추가적인 에너지와 힘을 가져다주죠. 시합 전에 선수들이 이러한 음식을 먹는 모습을 종종 볼 수 있는 이유가 바로 그 때문입니다. 탄수화물이 없으면 충분한 에너지를 내지 못할 것입니다.

Listening Skills

1 vest - (best)   2 (load) - road
3 (rice) - lice   4 carve - (carb)

• **Exercise 4** • —————————————————— p.115

정답 Ⓐ

스크립트 🎧 07-09

M Professor: Let's <u>talk</u> <u>about</u> <u>potassium</u> for a bit. Bananas are a <u>fine</u> source of this <u>important</u> nutrient. So try to eat a lot of them. Potassium <u>helps</u> <u>keep</u> the body—<u>even</u> a person's life— in balance. Potassium, um, also <u>helps</u> with <u>digestion</u>. Oh, there's something else. It <u>allows</u> the muscles <u>to</u> work <u>as</u> <u>well</u> <u>as</u> they can. And just <u>in</u> <u>case</u> you don't like bananas . . . Most vegetables and meats <u>contain</u> it, too. So you can <u>eat</u> them <u>to</u> <u>get</u> potassium as well.

해석

M Professor: 칼륨에 대한 이야기를 해보죠. 바나나에 이 중요한 영양소가 많이 들어 있습니다. 그러니 바나나를 많이 먹도록 하세요. 칼륨은 신체가, 사람의 인생까지도, 균형을 유지하도록 도와줍니다. 칼륨은, 음, 또한 소화를 돕습니다. 오, 또 있어요. 칼륨은 우리의 근육이 최대한 잘 기능할 수 있도록 돕습니다. 그리고 여러분이 바나나를 좋아하지 않는 경우를 위해 말씀을 드리면… 대부분의 채소와 육류에도 칼륨이 들어있습니다. 따라서 이들을 먹어도 칼륨을 섭취할 수가 있죠.

Listening Skills

1 ⓛot - not   2 ⓕine - file
3 lice - ⓝice   4 knife - ⓛife

• **Exercise 5** • —————————————————— p.116

정답 Q1 Ⓓ   Q2 Advantage: ①, ③, ④ Disadvantage: ②

스크립트 🎧 07-11

W Professor: Nowadays, many people <u>eat</u> <u>poorly</u>. They <u>consume</u> lots of fast food. They eat junk food and drink sodas. As a result, they don't get their <u>daily</u> <u>requirement</u> of vitamins and minerals. <u>Fortunately</u>, people can <u>take</u> <u>various</u> supplements. These <u>provide</u> people with the <u>proper</u> amount of vitamins and <u>minerals</u>. Now, uh, there are all <u>kinds</u> of <u>supplements</u>. Some people <u>take</u> multivitamins, which <u>contain</u> several different vitamins their bodies need. Others just <u>take</u> vitamin C, zinc, or calcium, for example.
What are the <u>benefits</u>? There are many. Supplements can make people <u>healthier</u>. They can help people <u>manage</u> their weight. Some can <u>prevent</u> <u>diseases</u> such as cancer. Of course, some people <u>take</u> <u>too</u> many supplements, which can <u>harm</u> their bodies. But <u>if</u> you <u>take</u> supplements in <u>moderation</u>, you'll be <u>fine</u>.

해석

W Professor: 오늘날 많은 사람들이 식사를 제대로 하지 않습니다. 패스트푸드를 많이 먹죠. 정크푸드를 먹고 탄산음료를 마십니다. 그 결과, 하루에 필요한 비타민과 미네랄을 섭취하지 못하고 있어요.
다행히도 다양한 보충제를 먹을 수가 있습니다. 이들은 사람들에게 적절한 양의 비타민과 미네랄을 제공해주어요. 현재, 어, 온갖 종류의 보충제들이 존재합니다. 어떤 사람들은, 그들의 몸에 필요한 서로 다른 비타민이 포함되어 있는, 종합 비타민을 섭취합니다. 다른 사람들은, 예컨대 비타민C, 아연 또는 칼슘만 섭취하기도 하죠.
보충제의 이점은 무엇일까요? 많습니다. 보충제는 사람들을 더 건강하게 만들어줄 수 있어요. 체중 관리에 도움을 줄 수도 있고요. 어떤 것들은 암과 같은 질병을 예방할 수 있도록 합니다. 물론, 보충제를 너무 많이 먹는 사람들도 있는데, 그러면 신체에 해가 될 수도 있어요. 하지만 적당히 보충제를 먹는 것은 괜찮습니다.

Listening Skills

1 ⓕast - past   2 ⓛots - rots
3 poor - ⓕor   4 pine - ⓕine

• **Exercise 6** • —————————————————— p.117

정답 Q1 Ⓐ   Q2 Tomatoes: ④ Carrot: ② Bean: ③ Walnut: ①

스크립트 🎧 07-13

M Professor: I <u>made</u> a list of <u>eight</u> foods. We <u>should</u> <u>try</u> to eat these foods as <u>often</u> as <u>possible</u>. The first is <u>spinach</u>. Maybe many of you don't <u>like its taste</u>. Still, it is good for the muscles. Next is yogurt. It <u>fights</u> cancer. Another is tomatoes. They <u>help</u> the body fight <u>diseases</u>. What else . . . ? Oh, carrots. They also fight cancer and are <u>good</u> <u>for</u> vision. Next are blueberries and blackberries. These <u>increase</u> brain activity. They <u>are</u> <u>good</u> <u>for</u> memory, too.
Of course, I <u>should</u> not <u>leave</u> out beans. Beans are <u>good</u> <u>for</u> many things, <u>especially</u> the heart. What <u>about</u> walnuts? I love walnuts. They are <u>high</u> in protein. They have just <u>as</u> <u>much</u> protein as steak and chicken. And last on my list is oats. They are <u>high</u> in <u>fiber</u> and <u>protect</u> the heart.

해석

M Professor: 제가 8개의 식품 목록을 만들었어요. 이 음식들은 가능한 자주 먹어야 하죠. 첫번째는 시금치입니다. 아마도 여러분 중 많은 사람들이 시금치 맛을 좋아하지 않을 거예요. 그러나 시금치는 근육에 좋습니다.
다음은 요구르트입니다. 요구르트는 암과 싸우죠. 다음 것은 토마토예요. 토마토는 우리 몸이 질병과 싸울 수 있도록 만듭니다. 또 무엇이 있을까요…? 오, 당근이 있었죠. 당근도 역시 암과 싸우고 좋은 시력을 유지하게 해줍니다. 그 다음은 블루베리와 블랙베리입니다. 이들은 두뇌 활동을 활발하게 만들어요. 기억력에도 좋습니다.
물론, 콩을 빠뜨려서는 안 되죠. 콩은 많은 점에서 좋은데, 특히 심장에 좋습니다. 호두는 어떨까요?. 저는 호두를 정말 좋아해요. 고단백질 식품이에요. 스테이크와 치킨에 들어있는 양과 같은 단백질이 들어 있습니다. 그리고 목록의 마지막에 있는 것은 귀리입니다. 귀리는 섬유질이 풍부하고 심장을 보호합니다.

Listening Skills

1 when - ⓦell   2 ⓛist - wrist
3 ⓒancer - cancel   4 ⓛeave - reeve

• **Exercise 7** • p.118

정답 Q1 Ⓒ Q2 Advantage: ①, ② Disadvantage: ③, ④
스크립트 🎧 07-15

W Professor: Vegetarians do not eat meat. Some don't even eat fish. There are advantages and disadvantages to being a vegetarian. Let me see . . . One main advantage is that vegetarians experience fewer diseases in general. Meat eaters have a higher risk of diseases like heart disease and cancer, to name a few. Vegetarians also have less cholesterol in their bodies. Their diets are high in most vitamins and minerals, too. Of course, they are rarely fat like people who eat, well, fast foods.

But there are some disadvantages, too. Vegetarian diets are usually low in protein, calcium, and iron. These are needed for strong bones and healthy muscles. Sometimes vegetarians must take extra vitamins. These help them get enough energy every day. Lots of vegetarians eat plenty of tofu, too. Tofu is high in protein.

해석

W Professor: 채식주의자들은 고기를 먹지 않습니다. 일부는 생선도 먹지 않아요. 채식주의자가 되는 것에는 장단점이 있습니다. 봅시다… 한 가지 주된 장점은 대체로 채식주의자들이 병에 덜 걸린다는 것이에요. 고기를 먹는 사람들은, 몇 가지만 얘기하면, 심장병이나 암과 같은 질병에 걸릴 위험성이 더 높습니다. 또한 채식주의자들의 체내에는 콜레스테롤을 적게 들어 있어요. 또한 그들의 식단에는 대부분의 비타민과 미네랄이 풍부하게 들어 있죠. 당연하게도 채식주의자들이 패스트푸드를 먹는 사람만큼 뚱뚱한 경우는 거의 없습니다.

그러나 몇가지 단점도 있습니다. 채식주의자의 식단에는 보통 단백질, 칼슘, 그리고 철분이 부족합니다. 이들은 튼튼한 뼈와 건강한 근육에 필요한 것이에요. 채식주의자들은 비타민을 따로 섭취해야 하는 경우가 많아요. 비타민은 이들이 매일 충분한 에너지를 얻을 수 있도록 해주죠. 많은 채식주의자들은 두부도 많이 먹습니다. 고단백질 식품이니까요.

Listening Skills

1 (name) - lame   2 (main) - mail
3 (low) - no   4 (fast) - past

• **Exercise 8** • p.119

정답 Q1 Ⓑ Q2 Frying: ②, ④ Streaming: ①, ③
스크립트 🎧 07-17

M Professor: There are many different types of cooking methods. But you need to remember that the way you cook food affects its nutritional value.

Let's start with frying. Fried food is cooked in oil. Most of the time, frying requires plenty of oil. Well, fried food tastes delicious, but it's not good for your body. All that oil in the food can make you gain weight. It can cause heart disease and other problems, too. I suggest cutting back on fried food.

Instead, I suggest steaming food. Steaming uses the steam from boiling water to cook foods such as vegetables. This is one of the healthiest cooking methods. Steamed foods often keep their nutrients. The fibers in vegetables get softened, too, so they are easier for the body to digest. Steamed foods taste terrific as well.

해석

M Professor: 여러 가지 종류의 요리법들이 있습니다. 하지만 여러분들은 음식을 요리하는 방법이 영양학적 가치에 영향을 미친다는 점을 기억해야 합니다.

일단 튀김부터 이야기해 보죠. 튀긴 음식은 기름으로 요리됩니다. 대부분의 경우 튀김을 할 때에는 많은 양의 기름이 필요해요. 튀긴 음식은 맛있지만 몸에 좋지는 않습니다. 음식에 들어 있는 기름은 체중을 증가시킬 수 있습니다. 이는 심장병 및 기타 문제들을 일으킬 수 있어요. 튀긴 음식은 줄이는 편이 좋습니다.

대신, 저는 찌는 음식을 추천합니다. 찜은 끓는 물에서 나오는 증기를 이용해 야채와 같은 음식을 요리하는 것입니다. 건강에 가장 좋은 요리법 중 하나죠. 찐 음식의 경우 영양소가 그대로 유지되는 경우가 많아요. 야채의 섬유질도 부드러워져서 신체가 더 쉽게 소화할 수 있습니다. 찐 음식은 맛도 훌륭하죠.

Listening Skills

1 prying - (frying)   2 (but) - putt
3 (gain) - cane   4 pack - (back)

Vocabulary Review p.120

A 1 moderation
      2 weight
      3 risk
      4 consume
      5 vision

B 1 Ⓐ   2 Ⓑ   3 Ⓒ   4 Ⓐ   5 Ⓑ

C 1 Ⓐ   2 Ⓑ   3 Ⓒ   4 Ⓒ   5 Ⓐ

D 1 stay away
      2 rarely
      3 advantage
      4 nutritional
      5 important

Practice Test p.122

1 Ⓒ   2 Ⓒ   3 Pro: ②, ④ Con: ①, ③   4 Ⓒ

스크립트 🎧 07-19

M Professor: The fact is that people rely on caffeine every day. Look at all the soft drinks and coffee we drink. One reason is that we like the taste, uh, you know, the flavor.

But another reason is the caffeine. Caffeine gives us a boost. It keeps us awake and alert. I read one article that said that over ninety percent of Americans consume caffeine every single day. Now, um, caffeine is a natural stimulant. This means it increases activity in the nervous system. Of course, um, there are some side effects. For example, Mr. Smith drinks three or four cups of coffee every day. However, he decides to cut back on his coffee. So he may have side effects such as headaches and tiredness. Now, um, another negative effect of caffeine can be sleep problems. For example, a student drinks six colas during a prime-time movie. That night, she can't fall asleep. The reason is that the caffeine in her system is still working. So it's keeping her from sleeping. In addition, too much caffeine makes people jumpy or nervous.

해석

M Professor: 사람들이 매일 카페인에 의존하고 있다는 것은 사실입니다. 우리가 마시는 청량음료와 커피를 보세요. 한 가지 이유는 우리가 그 맛을, 어, 아시다시피 풍미를 좋아하기 때문이죠.

하지만 또 다른 이유는 카페인 때문입니다. 카페인은 우리에게 기운을 주죠. 우리를 깨어 있게 만들고 정신을 차리게 해주어요. 저는 미국인의 90% 이상이 거의 매일 카페인을 섭취하고 있다는 기사를 읽은 적이 있습니다. 자, 음, 카페인은 천연 각성제입니다. 이는 카페인이 신경계의 활동을 증가시킨다는 점을 의미합니다. 물론, 음, 부작용도 있습니다. 예를 들어 스미스 씨는 매일 서너 잔의 커피를 마십니다. 그러나 커피를 줄이겠다는 결심을 하죠. 그래서 두통 및 피로감과 같은 부작용을 겪을 수도 있습니다.

자, 카페인의 또 다른 부정적인 효과는 수면 문제일 것입니다. 예를 들어 한 학생이 황금 시간대의 영화를 보면서 6잔의 콜라를 마신다고 해보죠. 그날 밤에는 잠을 잘 수가 없습니다. 그 이유는 그녀의 체내에서 카페인이 여전히 작용하고 있기 때문이에요. 그래서 수면을 방해하는 것이죠. 또한 카페인을 너무 많이 섭취하면 불안감과 긴장감을 느낄 수 있습니다.

CHAPTER 8 Endangered Animals

Understanding TOEFL Question Types & Listening Skills

p.126

1 Question Types ▶ Sample Question

Ⓒ

스크립트  08-01

W Professor: The gray wolf is a beautiful animal. It is normally three feet high and four feet long. One foot is a bit more than thirty centimeters. Hunters nearly made it extinct in the 1900s. Today, the gray wolf is protected. Still, it leads a harsh life. It sometimes struggles to find food. It fights with other wolves and predators. Most gray wolves live in the wild for only about six to eight years.

해석

W Professor: 회색늑대는 멋진 동물이에요. 보통 키가 3에서 4피트 정도이죠. 한 발의 크기는 30cm가 약간 넘습니다. 1900년대에 사냥꾼들이 이들을 거의 멸종시켰어요. 오늘날 회색늑대는 보호를 받고 있습니다. 하지만 힘든 삶을 살고 있죠. 음식을 찾기 위해 고군분투하는 경우가 많습니다. 다른 늑대와 포식자들과도 싸움을 하죠. 대부분의 회색늑대들은 야생에서 6년에서 8년 정도만 삽니다.

2 Listening Skills ▶ Check-Up

1 One foot is a bit more than thirty centimeters.
2 Hunters nearly made it extinct in the 1900s.
3 Most gray wolves live in the wild for only about six to eight years.

• Exercise 1 • ─────────── p.128

정답 Ⓒ

스크립트 08-03

M Professor: The third-largest land animal is the hippopotamus. It can weigh more than 7,000 pounds. It can also be around ten feet long. And it can grow up to five feet high at the shoulder. Hippos prefer to stay in the water. These endangered animals can be quite dangerous though. They are aggressive, can run fast, and will attack people and even boats entering their territory.

해석

M Professor: 세 번째로 크기가 큰 육지 동물은 하마입니다. 무게가 7,000파운드 이상 나갈 수도 있죠. 또한 길이가 약 10피트 정도일 수도 있어요. 그리고 어깨 높이가 5피트에 이를 때까지 자랄 수 있습니다. 하마들은 물속에서 지내는 것을 좋아합니다. 하지만 이 멸종 위기에 처한 동물들은 꽤 위험할 수 있어요. 이들은 공격적이고, 빠르게 달릴 수 있으며, 그리고 자신의 영역을 침범하는 사람과 보트를 공격하려고 합니다.

Listening Skills

1 It can weigh more than 7,000 pounds.
2 It can also be around ten feet long.
3 And it can grow up to five feet high at the shoulder.

• Exercise 2 • ———————————————— p.129

정답 Ⓐ

스크립트 🎧 08-05

M Professor: The bald eagle is a <u>magnificent</u> bird. Its white <u>head</u> and brown feathers make it look <u>especially</u> nice. It's too bad that hunters <u>almost</u> <u>killed</u> them all. But they are making a <u>comeback</u> today.
Let me talk about its size. This is a big bird. <u>Females</u> are often twenty-five percent <u>larger</u> than <u>males</u>. For example, the <u>average</u> female's wingspan is seven feet. That's about 213 centimeters. The average female's weight is <u>around</u> thirteen pounds. That's <u>about</u> 5.8 kilograms. A male, however, <u>normally</u> <u>weighs</u> around nine pounds.

해석

M Professor: 대머리독수리는 굉장한 새입니다. 하얀 머리와 갈색 깃털 때문에 특히 멋지게 보이죠. 사냥꾼들이 이들을 거의 다 죽였다는 점이 참으로 유감스럽습니다. 하지만 오늘날 그 수가 회복되고 있습니다.
크기에 대해서 말씀을 드리죠. 이 새는 크기가 큽니다. 암컷이 종종 수컷보다 25% 정도 더 크고요. 예를 들어 암컷의 날개의 길이는 평균적으로 7피트입니다. 대략 213cm이죠. 암컷의 평균 무게는 보통 13파운드 정도입니다. 약 5.8kg이에요. 그러나 수컷은 보통 9파운드 정도 나갑니다.

Listening Skills

1 That's about 213 centimeters.
2 Females are often twenty-five percent larger than males.
3 The average female's weight is around thirteen pounds. That's about 5.8 kilograms.

• Exercise 3 • ———————————————— p.130

정답 Ⓑ

스크립트 🎧 08-07

W Professor: The blue whale is the <u>largest</u> animal <u>ever</u> to live. This <u>even</u> <u>includes</u> the dinosaurs. Some of these animals <u>can</u> <u>reach</u> 100 feet in <u>length</u>. Their average <u>length</u> is about seventy feet. And listen to this . . . Most adult blue whales <u>weigh</u> about ninety tons. It's <u>unfortunate</u> that whale hunting <u>nearly</u> made them <u>extinct</u>. However, in 1966, they <u>became</u> a <u>protected</u> species. So their numbers <u>started</u> to increase. Still, <u>experts</u> <u>estimate</u> there are only around 10,000 in the world's oceans.

해석

W Professor: 흰긴수염고래는 역사상 가장 큰 동물입니다. 공룡도 포함해서요. 일부 흰긴수염고래의 경우 길이가 100피트에 이르기도 해요. 평균 길이는 70피트 정도이고요. 그리고 잘 들어보시면… 대부분의 다 자란 흰긴수염고래는 몸무게가 90톤에 달합니다. 이들은 안타깝게도 포경으로 인해 거의 멸종 상태에 있습니다. 하지만 1966년에 보호종으로 지정되었어요. 그래서 그 수가 증가하기 시작했습니다. 하지만 전문가들은 전 세계의 바다에 불과 10,000마리만 존재한다고 추정하고 있습니다.

Listening Skills

1 Their average length is about seventy feet.
2 However, in 1966, they became a protected species.
3 Still, experts estimate there are only around 10,000 in the world's oceans.

• Exercise 4 • ———————————————— p.131

정답 Ⓑ

스크립트 🎧 08-09

M Professor: The grizzly bear <u>lives</u> in the mountains of North America. It is a <u>threatened</u> species. This <u>means</u> that the grizzly bear's numbers are at <u>dangerously</u> low levels. But they are <u>slowly</u> beginning to increase. Still, it is <u>legal</u> to hunt them in Alaska and Canada.
Grizzlies are big, powerful bears. When they are <u>standing</u>, they can be about 2.4 meters in <u>height</u>. Males weigh two times <u>as</u> <u>much as</u> females. Adult males <u>average</u> about 272 kilograms in <u>weight</u>.

해석

M Professor: 회색곰은 북아메리카 산악 지역에서 서식합니다. 멸종위기에 처한 종이죠. 이는 그들의 개체수가 위험한 수준에 이르렀다는 점을 의미합니다. 하지만 그 수가 서서히 증가하기 시작했어요. 하지만 알래스카와 캐나다에서는 회색곰을 사냥하는 것이 합법입니다.
회색곰은 크기가 크고 힘이 센 곰입니다. 서 있는 경우 키가 2.4m에 달할 수도 있죠. 수컷의 몸무게는 암컷보다 2배 더 나갑니다. 다 자란 수컷은 평균 몸무게는 대략 272kg이에요.

Listening Skills

1 When they are standing, they can be about 2.4 meters in height.
2 Males weigh two times as much as females.
3 Adult males average about 272 kilograms in weight.

• Exercise 5 • ———————————————— p.132

정답 Q1 Ⓐ   Q2 Ⓓ

스크립트 🎧 08-11

W Professor: You probably <u>think</u> that dolphins only <u>live</u> in salt water, right? Well, if you do, you're wrong. The pink river dolphin, or boto, <u>lives</u> in <u>fresh</u> water. This dolphin can be <u>found</u> mainly in the Amazon and Orinoco rivers in South America.
The pink river dolphin is the <u>largest</u> river dolphin <u>species</u> in the world. It <u>grows</u> to be around 8.2 meters in length. Males can <u>weigh</u> more than 180 kilograms. That's a big mammal, huh? Some of them <u>can</u> also <u>live</u> in the <u>wild</u> for <u>around</u> thirty years.

There are a large number of these dolphins in the wild. However, they are still considered a vulnerable species. The problem is that the water in some places they live is polluted. In addition, dams are interfering with the areas where many of these animals live.

해석

W Professor: 여러분은 아마도 돌고래가 바닷물에서만 산다고 생각할 거예요, 그렇죠? 음, 만약 그렇게 생각한다면, 틀렸습니다. 분홍 강돌고래는, 혹은 보토는 민물에서 서식합니다. 이 돌고래는 주로 남아메리카의 아마존강과 오리노코강에서 찾아볼 수 있어요.

분홍 돌고래는 세계에서 가장 큰 강돌고래 종입니다. 자라면 길이가 약 8.2미터에 이르죠. 수컷의 몸무게는 180kg 이상 나갈 수도 있습니다. 거대한 포유류죠, 그렇죠? 또한 이들 중 일부는 약 30년 동안 야생에서 살 수 있습니다.

이들 돌고래는 야생에 많이 있습니다. 하지만 여전히 취약한 종으로 여겨지고 있어요. 문제는 그들이 사는 일부 지역의 물이 오염되었다는 점입니다. 또한 이들 동물이 살고 있는 많은 지역에서 댐이 방해가 되고 있습니다.

Listening Skills

1 It grows to be around 8.2 meters in length.
2 Males can weigh more than 180 kilograms.
3 Some of them can also live in the wild for around thirty years.

• Exercise 6 • p.133

정답 Q1 Ⓐ Q2 Ⓑ

스크립트 🎧 08-13

M Professor: Pandas are among the most loved animals on the planet. They are often the most popular attractions at zoos. Adults can weigh around 117 kilograms.

They are one of the most endangered species, too. These cute, furry, playful bears could become extinct soon. Today, you can only find them in the wild in China. In 2005, there were 1,596 pandas in the wild. There, hunters kill them for their fur and paws. They once lived in Burma and Vietnam. But they became extinct in those areas because of hunters.

Pandas are also losing their habitats. And get this . . . They spend about fourteen hours a day eating bamboo. Most wild pandas can live to be about fifteen years old. They can live to about thirty in zoos though.

해석

M Professor: 판다는 지구에서 가장 많은 사랑을 받는 동물 중 하나입니다. 동물원에서 종종 가장 인기가 있는 동물이죠. 다 자란 판다의 몸무게는 약 117kg에 달할 수도 있어요.

이들은 또한 가장 큰 멸종 위기에 처한 종이기도 합니다. 이 귀엽고, 털 많고, 놀기 좋아하는 곰들은 곧 멸종할 수도 있습니다. 오늘날 우리는 중국의 야생에서만 판다를 볼 수가 있어요. 2005년 야생에는 1,596마리가 남아 있었습니다. 이때 사냥꾼들이 판다의 가죽과 발을 얻기 위해 이들을 죽였습니다. 한때는 버마와 베트남에서도 서식을 했어요. 하지만 사냥꾼들 때문에 이들 지역에서는 멸종을 했습니다.

또한 판다는 서식지도 잃고 있습니다. 그리고 생각해보세요… 이들은 하루에 14시간 동안 대나무를 먹습니다. 대부분의 야생 판다는 약 15살까지 살 수가 있죠. 그러나 동물원에서는 30살까지도 살 수가 있습니다.

Listening Skills

1 Adults can weigh around 117 kilograms.
2 In 2005, there were 1,596 pandas in the wild.
3 They can live to be about thirty in zoos though.

• Exercise 7 • p.134

정답 Q1 Ⓓ Q2 Ⓒ

스크립트 🎧 08-15

M Professor: Rhinos are on the list of endangered species. A long time ago, there were more than twenty species of rhinos. Today, there are only five remaining. Experts estimate there are around 30,000 rhinos left on the Earth. In captivity, there are more than 7,500. The two main species are the African and Asian rhino.

The main threat to rhinos comes from poaching and the loss of habitat. Poachers illegally hunt and kill rhinos for their horns. The African rhino has two horns. The Asian rhino has one. Many projects to save rhinos are effective. Still, rhinos need more protection.

Some of you might know that rhinos are really tough. Well, they are. They are built like tanks. They are also great swimmers and runners. Most rhinos can run around forty miles per hour. That's very fast for such a big beast.

해석

M Professor: 코뿔소는 멸종 위기종의 목록에 있습니다. 오래 전에는 20여 종 이상의 코뿔소가 있었죠. 지금은 겨우 5종뿐입니다. 전문가들은 지구상에 30,000마리의 코뿔소 밖에 남아 있지 않다고 추산합니다. 사육되고 있는 개체수는 7,500마리 이상이고요. 주된 두 가지 종은 아프리카 코뿔소와 아시아 코뿔소 입니다.

코뿔소에게 주로 위협이 되는 것은 밀렵과 서식지의 감소입니다. 밀렵꾼들은 뿔을 얻기 위해 불법적으로 이들을 사냥을 해서 죽입니다. 아프리카 코뿔소는 2개의 뿔을 가지고 있어요. 아시아 코뿔소는 한 개를 가지고 있죠. 코뿔소를 구하기 위한 많은 프로젝트들이 효과를 보이고 있습니다. 하지만 코뿔소는 더 많은 보호를 필요로 합니다.

여러분 중 몇몇은 코뿔소가 정말로 거칠다는 점을 알고 있을 거예요. 음, 그렇습니다. 코뿔소의 몸집은 탱크와 비슷합니다. 또한 수영과 달리기에도 능하고요. 대부분의 코뿔소는 한 시간에 40마일을 달릴 수 있습니다. 그처럼 큰 짐승에게는 매우 빠른 속도죠.

Listening Skills

1 Experts estimate there are around 30,000 rhinos left on the Earth.
2 Most rhinos can run around forty miles per hour.
3 In captivity, there are more than 7,500.

- **Exercise 8** — p.135

정답 Q1 Ⓓ Q2 Ⓓ

스크립트 🎧 08-17

W Professor: The Siberian tiger is the <u>biggest</u> tiger. It can <u>weigh</u> more than 670 pounds. However, the tiger has a <u>very</u> <u>sad</u> story. Just <u>around</u> 100 years ago, there were tigers <u>everywhere</u> in Asia. They <u>lived</u> in Nepal, China, India, Southeast Asia, and <u>other</u> places. But today, in many of these countries, the tiger is extinct.
<u>Experts</u> think there are only <u>about</u> 5,000 tigers <u>left</u> in the wild now. There were more than 100,000 tigers 100 years ago. <u>How</u> shocking! But it is a very sad <u>reality</u>. Hunters <u>shoot</u> and <u>trap</u> them to sell their fur. But that's not all. Hunters sell the tiger meat, bones, and other <u>body parts</u>, too. They <u>even</u> <u>capture</u> tiger cubs to sell as pets. I <u>cannot</u> <u>believe</u> people <u>actually</u> buy tiger cubs. <u>How</u> terrible!

해석

W Professor: 시베리아 호랑이는 가장 큰 호랑이입니다. 무게가 670파운드 이상 나갈 수도 있죠. 하지만 이 호랑이는 매우 슬픈 이야기를 지니고 있어요. 약 100년 전에는 아시아의 대부분 지역에서 호랑이가 살고 있었습니다. 네팔, 중국, 인도, 동남 아시아, 그리고 그 밖의 지역에서도 살았죠. 하지만 오늘날 이들 지역 중 많은 곳에서 호랑이는 멸종되었습니다.
전문가들은 현재 약 5,000마리만이 야생에서 살고 있다고 생각합니다. 100년 전에는 10만 마리 이상의 호랑이들이 살고 있었죠. 너무나도 충격적입니다! 하지만 슬픈 현실입니다. 사냥꾼들은 털을 팔기 위해 이들에게 총과 덫을 사용했어요. 하지만 그것만이 아닙니다. 사냥꾼들은 호랑이의 고기, 뼈, 그리고 기타 신체들도 팔았습니다. 애완동물로 팔기 위해 새끼 호랑이들까지 포획을 했어요. 사람들이 실제로 새끼 호랑이들을 산다니 것을 믿을 수가 없습니다. 너무나 끔찍해요!

Listening Skills

1 It can weigh more than <u>670</u> pounds.
2 There were more than <u>100,000</u> tigers <u>100</u> years ago.
3 Experts think there are only about <u>5,000</u> tigers left in the wild now.

Vocabulary Review — p.136

A
1 extinct
2 threatened
3 imagine
4 habitat
5 aggressive

B 1 Ⓒ 2 Ⓓ 3 Ⓒ 4 Ⓐ 5 Ⓑ

C 1 Ⓑ 2 Ⓓ 3 Ⓐ 4 Ⓒ 5 Ⓐ

D
1 paws
2 wingsapn
3 comeback
4 polluted
5 protected

Practice Test — p.138

1 Ⓒ   2 Bears: ①, ② Others: ③, ④   3 Ⓑ   4 Ⓒ

스크립트 🎧 08-19

M Professor: Animals <u>need</u> to <u>get</u> fat <u>in</u> <u>order</u> to <u>survive</u>. Many animals <u>sleep</u> a long time <u>during</u> the year. We call this <u>hibernation</u>.
<u>Certain</u> animals <u>fatten</u> themselves up to <u>survive</u>. Why? Well, in winter, food can <u>become</u> <u>scarce</u>, so it's hard to find. So animals eat as much as they can before winter <u>comes</u>. They eat and <u>store</u> it as fat in their bodies. <u>Hibernation</u> also <u>allows</u> animals <u>to conserve</u> energy.
Now, please <u>follow</u> closely. During hibernation, the animal's body <u>temperature</u> drops. This <u>allows</u> the animal <u>to burn</u> less energy even while it sleeps. We all know that bears <u>hibernate</u> during winter. In fact, <u>many</u> <u>kinds</u> of bears hibernate. They go into a <u>den</u>, which is usually a cave or <u>even</u> an old tree trunk, and then sleep <u>through</u> winter. Many bears can spend more than three months hibernating. They do not <u>wake</u>, <u>eat</u>, or <u>move</u> about during this time. Isn't that amazing? Other hibernating animals like raccoons <u>must</u> <u>wake</u> <u>often</u> to eat stored food or, um, to <u>relieve</u> themselves. Bears, however, do not.

해석

M Professor: 동물들은 살아남기 위해 지방을 가지고 있어야 합니다. 많은 동물들이 1년 중 긴 시간 동안 잠을 잡니다. 우리는 이를 동면이라고 부르죠.
어떤 동물들은 살아남기 위해 지방을 축적합니다. 왜일까요? 음, 겨울에는 먹을 것이 부족해지기 때문에 먹이를 구하기가 어렵습니다. 그래서 동물들은 겨울이 오기 전에 가능한 많은 먹이를 먹습니다. 먹이를 먹어서 몸에 지방을 축적합니다. 또한 동면을 함으로써 동물들은 에너지를 보존할 수 있습니다.
자, 잘 들으세요. 동면 상태에서는 동물의 체온이 낮아집니다. 이렇게 함으로써 동물들은 잠을 자는 동안 에너지를 덜 소비하게 되죠. 우리 모두는 곰들이 겨울에 동면한다는 점을 알고 있습니다. 실제로 많은 종류의 곰들이 동면을 하죠. 동굴이나 오래된 나무 몸통과 같은 굴에 들어가 겨울 동안 잠을 잡니다. 많은 곰들이 석 달 넘게 겨울잠을 잡니다. 이 기간 동안에는 잠에서 깨지도 않고, 음식을 먹지도 않으며, 몸을 움직이지도 않습니다. 놀랍지 않나요? 라쿤과 같은 다른 동면 동물들은 저장해 놓은 먹이를 먹거나, 음, 휴식을 취하기 위해 자주 잠을 깨야만 하죠. 그러나 곰은 그렇지가 않습니다.

Actual Test

Actual Test 1
p.142

1 Ⓐ   2 Ⓒ   3 Ⓓ   4 Ⓐ   5 Ⓐ   6 Ⓑ
7 Weather: 1, 4   Climate: 2, 3

스크립트 🎧 09-01

W Student: Hello, Professor Madison. May I speak with you for a moment?
M Professor: Sure, Wendy. What's on your mind?
W: It's the midterm exam.
M: Ah, yeah. You didn't do too well on it, did you?
W: Not at all. I was actually really sick last week.
M: I'm sorry. Are you feeling better now?
W: Yes, I'm okay. So, uh . . . I wonder if . . .
M: Yes?
W: Could I retake the test? I mean, uh, I was sick.
M: I'm really sorry, but I can't let you do that.
W: Are you sure?
M: Yes. It's a school rule. Retests are not allowed. But . . .
W: But what?
M: I can give you a bonus assignment. Are you interested in that?
W: Definitely. That would be great.

해석

W Student: 안녕하세요, 매디슨 교수님. 잠깐 말씀을 나눌 수 있으신가요?
M Professor: 물론이에요, 웬디. 무슨 일인가요?
W: 중간고사 때문에요.
M: 아, 그래요. 중간고사를 그다지 잘 보지 못했군요, 그렇죠?
W: 완전 못 봤어요. 사실 지난 주에 정말로 아팠거든요.
M: 유감이에요. 지금은 몸이 괜찮은가요?
W: 네, 괜찮아요. 그래서, 어… 궁금한 것이…
M: 네?
W: 제가 시험을 다시 볼 수는 없을까요? 제 말은, 어, 제가 아팠잖아요.
M: 정말로 유감이지만 그럴 수는 없어요.
W: 확실한가요?
M: 네, 학교 방침이거든요. 재시험은 허락되지 않죠. 하지만…
W: 하지만 무엇인가요?
M: 보너스 과제를 줄 수는 있어요. 관심이 있나요?
W: 그럼요. 그러면 정말 좋을 것 같아요.

스크립트 🎧 09-02

M Professor: We need to discuss something important. You will often hear two words in my class this semester. The words are weather and climate. Most people believe they're the same. However, that isn't true. Let me explain the difference.
Weather refers to specific conditions in the atmosphere. For instance, it could be sunny on a hot day. Or it could be snowy on a cold and cloudy day. Weather refers to events that happen in just a few hours. It could also refer to events that happen in a few days or even weeks. Weather therefore refers to short-term events.
What about climate? Well, climate refers to the average weather conditions over a long period of time. How long? Normally, it's at least thirty years. It could be longer though. For example, we can talk about the average climate during the time of the dinosaurs. That period covers millions of years.
Why is it important to know the difference? Hmm . . . Here is one reason. During summer, the weather might get very hot for a few days. Then, many people start claiming the Earth is getting hotter. Sorry, but you can't tell that from just a few days of weather. You have to look at long-term data instead. You know, the climate. Try to remember this information all semester long. Okay?

해석

M Professor: 중요한 내용을 논의하도록 하죠. 여러분들은 이번 학기 제 수업에서 두 개의 단어를 자주 듣게 될 거에요. 바로 날씨와 기후이죠. 대부분의 사람들은 이들이 같은 것이라고 생각합니다. 하지만 그렇지가 않아요. 그 차이점을 설명해 드리죠.
날씨는 대기의 특별한 상태를 가리킵니다. 예를 들어 더운 날에 맑을 수가 있습니다. 혹은 춥고 흐린 날에 눈이 내릴 수도 있죠. 날씨는 몇 시간 동안 일어나는 현상을 가리킵니다. 또한 며칠이나 심지어 몇 주 동안 일어나는 현상을 가리킬 수도 있어요. 따라서 날씨는 단기적인 현상을 가리킵니다.
기후는 어떨까요? 음, 기후는 장기간에 걸친, 날씨의 평균적인 상태를 가리킵니다. 얼마나 오랫동안일까요? 보통 최소 30년입니다. 하지만 더 길 수도 있어요. 예를 들어 우리는 공룡의 시대의 평균적인 기후에 대해 이야기할 수 있습니다. 이러한 기간은 수백만 년에 달하죠.
차이점을 아는 것이 왜 중요할까요? 흠… 한 가지 이유를 알려 드릴게요. 여름에는 날씨가 며칠 내에 매우 더워질 수 있습니다. 그러면 많은 사람들이 지구가 점점 더 더워지고 있다고 주장하기 시작하죠. 미안하지만 며칠간의 날씨로 그러한 점을 확인할 수는 없습니다. 대신 장기적인 데이터를 살펴보아야 하죠. 아시다시피, 기후를요. 이러한 내용은 모두 학기 내내 기억하고 있어야 합니다. 아시겠죠?

Actual Test 2
p.146

1 Ⓑ   2 Ⓐ   3 Ⓐ   4 Ⓑ   5 Ⓑ   6 Ⓒ   7 Ⓓ

스크립트 🎧 09-03

W Librarian: Good morning. How can I help you?
M Student: Hello. I'm looking for Ms. Julie Samuels.
W: That's me. And you are . . . ?
M: My name is David Thompson. I called you yesterday.
W: Ah, yes, Mr. Thompson. We spoke about a job, right?
M: That's right. I was told you have a position available here.
W: You are correct. Do you have any experience working in a library?
M: Actually, yes. I used to volunteer at my local library.
W: What did you do there?
M: I shelved books. I helped people find material. I checked out books, too.

W: That's exactly what you would do here.
M: Great. Um . . . does that mean I'm hired?
W: It depends. There are two work shifts. One is one Monday afternoon. The other is on Friday evening.
M: I'm free both days.
W: Come with me then. You need to fill out some paperwork.
M: Sounds good. Thanks a lot, Ms. Samuels.

해석

W Librarian: 안녕하세요. 어떻게 도와 드릴까요?
M Student: 안녕하세요. 줄리 사무엘스 씨를 찾고 있어요.
W: 저에요. 그러면 학생은…?
M: 제 이름은 데이비드 톰슨입니다. 어제 저에게 전화를 하셨죠.
W: 아, 그래요, 톰슨 군. 일자리에 대해 이야기를 나눴죠, 그렇죠?
M: 맞아요. 이곳에 일자리가 있다고 말씀해 주셨어요.
W: 그래요. 도서관에서 일을 해 본 경험이 있나요?
M: 사실 있어요. 동네 도서관에서 자원봉사를 한 적이 있어요.
W: 그곳에서 어떤 일을 했나요?
M: 선반에 책을 꽂아두었어요. 사람들이 자료 찾는 일도 도왔고요. 책을 대출해 주는 일도 했어요.
W: 정확히 이곳에서 하게 될 일들이군요.
M: 잘 되었네요. 음… 제가 고용되었다는 말씀이신가요?
W: 상황에 따라서요. 근무 시간대가 두 개가 있어요. 하나는 월요일 오후에 있죠. 다른 자리는 금요일 저녁에 있고요.
M: 두 시간대 모두 가능합니다.
W: 그러면 저를 따라 오세요. 몇 가지 서류를 작성해야 하거든요.
M: 좋습니다. 정말 감사합니다, 사무엘스 선생님.

스크립트 🎧 09-04

W Professor: In the past, many teachers relied on rote learning. In fact, many still use it today. Rote learning involves memorization. Students repeat information again and again. This lets them memorize it. Rote learning is very effective. But it's not the only learning method. It's also not the best method for some students.
One woman developed her own learning method. Her name was Maria Montessori. She came up with the Montessori Method. Montessori believed children needed to develop at different paces. Some were fast learners. Others were slow learners. In traditional classrooms, this was a problem. Why? Well, teachers went too slowly for the best students. And teachers went too fast for the worst students.
Montessori wanted students to learn at their own pace. She wanted them to focus on developing their own natural abilities, too. The students who learned with her method were given a lot of independence.
Montessori thought play was important. In fact, she said, "Play is work." She also liked hands-on learning. Her classrooms had toys and other materials. Teachers encouraged students to use them. That way, students could learn. Teachers also had students do practical activities, such as sweeping and cleaning. This method is not for all students. But it has been effective for many. I wonder . . . Did any of you learn with the Montessori Method?

해석

W Professor: 과거에는 많은 교사들이 암기 학습에 의존했습니다. 사실 오늘날에도 많은 교사들이 암기 학습을 이용하고 있죠. 암기 교육은 외우는 것과 관련이 있습니다. 학생들은 계속해서 반복적으로 학습을 합니다. 이로써 암기가 되는 것이죠. 암기 학습은 매우 효과적입니다. 하지만 이것이 유일한 학습법은 아니에요. 또한 일부 학생들에게는 최선의 학습법도 아니에요.
한 여성이 독자적인 학습법을 만들었습니다. 그녀의 이름은 마리아 몬테소리였어요. 그녀는 몬테소리 학습법을 생각해 냈어요. 몬테소리는 아이들이 서로 다른 속도로 발달해야 한다고 믿었어요. 일부 학생들은 배우는 것이 빨랐습니다. 배우는 것이 느린 학생들도 있었고요. 전통적인 교실에서는 이러한 점이 문제였습니다. 왜일까요? 음, 가장 성적이 좋은 학생들에게는 교사들의 수업이 너무 느렸습니다. 그리고 가장 성적이 나쁜 학생들에게는 너무 빨랐죠.
몬테소리는 학생들이 각자의 속도로 배우기를 바랐어요. 또한 학생들이 자신의 타고난 능력을 향상시키는데 집중하기를 바랐죠. 그녀의 학습법으로 학습한 학생들은 독립심을 기를 수 있었습니다.
몬테소리는 놀이가 중요하다고 생각했어요. 실제로 "놀이가 공부다"라는 말을 하기도 했죠. 또한 직접 해 보는 학습을 선호했습니다. 그녀의 교실에는 장난감 같은 것들이 있었어요. 교사들은 학생들에게 이를 사용할 것을 권장했고요. 그러한 방식으로 학생들은 배울 수가 있었습니다. 또한 교사들은 학생들이, 빗자루질과 청소와 같은, 실용적인 활동을 하도록 시켰죠.
이러한 방법이 모든 학생들을 위한 것은 아닙니다. 하지만 다수의 학생들에게 효과적이었어요. 궁금한 것이 있는데… 여러분 중에서 몬테소리 학습법으로 배워 본 사람이 있나요?

Actual Test 3 p.150

1 ⓒ 2 ⓓ 3 ⓓ 4 ⓒ 5 ⓐ 6 ⓒ 7 ⓑ

스크립트 🎧 09-05

W Professor: Good afternoon, Matt. How can I help you?
M Student: Hello, Professor Arnold. I just saw the class list for next semester.
W: Oh? What are you going to take?
M: I'd really like to take your seminar on medieval history.
W: You're a junior, right?
M: That's correct. Is that a problem?
W: Well, seniors usually take up all the spots in seminars.
M: How many students can sign up for it?
W: Only fifteen. And those spots fill up very fast.
M: So I probably won't be able to register for it, right?
W: That's correct. Sorry about that.
M: That's a shame. I was really looking forward to it.
W: Don't worry too much. I have some good news for you.
M: What's that?
W: I'm going to teach the same seminar next year, too.
M: That's wonderful news. I'm really looking forward to it.

해석

W Professor: 좋은 아침이에요, 매트. 어떻게 도와 줄까요?
M Student: 안녕하세요, 아놀드 교수님. 조금 전에 다음 학기 수업 리스트를 보았어요.
W: 오? 어떤 수업을 들을 예정이죠?
M: 저는 중세 역사에 관한 교수님의 세미나 수업을 정말로 듣고 싶어요.

W: 3학년이죠, 그렇죠?
M: 맞아요. 그것이 문제가 되나요?
W: 음, 세미나 수업은 보통 4학년 학생들에 의해 자리가 채워지죠.
M: 얼마나 많은 학생들이 등록을 할 수 있나요?
W: 15명뿐이에요. 그리고 매우 빨리 자리가 채워져요.
M: 그러면 아마도 저는 등록을 할 수가 없겠군요, 그런가요?
W: 맞아요. 그에 대해서는 유감이에요.
M: 안타깝네요. 저는 정말로 그 수업을 고대하고 있었거든요.
W: 너무 걱정하지는 말아요. 좋은 소식이 있으니까요.
M: 무슨 소식이요?
W: 내년에도 제가 똑같은 수업을 하게 될 거예요.
M: 정말 멋진 소식이군요. 정말로 기대가 되어요.

스크립트 🎧 09-06

W Professor: That piece of music was from one of my favorite composers. Does anyone know it . . . ? No . . . ? That's too bad. It was from a work of orchestral music called *Water Music*. The composer was George Frideric Handel.

Handel was born in 1685. That was the same year Johann Sebastian Bach was born. Sadly, the two great composers never met. Handel died in 1759. He lived during the Baroque Period. He was one of that period's best composers.

Most people know Handel for his oratorios. An oratorio is a long musical work which usually has a religious theme. It features an orchestra. It also has solo singers as well as a chorus. Handel's most famous work was the *Messiah*, an oratorio. It tells the story of Jesus Christ. Amazingly, Handel wrote the entire oratorio in just twenty-four days. The *Messiah* became an instant hit. The "Hallelujah Chorus" is the best-known piece of music in it. According to stories, King George II of England was very moved by the performance. So he stood up during the "Hallelujah Chorus." Since then, audiences around the world have done the same.

Handel did not just write oratorios though. He wrote operas, too. In fact, he composed more than forty of them. One popular opera of his was *Orlando*. *Music for the Royal Fireworks* was another popular work of Handel's.

해석

W Professor: 제가 제일 좋아하는 작곡가의 작품 중 하나였습니다. 아는 사람이 있나요…? 없나요…? 안타깝군요. *수상음악*이라고 불리는 관현악곡의 일부였어요. 작곡가는 게오르그 프리데릭 헨델이었고요.

헨델은 1685년에 태어났습니다. 요한 세바스찬 바흐가 태어난 해와 같은 해였죠. 안타깝게도 이 두 위대한 작곡가는 한 번도 만난 적이 없었습니다. 헨델은 1759년에 사망했어요. 그는 바로크 시대에 살았죠. 이 시기 최고의 작곡가 중 한 명이었습니다.

대부분의 사람들은 성가곡 때문에 헨델을 알고 있습니다. 성가곡이란 보통 종교적인 주제를 지니고 있는 긴 음악 작품이에요. 오케스트라로 연주되는 것이 특징이죠. 솔로 가수들로 이루어질 수도 있고 코러스로 이루어질 수도 있어요. 헨델의 가장 유명한 작품은 *메시아*라는 성가곡이었습니다. 이는 예수 그리스도의 이야기를 들려주어요. 놀랍게도 헨델은 단 24일만에 이 성가곡을 썼습니다. *메시아*는 발표되자마자 히트를 쳤어요. 그 중 "할렐루야 코러스" 부분이 가장 유명합니다. 이야기에 따르면 영국의 왕 조지 2세는 공연을 보고 매우 감동을 받았다고 합니다. 그래서 "할렐루야 코러스"가 불리는 동안 일어서 있었어요. 그 이후로 전 세계 관객들은 똑같은 동작을 하고 있습니다.

하지만 헨델이 성가곡만 쓴 것은 아니었어요. 오페라도 썼습니다. 실제로 40곡 이상의 오페라를 작곡했어요. 그의 유명한 오페라 중 하나는 *오를란도*였습니다. *왕궁의 불꽃놀이 음악*도 헨델의 오페라 중 유명한 작품이었고요.